IN CASE OF FIRE

THE ILLUSTRATED HISTORY AND MODERN ROLE
OF THE LONDON FIRE BRIGADE

JEREMY MILLS
PUBLISHING LIMITED

IN CASE OF FIRE

THE ILLUSTRATED HISTORY AND MODERN ROLE OF THE LONDON FIRE BRIGADE

NEIL WALLINGTON

JEREMY MILLS
PUBLISHING LIMITED

LONDON FIRE BRIGADE
making London a safer city

Royal Foreword

by HRH Prince Michael of Kent

There can be few organisations anywhere that demand more respect from the public than the London Fire Brigade. A great deal of research has gone into this fascinating book. It explains in detail the history of firefighting, gives descriptions of some of the major fires and emergencies in London over the years, and explains the scope of the important work currently being undertaken by the Brigade to make our capital city a safer place.

I recommend 'In Case of Fire' as essential reading for anyone wanting to learn more about the London Fire Brigade, its brave personnel and their often unsung service to the community.

Introduction

by **Ken Knight** CBE, QFSM, MIFireE, CCMI
Commissioner, LFEPA

What you will see in this book is how, time after time, London's fire-fighters have risen to meet the challenges that have faced them. As you turn the pages you will read over and again of the bravery and fortitude of London's firefighters, often in the most extreme of conditions and sometimes with only basic equipment to protect them. You will read that, on occasions, they have sadly paid the ultimate sacrifice in their efforts to serve the people of London.

Over a number of years welcome fire safety legislation has been introduced and enforced and the huge commercial and industrial blazes that were once a regular occurrence are now an occasional, sometimes rare, event. Similarly, the benefits of new technology mean that we are better able to understand the nature of fire, we have better equipment at our disposal with which to fight fire and our firefighters are able to carry out their work with the benefit of safer and more efficient personal protection and also undertake the wider rescue role expected of a modern fire and rescue service.

Now we see different types of challenge. We know that to build on the successes of fire safety in the workplace and drive down still further the numbers of those killed and injured in fire, we need to turn our attention to fire in the home where most fire deaths now occur. To do so we continue to work closely with partner organisations and with the communities themselves to identify those most at risk.

Fire deaths in London are falling, but we cannot be complacent. Only if they continue to fall can we say we are meeting our principal aim of making London a safer city.

Ken Knight

Ken Knight CBE, QFSM, MIFireE, CCMI
London Fire Commissioner
June 2005

Published by Jeremy Mills Publishing Limited, The Red House,
22 Occupation Road, Lindley, Huddersfield HD3 3BD, UK
www.jeremymillspublishing.co.uk

With the official support of The London Fire Brigade

This edition first published 2005

Layout and design © Jeremy Mills Publishing Limited
Text © Neil Wallington

ISBN 0-9546484-6-3

A CIP catalogue record for this book is available from the
British Library.

Typeset in Century Schoolbook and Gill Sans by
Concept, Huddersfield, UK (01484 312602)

Printed by SNP (International) Ltd

Contents

Prologue

I cannot quite remember just when as a youngster my mind first became set upon becoming a firefighter, but for sure, the family influence played a part. An uncle who joined the Auxiliary Fire Service (AFS) before the Second World War went on to survive the 1940–41 London Blitz, and then the subsequent period of the Flying Bombs and V2 rockets. Another family friend also joined the pre-war Auxiliary Fire Service and he too saw plenty of active service throughout the London firemen's war.

Unfortunately, by the time I was old enough at eighteen years of age to apply to join the London Fire Brigade, there was a long waiting list for the selection and recruitment process. Not to be denied my ambition, I temporarily joined my local part-time Auxiliary Fire Service in Croydon. This Second World War reserve fire service had been reformed across the country in the early 1950s as a Cold War precaution against the threat of nuclear war and its likely effects. I hoped that experience as an 'Auxiliary' would enhance my application to join the LFB when it finally came to the top of the pile.

London firefighters rigged in full protective clothing are briefed during a recent decontamination exercise at the Bank Underground station.

A brass helmeted firemen with two typical grey horses that pulled London's fire engines for over half a century. Bred and specially trained for their fire brigade work, these fine and much loved steeds worked in pairs and gave valiant and reliable service from the 1870s until the last horses were pensioned off in 1921.

As it happened, plans for the shape of the proposed Greater London Council and its huge administrative area first became public in 1963. In these plans the enlarged London Fire Brigade would see its existing sixty fire stations merge with those of the Middlesex County Brigade and the smaller county borough Brigades of Croydon, East Ham, and West Ham, together with parts of the Essex, Hertfordshire, Surrey and Kent. The new Greater London Council would come into being on 1 April 1965 and bring about a new London Fire Brigade with 124 fire stations located across some 620 square miles. This merger would produce the greatest urban area ever covered by any single fire brigade anywhere in the world. But I still had to wait to join. . . .

Then, somewhat unexpectedly, several fireman vacancies came up in the professional 200 strong Croydon Fire Brigade and I applied knowing full well that by April 1965, the Croydon force would be part of the Greater London Fire Brigade. After a successful selection procedure I was sent on the LFB recruits basic course at Southwark Training Centre, where I underwent three months of unrelenting physical and mental sweat and toil over the thirteen weeks of the course. Then, emerging into the outside

> *Sadly, it was not long before I saw
> my first fire fatality...*

world as a newly-qualified probationary firemen and posted to my first fire station, I faced the excitement of being a member of a crew responding to 999 calls.

I soon found that life in the London Fire Brigade was every bit as rewarding as I had imagined it to be. Those first rides to emergencies on the gleaming red fire engines were full of anticipation and adrenalin. Sadly, it was not long before I saw my first fire fatality and experienced at first hand the physical and mental pain of those that suffer a fire, even a small outbreak. As my Leading Fireman said to me in my first weeks on the station: 'Never forget it's a different set of people involved every time'. He had served through the Blitz years and his philosophy was simple, yet spot on.

As a probationary fireman, my personal witness to considerable human suffering at fire and accident scenes was offset by the special esprit-de-corps of the fire service and its close teamwork atmosphere. With crews working a three watch rota, the LFB was a very busy operational brigade. This was especially so in the Inner London area, to where I was soon able to engineer a transfer in order to gain more firefighting and rescue experience. Thus I found myself in the LFB's high risk 'A' Division whose ten fire stations covered the West End and central part of the capital. Here, over the next fourteen years I was to learn my profession whilst serving in several historic fire stations. Some of these went back to the Victorian days when the Prince of Wales had had a fire uniform kept ready at Chandos Street fire station near Covent Garden, and would occasionally ride to fires along with the brass-helmeted crews on galloping horsedrawn steamer pumps.

Since the first professional brigade was set up in 1833, London's fire-fighters have been called to deal with many fires that have developed into major conflagrations, saved many thousand of lives and dealt with the aftermath of major accident scenes. The 18th and 19th century era of the London Brigade was a time when man's struggle against uncontrolled fire was primarily a battle of physical strength. Successive Chief Officers

The funeral of an LFB hero. The coffin of Station Officer Colin Townsley who lost his life whilst carrying out rescues at the Kings Cross fire tragedy on 18 November 1987 is borne to his final resting place by Soho's flower-bedecked turntable ladder. The guard of honour was made up of hundreds of London firefighters and representatives of almost every other brigade across the United Kingdom. (*The Independent*)

James Braidwood and Captain Eyre Massey Shaw, set new international standards in firefighting through their leadership qualities, pioneering techniques and beliefs.

The long days and nights of the London Blitz is another chapter of LFB history that showed the amazing resilience, courage and fortitude of the men and women of the Brigade, especially during the high explosive and incendiary raiding that lasted during one period for fifty seven continuous fiery nights.

The challenges of the 21st century for the modern day London Fire Brigade are, of course, very different, and through the pages of *In Case of Fire* I have tried to describe something of how the LFB aims to protect London's population from new threats. For the modern enemy is not just fire, although in comparison with my time, the personnel of the modern LFB nowadays are taking wider initiatives to make London a safer city by their fire safety work amid the community in the various boroughs.

The new threats are not just about global terrorism. The enormous increase in everyday non-fire rescue work such as extrication rescue work at road accidents, and the sudden and unexpected effects of freak weather bring a varied '999' emergency workload. The LFB has to equip, train and maintain an immediate readiness to face whatever these

“ *Every firefighter knows that it is not
fire itself that kills, but the toxic smoke
from the combustion process.* ”

new challenges might bring to those who serve in the modern Brigade. Fortunately, science and technology is progressively coming to the aid of firefighters everywhere, with new state-of-the-art equipment.

But new equipment is only part of the equation and it is personal qualities that set firefighters apart as very special people. Surely any organised group who train and equip themselves to save life and property from the ravages of fire must have a selfless commitment to their fellow beings, and not a small measure of physical and mental courage. For fire will always be an unforgiving and unpredictable animal, being both man's oldest friend and enemy. Every firefighter knows that it is not fire itself that kills, but the toxic smoke from the combustion process. Even in relatively small volumes in a confined space, smoke is always the principal evil.

When an outbreak of fire is first discovered, most people flee in the opposite direction from the danger, out of the building and hopefully into the safety of fresh air. Not so the firefighting teams, who head into the thick smoke and danger to carry out rescues, locate the fire and tackle the beast at very close quarters.

Even as I started drafting the early pages of *In Case of Fire*, two London firefighters, Adam Meere aged 27, and Bill Faust, 35, both based at Whitechapel fire station, lost their lives following firefighting operations inside a burning premises in Bethnal Green, east London. Their deaths were another stark reminder that a modern day firefighters' calling is every bit as demanding as for those who served during the days of horse-drawn fire engines and brass helmets, or the men who faced the nightly horrors of the London Blitz.

In Case of Fire recalls some of the many events, great and small, not only during 100 years of the London Fire Brigade, but also across the time of its two precursors, the London Fire Engine Establishment, and the Metropolitan Fire Brigade.

This book is also my personal tribute to an army of London firefighters, both past and present, who over some 170 years of service in

both peacetime and war, have protected the population of London from the ravages of fire and a wide range of other emergencies. The London Fire Brigade is one of the world's premier fire and rescue brigades, and all those who have donned the uniform of the LFB can feel part of a long heritage of which both they and every Londoner can be justifiably proud.

Neil Wallington
Kirkby Underwood,
Bourne,
Lincolnshire
May 2005

LFB crews in action during a recent serious nightime fire in East London.

CHAPTER ONE

Genesis: The First Firefighting Efforts

Organised firefighting in London can be traced back into history far further than many people imagine. The Romans were the first to provide some basic fire protection measures using slave labour. Not surprisingly, this proved quite ineffective when put to the occasional test and it was not until there occurred a huge fire in Rome in AD6, when over a quarter of the centre of the city was destroyed, that more organised fire safety measures were taken.

These improvements were built around the formation of a new group of firefighters called *Vigiles*. These early firefighters lived in barracks with a high level of comfort that included baths and were highly regarded by Roman society. The *Vigiles* were formed into three operating forces.

The first of these *Vigiles* groups organised disciplined double-line bucket chains, one bringing water to the fire, the other returning the empty buckets. The second section worked the primitive hand held water squirts of that time, ineffective though they probably were. Finally, the remaining *Vigiles* had the dangerous physical task of trying to pull down parts of walls, ceilings and the roofs of burning buildings to create some sort of fire break. To aid these tasks, the *Vigiles* carried ladders and hooks mounted on the end of long poles.

As the Roman Empire spread, it is most probable that cities such as London (Londinium) would have been protected from fire by a corps of *Vigiles*. However, following the fall of the Roman Empire, the progress and awareness of the dangers from fire were lost and when fires did break out, whatever firefighting that did take place in London must have been disorganised and largely ineffective — fires burning themselves out having consumed all before the flames.

> *Organised firefighting in London can be traced back into history far further than many people imagine.*

A contemporary print of a 15th century fire scene showing bucket chains at work and hooks mounted on long poles being used to try and create a firebreak in the burning thatch.

Most buildings in London at that time were of wooden construction with thatched roofs and, with the widespread use of candles and cooking over open fires inside dwellings, the risk of fire in early London was immense. Two particularly huge conflagrations occurred in 798 and 982, and in 989 a small outbreak in Aldgate soon spread unchecked to 'burn down houses and churches all the way to Ludgate, together with the stately fabric of St. Paul's'.

Early on during the reign of William the Conqueror, the King attempted to raise the level of London's fire protection. He enacted a couvre-feu (curfew) requiring all persons to extinguish their domestic fires and lights at nightfall in an attempt to reduce the outbreak of fire, often caused when sparks from a cooking area of a house or a candle fell into highly combustible straw scattered around as a floor covering. However, this curfew was unpopular and although large fires causing death, injury and widespread damage still broke out, including one in 1086 that devastated a large area of the city, William's son, Henry I, abolished the requirement in 1100.

> 66 *Then followed almost five centuries where fire prevention measures were never a high priority.* 99

A 1556 Act of Parliament required London's streets to be patrolled by a 'bellman' to ring a pre-darkness warning calling out '*Take care of your fire and candle, be charitable to the poor and pray for the dead*'.

A view showing a dwelling fire c.1600 with three men using a fire squirt to try to douse the flames. These squirts had to be refilled from buckets and were clearly laborious and ineffective in use.

Then followed almost five centuries where fire prevention measures were never a high priority, despite various local bylaws being put in place. In one of these, the first Lord Mayor of London, Henry Fitzalwin, decreed that all new building in the City of London district should be constructed of stone and roofed with slate or clay tiles. But fires still broke out and caused major loss of life and damage. In 1212, a small fire in a dwelling on London Bridge, built almost entirely of wood, spread quickly into properties on both north and south banks of the Thames. Over 3,000 lost their lives in the smoke and panic that ensued.

Despite these tragedies London continued to grow, although little progress was being made to improve fire safety and to provide some sort of organised firefighting arrangements. By this time, the first primitive fire engines began to appear. These were the result of engineers mounting a

large hand held brass fire squirt upon a set of wheels. The squirt was fed from a water tank within the frame which was topped up by a bucket chain. The ensuing intermittent water jet was pretty poor and relied upon the physical effort directly imparted to the squirt plunger. Records show that such early fire engines were used at a large blaze in 1633, which once again broke out amid the cramped buildings on London Bridge.

This rare bargeboard shows two watermen/firemen of the Phoenix Company and scenes from the River Thames and the City of London.

ELIZABETH, Widow of ADAM NUTTALL, of *Long-acre*, *London*,

Engine Maker to all his MAJESTY's Public Offices, Dock-Yards, Forts and Garrisons, &c. belonging to his MAJESTY's Royal Navy.

CONTINUES to make and fell Engines of all forts for extinguishing of Fires and watering Gardens, which play with a conftant ftream and prodigious force a large bore of water clofely collected together, and thereby fooner extinguifh the flames in Buildings, than any Engines hitherto contrived. The Engines I make, have a fuction-pipe feven feet long, or longer if required, to feed themfelves with water from any pond, river, well, channel, or main where it may ftand, and has twice the room to pour in water, where the fuction-pipe cannot be applied, than any other Engines, whofe levers work at the fides of the ciftern.

I make five different fizes of thefe Engines, and three fmaller for watering of Gardens, two of which are in cifterns to be carried like a chair, or run upon wheels if required, and by having a fan fixed on the branch, will fprinkle the water like rain; and thefe fmall Engines are likewife exceeding ufeful at fires, being handy to be carried where a fire begins, and thereby fpeedily extinguifh it; and by having a convenient length of leather pipe, the fcrews whereof fit each other, they will be rendered much more beneficial, inafmuch as the water may be thereby conveyed through any narrow paffage, or up the ftair-cafe, or in at the window of any houfe, and by that means prevent the fire's fpreading any farther.

All that is poffible to be required of an Engine is performed by mine, the parts being made of the beft and moft fubftantial materials; the cifterns are made of good large *Englifh* Oak quartered and well feafoned, the joints of the cifterns are lined with copper and nailed with brafs nails, and the wheels are compleatly fhod with iron.

The largeft of thefe Engines may not only be drawn through a paffage three feet and half wide, but may be worked in the fame either by fuction or out of the ciftern, there being room to pour in water by four buckets at a time, through large copper ftrainers, which thofe Engines work'd by treddles cannot. The fmaller fort are proportionably narrower, may be turned about at either end, and will ftand firm on uneven ground.

The preference given to thefe Engines for many years by the Hon. the Commiffioners of his Majefty's Navy, and feveral other ingenious mathematicians, well fkill'd in the principles of mechanical powers, fufficiently teftifies their allowing them to be the beft; and that it is, and always has been the conftant and chief ftudy of a good mechanick to reduce friction as much as poffible in all machines, and particularly in Engines, but more efpecially thofe defigned to work in falt water, cannot be controverted; and the fatal confequence of the contrary fyftem hath lately been fufficiently demonftrated by Engines, whofe moving parts have been many, and friction great, they having been in a fhort time rendered incapable of working, and confequently entirely ufelefs. The many improvements lately made in Engines for working in falt water, and otherwife, are worthy of notice and encouragement, as I will maintain they will work many years without wanting the leaft repair, whereas Engines that have racks and chains become ufelefs in a fhort time, and liable fo to be when moft wanted.

CHAPTER TWO

The Great Fire of 1666

The fire broke out on 2 September 1666 in Pudding Lane, a narrow street off Eastcheap, in a shop belonging to the King's baker, a Mr. Thomas Farynor. He awoke at about 2 am to find smoke drifting into his house above the shop below and was able to make his escape with his family through a window onto an adjacent roof.

The fire rapidly spread out of the Farynor's bakery into stocks of hay and fodder stored in adjoining alleyways and despite the efforts of a large number of volunteers who provided a bucket chain, the fire was quickly out of control, progressively taking hold of the closely packed properties in its path. By early morning, the fire had spread in three directions although it was largely restricted by the Thames on its southern flank.

However, the fire did creep southwards onto London Bridge but, fortuitously, it was stopped from crossing the Thames by a large gap in

A German print of the 1666 Great Fire of London that highlights some of the thousands of buildings destroyed by the uncontrolled fire spread across a widespread area of the capital alongside the Thames.

The Great Fire and its Chain of Command

About one hour after the outbreak of fire in Pudding Lane had first been discovered, the Lord Mayor, Sir Thomas Bludworth, was called from his slumbers to see the fast spreading flames. Taking a carriage to view the fire scene close to the northern side of London Bridge, Bludworth was dismissive of the obviously perilous situation. He was quoted as saying: '*Pish! A woman might piss it out*' and promptly returned to his bed. Samuel Pepys, the diarist, called Bludworth '*a silly man, I think*'. Pepys' diaries reveal that he too underestimated the potential damage that the fire was going to cause. Even as Pepys was committing his thoughts to paper, the fire was progressively growing in intensity, spreading to consume more combustible buildings with flames leaping across alleyways and streets by the minute.

By noon that day, the fire covered an area of about half a square mile along a frontage of riverside warehouses and dwellings. In the early afternoon, the Lord Mayor paid his second visit. This time he came on horseback looking dishevelled and tired, complaining to his aides that nobody seemed to respond to his orders to demolish buildings in the path of the advancing flames.

In fact it had been the King, Charles II, who had issued stern instructions to Bludworth to organise firebreaks by demolishing buildings. However, it seemed that chaos prevailed everywhere amid the smoke and cascades of flying sparks, many of which were drifting downwind on the updraft of the fire only to settle and ignite the thatched roofs of unaffected properties some distances away. Traders and householders jammed the streets as they tried to remove their goods and belongings, and looters were already at work.

At about 9 am on the second morning of the fire, Charles II could see that the Lord Mayor was apparently unable to take charge of the situation and finally ordered the Duke of York to take over control of firefighting operations. It seems that from then on,

some form of positive action started to be taken. By noon, a number of front line posts had been set up manned by companies of the Guards, although the fire still continued to spread into new areas of the capital. During the early evening, the King himself came to witness the firefighting efforts, later returning several times to various points along the fire front, to throw coins at the hundreds of volunteer firemen, pumpers and those manning bucket chains to generally encourage them in their physical labours.

By the evening of the 4 September, the third night of the fire, the Duke of York's efforts appeared to be having some effect. He had earlier drafted into the City large numbers of sailors and dockyard labourers and they had gone to work with gunpowder charges to demolish buildings in whole rows of streets in the path of the fire. As a result, the fire could not cross these gaps and its advance began to be halted during the early hours of the following morning. Although the huge amount of charred debris across the devastated areas continued to smoulder for weeks afterwards, the radical use of explosives had finally arrested the angry flames.

Samuel Pepys recorded the end of the Great Fire of 1666 with this cryptic diary entry on the 5 September: '*Up by five o'clock; and blessed be to God! Find all's well!*' And unsurprisingly, within a month of the Great Fire, Sir Thomas Bludworth, the Lord Mayor relinquished his post, no doubt wishing that he had taken the outbreak somewhat more seriously in the first place.

Up to the time of the Great Fire of London, the development of effective firefighting equipment had been slow, relying almost entirely upon physical human effort through the use of bucket chains and firebreaks. Amongst all the enormous destruction wreaked by its flames, the 1666 Great Fire proved to be something of a turning point, serving as the catalyst in the efforts to provide London with a credible and reliable firefighting force.

66 *The cause of the Great Fire of London has never been clearly established.* 99

terraced properties on the bridge caused by the 1633 fire. Had this gap not been present, the Great Fire would undoubtedly have spread into the South Bank and Southwark areas of the Thames near to the Globe Theatre.

On the north side, despite the demolition of a number of unaffected buildings to provide firebreaks, the huge conflagration burned on and was not halted until late evening on the 5 September. The total area of the City of London destroyed by the Great Fire was in excess of one square mile. This was, in fact, greater than the damage inflicted on the same area by the Luftwaffe during the intense Blitz raids of 1940–41. Amid the charred and smouldering ruins of the City lay 87 churches (including St. Paul's), 52 livery halls and other public premises, and over 13,000 dwellings. The fire made over 100,000 Londoners homeless and, amazingly, only six deaths were publicly recorded, although it is probable that this figure was in reality much higher.

The cause of the Great Fire of London has never been clearly established. Thomas Farynor denied any carelessness on his part and there were suspicions of persons of Dutch origin. Eventually, a French youth, Robert Hubert, confessed to starting the fire, even though it was later established he was not in London at the time of the fire. He was tried, found guilty and executed. Some months later, a Parliamentary inquiry found that the fire had been the result of *the hand of God*.

Interestingly, some archaeological excavations around the site of Farynor's shop during the 1980s found that his neighbour had a store containing barrels of pitch close by the baker's shop. It is probable that the spread of fire was rapidly aided by the proximity of such combustible material. Back in 1666, the fiscal loss of the Great Fire was put at £10 million, an enormous sum for those times, and one that served to underline the dire social and economic effect of uncontrolled fire. There was a strong feeling, particularly in commercial quarters that something would have to be done to prevent such catastrophic fire damage from ever happening again in London.

A 16th century leather fire bucket.

Two examples of primitive fire extinguishers. These were water filled glass spheres that would shatter when thrown on an incipient outbreak of fire.

CHAPTER THREE

The First Insurance Brigades

One immediate and positive aftermath of the Great Fire was that the City's Court of Common Council required the twelve principal livery companies to initiate some immediate fire precautions. These included the provision of an engine, 30 leather buckets, three ladders, two hand squirts, sledges and pickaxes. In addition, many businesses were in ruins and even those that had survived with some damage sought restoration. Although marine insurance had been in place for some years, the insurance of buildings against fire was a new concept.

Nicolas Barbon was an entrepreneur and in 1667 he conceived the idea of an insurance office which in return for a subscription would insure against loss by fire. Other similar schemes were soon competing for business but Barbon had a head start with 4,000 subscribers. However, under pressure from several competitors, he announced a master stroke.

This Hogarth cartoon of 1750 clearly shows the chaos of the early years of insurance company fire brigades. Union Insurance Office firemen are portrayed trying hard to tackle the premises on fire whilst crews of rival brigades create various obstructions and generally interfere with firefighting operations.

Three examples of 18th century metal firemarks. These were affixed to the outer face of an insured premise to indicate which brigade would be required in event of fire. The various insurance offices are: left to right: the Norwich, the Sun and the Phoenix.

Barbon's company pledged to 'provide a group of men versed and experienced in extinguishing and preventing fire. ... Servants in livery with badges who are Thames watermen and other lusty persons who are always ready when any sudden fire happens, which they are very laborious and dextrous in quenching ...'.

For the very first time in London's history, a uniformed firefighting force was available although only to those property holders insured with Barbon's fire office. Naturally, it was not long before Barbon's competitors also began to provide teams of watermen firefighters in livery to protect their respective insured properties.

All these pioneer firefighters were employed on a part time basis but were given some basic instruction in the working of the primitive manual pumps of that time. It is interesting to note that their role was only to save property from the ravages of fire; they were not expected to save life through carrying out rescues.

By the beginning of the 18th century, steady advances were also being made in the means to fight outbreaks of fire. Manually pumped wheeled fire engines were now in common use but these still relied upon a constant

> 66 *Manually pumped wheeled fire engines were now in common use...* 99

Beer for the Pumpers

Manual fire pumps relied upon plenty of muscle power to provide a working firefighting jet of water. Volunteers had to stand up to ten in a line and bend their backs in unison to work the long handles on each side of the fire engine up and down in a continuous action. Naturally, this was very physically demanding work and at a large fire, pumping efforts could last for several hours or even more. volunteers soon discovered that singing or calling out from each side of the manual pumps greatly helped to get a good rhythm going. Soon after manual pumps had become established in the early 18th century, the insurance companies would try to ensure that there was always a plentiful supply of beer available to refresh the pumping volunteers. This had the effect of securing a reasonably reliable source of manpower when required, although if beer was not forthcoming, cries of '*Beer Oh! Beer Oh!*' would signal a stoppage until beer turned up at the scene.

supply of water into their tank from a reliable bucket chain. The fire-fighting water stream from these manuals came from a nozzle mounted on the top of the fire engine. Then the Van der Heiden brothers, both Dutch engineers, pioneered a manual fire engine which featured a leather suction hose that was able to draw water from a source such as a river, stream or pond. Leather hose, although very heavy to manhandle, now meant that a jet of water from the fire engine could be taken much closer to a burning building.

In 1721 Richard Newsham, a London button manufacturer with an interest in fire engines, designed a new and powerful manual pump. This had two double-acting pistons and a tall air vessel that ensured a continuous jet of water could be discharged. Newsham's pumping power was provided either by large handles along both sides of his fire engine or by foot treadles.

But despite the improvements in fire engine performance, the growing number of insurance brigades in London still faced considerable difficulty. Insured properties were marked by the placing of a metal fire mark on a

Two Sun Office firemen in their colourful uniforms, c.1760.

prominent face of a building to indicate which insurance company carried the risk. In event of a fire, it was the sole responsibility of that insurance brigade to tackle it. The burning building might be displaying a Phoenix Insurance company fire mark and if for example the first brigade to arrive on the scene was that of the Sun Insurance, they would simply stand by and watch the fire develop.

By the early 1700s, the number of insurance brigades had grown and instances were recorded where those firefighters who tried to tackle a burning premises insured with their company were openly obstructed in their efforts by firemen from rival insurance brigades. In the outer London areas, some parishes were beginning to provide a manual engine to give some fire cover although these were manned purely by local volunteers in the event of a fire. The situation was further complicated when an Act of Parliament was amended to provide a reward for the attendance at a fire by *any* person with a fire engine. This was a recipe for chaos and, indeed, hoses were slashed and fights regularly broke out at the scene of an outbreak with regard to who had the 'right' to tackle a blaze.

Another view of a Sun fireman, c.1805, showing a manual pump in the background being pumped by volunteers.

Inevitably, against this background, many fires took hold until the building burnt to the ground and few records show what the loss of life must have been. There are recorded cases of fires not being properly extinguished, only to reignite some hours later to cause further damage. In 1794, a huge fire in the Wapping district alongside the Thames destroyed 630 dwellings before it was checked, whilst another in an East India Company dockside warehouse saw a recorded loss of £1 million. It became increasingly clear that something had to be done to provide the ever-growing population of London with a more efficient firefighting service.

A fireman in the green uniform of the Royal Exchange insurance brigade c.1832. Behind him is one of the company's manual pumps in a similar livery.

Thus in 1791, three of the larger insurance companies, the Phoenix, the Royal Exchange, and the Sun decided to combine their fire brigades into a joint private fire service called 'The Fire Watch'. This combined brigade centred on fire stations in Southwark, Lincoln's Inn Fields, Great Swallow Street, Guildhall and Wellclose Square. The arrangement worked with some success until 1805, when the three participating companies complained of the escalating cost of providing such wide ranging fire cover, and the joint arrangement collapsed.

Throughout this period, London continued to develop its trade at a truly phenomenal rate. The Port of London warehouses and wharves were packed full of goods in transit, many of a highly combustible nature. The

66 *There are recorded cases of fires not being properly extinguished, only to reignite some hours later to cause further damage.* 99

capital's population also grew at an amazing rate as people were attracted from the rural areas to new jobs being generated in the thriving factories and businesses of all types. Rows and rows of terraced houses were being built to house the workers in slum conditions, especially in the East End. Restrictions on the size of commercial buildings and their storage were largely ignored and despite a ban on explosives in the City area, it was obviously ignored. In 1800, a fire in a warehouse near the Docks at Custom House reached sacks of gunpowder and the subsequent explosion demolished a wide area.

In the same year, a fire in sugar warehouses in Lower Thames Street spread so quickly that it set alight the rigging of ships moored alongside before they could cast off and pull out into the tideway. Damage was estimated at £300,000. The Drury Lane Theatre, having suffered a major fire in 1795, was struck again by flames in 1809, and so the fire damage and loss of life across London went on with monotonous regularity, at outbreaks large and small.

Against this background, there were more stirrings to try and create a more professional level of fire protection for London. Letters in *The Times* caused some interest in various quarters, but Parliament seemed pre-occupied with matters of the Empire and Ireland. Several unsuccessful attempts to combine the resources of insurance companies were made but by the 1820s with the risk of fire in London having never been so great, the state of the capital's fire protection was in serious decline. Arson too, was becoming a problem, as many unemployed men knew that when a brigade arrived at a fire, volunteer pumpers would be needed along with copious supplies of free beer.

Fortunately, dogged perseverance paid off when in 1830, Charles Bell Ford, the Company Secretary of the Sun Fire Office, proposed that ten of the largest insurance companies should combine to provide a single fire-fighting force for London. After much further argument regarding the shape of the new force, its fire stations and personnel, the London Fire Engine Establishment (LFEE) was born.

A recent view of some 18th and 19th century fire engines in the London Fire Brigade Museum at Southwark.

London's new fire brigade was formed by 80 existing firemen from the Alliance, Atlas, Globe, Imperial, London, Protector, Royal Exchange, Sun, Union, and Westminster insurance companies. Plans were laid for the new force to come into effect on 1 January 1833, initially based at 19 LFEE fire stations and two river stations on the Thames. The estimated annual cost of the LFEE was put at around £8,000, and as the first buds of spring emerged in 1832, the search was on for a suitable person to lead the capital's new professional fire brigade.

CHAPTER FOUR

Braidwood and the London Fire Engine Establishment

After considerable competition for the post of Superintendent of London's new firefighting force, the choice fell upon James Braidwood, the 32 year old Firemaster of the Edinburgh Fire Engine Establishment. Interestingly, the Scottish city had somewhat pre-empted moves in London, when in 1824 it merged most of its various insurance brigades into one municipally controlled firefighting force. James Braidwood was appointed to command the Edinburgh brigade from its inception and when he was first approached by the London authorities some eight years later, was probably the most experienced fire officer in the land.

Braidwood's father was a master builder and this provided James with a strong youthful interest in building construction and surveying. When he left school, he joined the Edinburgh volunteer fire brigade and soon became absorbed in the whole science of firefighting, its equipment

A print of a horsedrawn manual pump and fireman of the London Fire Engine Establishment (LFEE) c.1850.

A horsedrawn manual pump manufactured by Merryweather & Sons. This model was typical of the type used in London during the latter part of the 19th century.

and associated issues. By the time he became Firemaster of Edinburgh's new municipal brigade at the age of 24, Braidwood's reputation was that of a leader of men, with good organisational skills and an enthusiasm for new firefighting tactics.

Although the firemen of the Edinburgh Fire Engine Establishment were employed on a part-time basis, Braidwood placed a great emphasis on their level of training not previously seen. He regularly turned out his part-time crews in the middle of the night to pitch ladders and get jets of water to work on imaginary fires from pumps amid the most inaccessible inner city buildings in Edinburgh. Practice, practice, practice was Braidwood's byword. There is no doubt that the Edinburgh crews became highly adept at dealing with real fires, and soon developed a confidence and pride in their work, together with a high regard for their Firemaster.

Braidwood also found time to write extensively on firefighting practices and the design of firefighting equipment. He was particularly critical of 'long shot' tactics at fires, where vast quantities of water would be put into burning buildings in a haphazard manner. Braidwood encouraged his crews to get as close as possible to the fire scene, and to try and enter to extinguish the source of the fire, even if this was usually impossible in the late 1820s without breathing apparatus and robust protective clothing.

No doubt tempted by the challenge of leading London's new brigade and an annual salary of £400, Braidwood accepted the new post of Superintendent of the London Fire Engine Establishment (LFEE) and moved south in June 1832 to take up his post at the LFEE headquarters

"Braidwood's reputation was that of a leader of men, with good organisational skills and an enthusiasm for new firefighting tactics."

James Braidwood, the first Superintendent of the London Fire Engine Establishment at its foundation in 1833. He tragically died whilst still in office during firefighting operations at the huge Tooley Street riverside fire on 22 June 1861.

> *Braidwood constantly preached fire safety warnings to the community, especially warehouse owners...*

in Watling Street, not far from St. Paul's. From his office in the heart of London's commercial centre, Braidwood presided over an all-professional firefighting force consisting initially of 80 firemen based at 19 fire stations strategically placed across the capital. There were also two fireboats to protect the enormous fire risks within the ships and warehouses that lined the Thames for several miles on both banks. Throughout his years in command and despite regular major fires in dockland, Braidwood constantly preached fire safety warnings to the community, especially warehouse owners, to be aware of the risk of rapid fire spread amid their combustible contents. In particular, he encouraged builders to construct fire resisting walls and fit iron doors to create compartments within the vast open floors of new warehouses to restrict the passage of a fire.

One of his first acts as London's new fire chief was to produce a uniform for his firemen that for the first time had some rudiments of personal protection from the hazards of firefighting. Gone were the highly impractical liveried frock coats of the insurance firemen to be replaced by a thick

A Summons Most Royal

One of the most unusual callouts made by the London Fire Engine Establishment occurred during the evening of 19 March 1853 when a telegraph message from the Prince Consort, Prince Albert, was received at Braidwood's Watling Street Headquarters in the City. The telegraph told of a serious fire in progress at Windsor Castle caused by a small fire in the servants quarters getting out of control and spreading into the East Terrace. A battalion of Guards and nine local fire engines were already at work, so far to no avail. No persons had yet been injured, but the Queen and the royal family were in residence. Prince Albert requested Braidwood to attend upon the Castle.

London's fire chief lost no time in mobilising two of his most powerful pumps manned by some of his most experienced crews. They galloped through the cobbled streets and over the Thames to the nearby Waterloo station of the London and South Western Railway. Here Braidwood was directed to Nine Elms Depot at Battersea, some three miles away, where a special train with horse boxes was in steam waiting to take the London firefighters to Windsor as fast as possible.

> 66 *His firemen soon became known across the capital as 'Jim Bradys', a title that stuck to London firemen even up to the London Blitz.* 99

A fireman of the London Fire Engine Establishment poses for the photographer. This style of practical firefighting uniform was one of a number of improvements introduced by James Braidwood.

> ❝ *Parts of urban London were still without a fire station and these included Kensington and St. John's Wood.* ❞

The Hodges Private Fire Brigade

One of the most effective private fire brigades in London in the mid 19th century was that of the Hodges Gin Distillery in Lambeth, south London. Founded by 'Captain' Fred Hodges, it was primarily set up in 1851 to protect his highly profitable distillery premises, surrounded as it was by high fire risk including a fireworks factory, a candle works, and tallow factories. Consisting at first of two horse drawn manual pumps and forty employees acting as volunteer firemen, the Hodges brigade soon started responding to fire calls in the area around Lambeth, often arriving before the 'official' engines of the Braidwood's LFEE. Hodges even had an observation tower built from where one of his uniformed firemen kept a daytime watch for smoke over the capital's roofline. With a growing reputation for efficiency and plenty of money to spend on his growing enthusiasm, Hodges invested in the first steam pump in 1861 and this was built by Merryweather & Sons and appropriately named *Deluge*. This was the first steam powered fire engine to go into service in the London area and its arrival put Braidwood under even more pressure to introduce similar engines for the LFEE. Hodges ordered a second steamer shortly after the delivery of *Deluge*.

---

black serge tunic with belts and axe cases, leather helmet, and knee boots. Braidwood also issued silk neck scarves to prevent sparks from getting down necks. His firemen soon became known across the capital as 'Jim Bradys', a title that stuck to London firemen even up to the London Blitz. Braidwood also worked hard to improve the conditions of his crews who were initially paid 21 shillings per week with deductions for accommodation. There was promotion through the ranks and even a basic pension scheme. All recruits to the LFEE were drawn from the ranks of sailors who were strong, disciplined, and used to obeying orders.

Very soon, there was a waiting list to join the LFEE and more firemen were gradually taken on as Braidwood opened more fire stations to protect the steady growth of the metropolis, although this was not as rapid an expansion as Braidwood would have liked. Parts of urban London were still without a fire station and these included Kensington and St. John's Wood. However, by 1853, the LFEE could boast 110 professional firemen,

The following are the Stations at which there is constant attendance, Day and Night.

RATCLIFFE .... **Princes-square**
ST. MARY AXE....... **Jeffries-square**
FINSBURY .... **White-cross-street**
CHEAPSIDE .... { **Watling-street, No. 68, Double Station**
BLACKFRIARS ..... **Farringdon-street**
HOLBORN .... **French-horn-yard**
COVENT GARDEN .. **Bedfordbury**
OXFORD STREET .. **Wells-street**
GOLDEN SQUARE .. **King-street**
PORTMAN SQUARE, King-street, corner of **Baker-street**
WATERLOO BRIDGE ROAD, opposite the **Coburg Theatre**
SOUTHWARK BRIDGE ROAD, near **Union-street**
TOOLEY STREET... **Morgan's-lane**

———

The following are the Stations of the Extra Engines.

SHADWELL .... **Schoolhouse-lane**
WESTMINSTER...... **Horseferry-road**
LAMBETH .... **Edward-street, Ped-lar's-acre**
ROTHERHITHE .... **Broadway**——The Men appointed to this Engine have also the care of the Floating Engine.
Floating Engine, off **King's Stairs, Rotherhithe**

———

N.B. The Firemen will be clothed in an Uniform of Dark Grey, with their Numbers in Red on their left breasts. In the event of any of them acting improperly, it is requested that his Number be taken, and a complaint made forthwith to the Superintendent at the Chief Station, No. 68, Watling-street, or to the Secretaries of any of the Offices herein named.

Payne and Harris, Printers,
21, Gracechurch Street.

An original poster c.1833 that displays to the public where the first stations of the London Fire Engine Establishment were located.

The Destruction of the Royal Exchange by Fire on Jan.ʳ 10ᵗʰ 1838.
Drawn on Stone by mr WILLIAM HEATH from a sketch made by him on the spot.
This Print is by permission most respectfully Dedicated to Richard Lambert Jones Esqr.
(CHAIRMAN OF THE COMMITTEE FOR THE REBUILDING OF THE ROYAL EXCHANGE)

A print of the serious fire at the Royal Exchange, 10 January 1838. Note the large number of manual pumps at work.

25 horse drawn manual pumps and 28 hand-propelled manual pumps. In that year, the Brigade attended 900 fires, 261 of which caused major damage including several serious fires in dockland warehouses.

However, Braidwood did have several inexplicable backward traits. The most serious was his long resistance to the adoption of steam-powered pumps for the London brigade. Steam pumps had first appeared in 1829 when Braidwood was still in Edinburgh, and by 1850 were very well developed and reliable, with even the small models far outperforming the pumping capacity of the horse drawn manuals of the LFEE, no matter how many 'pumpers' were at work. Right from his early days as London's fire chief, Braidwood believed that there would be insufficient water to feed steamers and that their water jets would damage the fabric of buildings. He also resisted the use of the telegraph for mobilising and other purposes, continuing to rely on runners or horseback riders to carry urgent messages, for which they were paid a reward of a shilling from Brigade funds.

ONE MILE
CCCL FEET
FROM
108
FLEET STREET

This print shows one of the street escapes provided at strategic sites across central London by the Royal Society for the Protection of Life from Fire. By 1856, the Society had established some 85 street corner escape stations and this view shows the escape station at The Obelisk, in Blackfriars Road, SE1. Note the uniformed conductor, who with the aid of volunteers, would push the heavy escape ladder to the fire.

> 66 *Tragically, Braidwood's reign*
> *came to a sudden and violent end on*
> *Saturday 22 June 1861.* 99

The Royal Society for the Protection of Life from Fire

Despite Braidwood's success in setting up an efficient LFEE, its primary role remained, like that of the old insurance company brigades, to protect property and contents from the ravages of fire. Life saving, as such, was simply not a primary role.

By the mid-1830s, the number of fires to which the LFEE were called to deal with continued to grow and Braidwood still only had a relatively small number of firefighters considering the commercial growth of London. Although his firemen did carry out the occasional rescue of persons trapped by smoke and flames where possible, it was not surprising that London's death toll and numbers of those injured by fire continued to escalate.

This unacceptable situation led in 1836 to a group of London philanthropists founding The Royal Society for the Protection of Life from Fire. The Society started life with six 35 ft wooden wheeled ladders sited across Central London at sites close to the larger squares and churches. These escape stations were manned by a conductor or 'escape man' during the hours of darkness. When the LFEE were summoned to a fire, a runner would also alert the conductor at the nearest escape station. He would use a loud rattle to summons several volunteers to help him push the escape ladder to the scene of the blaze. There it would be quickly extended into the upper floors of a building in which persons might be trapped. Each escape ladder had an underslung canvas trough down which those being rescued could slide to safety. An additional folding ladder could be added to reach up to a height of 60 ft if needed.

Tragically, Braidwood's reign came to a sudden and violent end on Saturday 22 June 1861. In the late afternoon of that warm summer day, a small smouldering fire was discovered in a bale of cotton on the first floor of Scovell's six floor riverside warehouse in Tooley Street, Southwark, on the south bank of the Thames between London and Tower Bridges. By the time that the first fire engines from Watling Street were on the scene, other crammed floors of the warehouse contents including bales of cotton and hemp, tallow, oils, tea, sugar, and spices were fast becoming involved in fire.

Inside an hour, virtually all of the LFEE's fire engines were hard at work being pumped by hundreds of volunteers and Braidwood arrived to take personal command at about 5.30 pm. By then, under intense radiated heat

A contemporary view of the huge riverside fire at Tooley Street near Tower Bridge during which James Braidwood was killed. 22 June 1861.

and a hail of downwind sparks, the blaze had already jumped across a narrow side street to the adjoining Cotton's Wharf. By 7 pm, two further separate warehouses on the other riverside frontage of Scovell's warehouse were ablaze and before very long, about 1,000 yards of Thamesside frontage was burning furiously. Crowds of sightseers flocked to the area and packed onto London Bridge, completely blocking the roadway. This caused serious delays to re-inforcing engines and firemen from various private brigades and parishes galloping in from the outskirts of the London area, all no doubt keen to have some share of the LFEE's fiery action.

Sadly, the water jets from the LFEE manual pumps hardly reached the lower floors of the huge warehouses and had little cooling effect on the developing blaze. In fact, it was not until the new steam pump of the Hodges Brigade and those of several other private brigades booked in attendance at about 6.30 pm, that powerful and effective firefighting water jets at 100 pounds per square inch pressure were applied to the range of burning warehouses.

Around 7 pm Braidwood, accompanied by one of his officers, was moving amongst his crews down a smoke filled alleyway to the river when a cracking sound was heard. With a shouted warning, the group of firemen ran for their lives, and as they did so, a huge end wall of a warehouse crumbled above them and fell outwards. Braidwood and his officer were killed instantly under tons of red hot masonry and roof timbers. Their bodies were not recovered for three days and the Tooley Street fire was not fully extinguished for four weeks, by which time the insured damage had been calculated to be in excess of £2,000,000.

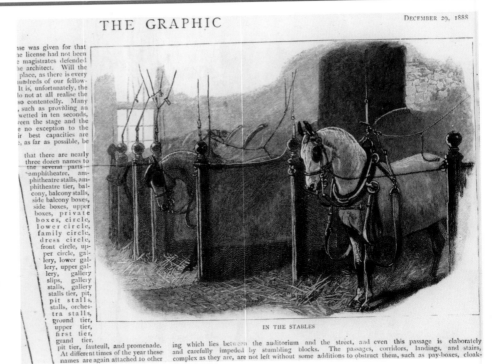

An article and illustration from *The Graphic* newspaper showing the stabling layout for the fire horses inside a London fire station, in stalls immediately behind to waiting fire engines.

Braidwood's funeral was a time for a great outpouring of grief by both the men of the LFEE and Londoners for their fire chief of 28 years standing. Queen Victoria sent her condolences to Braidwood's family and other similar expressions came in from fire brigades around the world. The funeral procession was a mile and a half long, and enormous crowds flocked the streets along its route. Shops were closed across the capital and the bells of churches in the City tolled all day long. A Staffordshire pottery even sold a special china figure in Braidwood's memory. But even as the mourning continued and with the governing committee of the LFEE still fearing that the escalating insurance liability from the Tooley Street conflagration would threaten the future of the LFEE, steps were soon put in hand to begin a search for a worthy and reliable successor to Braidwood.

CHAPTER FIVE

Captain Eyre Massey Shaw, Steam Engines and Brass Helmets

Following the tragic death of Braidwood at Tooley Street, the insurance companies were anxious to bring some stability to the leadership of the London Fire Engine Establishment (LFEE), and at the same time, placate the many businesses seriously affected by the vast material damage to buildings and stock caused by the Thameside conflagration.

No time was lost for in August 1861, the Board of the LFEE appointed the 33 year-old Captain Eyre Massey Shaw as London's new fire chief, on a salary of £750 per annum together with a provided house and other allowances. At Trinity College, Dublin, Shaw had studied engineering and science and at the time of his appointment, Shaw, a former army officer with the North Cork Rifles, was serving as the Chief Constable and Chief Officer of Belfast Fire Brigade. Although their origins were Scottish, the Shaw family had moved to Ireland in the 18th century; George Bernard Shaw was Massey Shaw's cousin.

It is perhaps remarkable that the LFEE Board chose Captain Massey Shaw for such a challenging post in the capital. He had only been in post as the Chief of the Belfast Brigade for little over a year, and his firefighting experience was therefore extremely limited. But the LFEE Board must have seen something very special in the Irishman. It might have been his physical appearance for Shaw was over six feet tall with blue eyes, a goatee beard and long moustache. This commanding presence also made an early impression on his London firemen who soon nicknamed him 'The Skipper' or 'The Long 'Un'. Massey Shaw quickly endeared himself to his crews as a courageous and self-assured front line leader at fires, fearsomely loyal to his men, yet demanding and strict in disciplinary matters.

> 66 *Captain Massey Shaw was destined to become even more famous a Chief Officer than Braidwood* 99

66 *Massey Shaw quickly endeared himself to his crews as a courageous and self-assured front line leader at fires...* 99

Captain (later Sir) Eyre Massey Shaw, the first Chief Officer of the Metropolitan Fire Brigade, pictured in 1866.

> 66 *It was not long before Shaw had also established a reputation as a tireless international advocate of fire prevention...* 99

Shaw at Work

Massey Shaw spent a considerable amount of his time visiting fire stations and personally taking his firemen at drill. Once when on a tour of the 'A' District of the West End in his carriage, Shaw arrived at a fire station just off Oxford Street to see the station telegraph spelling out: 'Watch out — the Long 'Un is out and about. He may look you up'. Shaw stood erect as he told the telegraph operator to send back: 'With thanks. Your message received. The Chief Officer'.

Shaw was also insistent upon the twice daily return of his fire station availability. On one occasion in the spring of 1870, he noticed that a street wheeled escape ladder stationed at Whitechapel Church had not been booked 'available'. When he asked the local Superintendent for a confirmation, Shaw was told that the escape was actually operational. However, no doubt wishing to make a point, the Chief Officer ordered the escape ladder to be pushed the two miles to his headquarters at Southwark so that he could see it. When two sweating firemen turned up about an hour later pushing the heavy escape, Shaw briefly inspected the ladder and then immediately made them turn round and head back to Whitechapel. The escape ladders weighed almost one ton and with plenty of uneven cobbled streets ahead of them on the return journey, the two firemen could not have been best pleased. But word got around the brigade pretty quickly that Shaw's daily availability return was sacrosanct and woe betide those who transgressed.

Over the next 30 years of his command of the London Brigade, Captain (later Sir) Massey Shaw was destined to become even more famous a Chief Officer than Braidwood, and certainly more charismatic. Right from the outset, Shaw took on an immense workload of attending fires, supervising drill and training sessions, chairing and attending meetings, and the constant lobbying and argument with politicians, both local and at Parliament for more funds to develop London's firefighting force. It was not long before Shaw had also established a reputation as a tireless international advocate of fire prevention and greater fire safety across the civilised world.

But even as Massey Shaw moved to take up his new appointment in London in 1861, more trouble was brewing for the LFEE and its supporting

" The pressure for change grew from many quarters. "

insurance companies, who by then totalled 30. In the aftermath of enormous financial claims of the Tooley Street blaze, many insurance companies promptly raised their premiums to cover their losses. In some cases premiums went up almost fourfold and merchants and businesses right across London protested vociferously, claiming that they should not have to bear the direct cost of London's fire brigade. The protesters argued that the newly constituted Metropolitan Board of Works — the first single municipal body for the 117 square miles of the London area — should take the overall responsibility for the fire brigade. It was power-fully pointed out that other British cities including Edinburgh, Glasgow, Manchester and Liverpool all had in place municipally funded brigades of some long standing and it was wrong that London did not follow suit.

The pressure for change grew from many quarters. Although it was accepted that the LFEE was a professional force, it was too small to satisfactorily protect the entire London area. In fact, the LFEE's 19 fire stations only covered an area of some 10 square miles radius of the City of London, even though this was, of course, the very high risk inner area of the capital.

Against this background in 1862 Parliament constituted a Select Committee to investigate and recommend the best way forward to provide a better and more economic method of protecting Greater London from the ravages of fire. Much discussion and argument followed for months; there was even talk of a combined police and fire service for London. How-ever, after much Parliamentary debate, the outcome in July 1865 was the Metropolitan Fire Brigade Act. This placed the responsibility for the organisation and funding of London's fire brigade with the Metropolitan Board of Works (MBW), the local government body that preceded the London County Council.

The new Brigade came into being on 1 January 1866 and with it came a change of name from the London Fire Engine Establishment to the Metropolitan Fire Brigade. For the Brigade's first year, it was funded by the MBW finance committee initiating a half-penny in the pound rate,

together with a maximum central government contribution of £10,000 per annum and annual contributions from the parishes. It did not please the insurance companies to have to fund up to £12,000 a year, but in addition, the MBW could, if necessary, borrow up to £40,000 per annum to assist the financing of the Metropolitan Fire Brigade.

During the various Parliamentary debates of 1862–64, Massey Shaw continuously lobbied government ministers, MP's and local councillors for a much expanded fire brigade to protect the enormous fire risks across the London area, both in the developing business and commercial sectors, and of the population in their cramped housing. Early on in this process, Shaw proposed enlarging the Brigade from 19 fire stations to 43 and increasing the firefighting establishment from 129 firemen to 232.

In January 1866, this was, in fact, broadly the shape of the new Metropolitan Fire Brigade that covered a larger area of London from Hammersmith in the west, to Bow in the east, and from Hampstead in the north to Tooting in the south. The Brigade area was organised into four districts. The 'A' district covered the West End; 'B' the City and Central areas; the 'C' the East End; and the 'D' was the area south of

Another contemporary drawing of a fire engine demonstration, c.1870, organised by Massey Shaw to which members of the gentry and their ladies were invited. In this view of great activity by the riverside near Southwark Bridge, there are massed steam pumps at work and on the right is a wheeled escape ladder bringing down volunteers from the roof of the building.

> ❝ *The first steam fire engine appeared on the scene in 1829 and by the 1850s steamers were becoming more common.* ❞

the Thames. Each station had an Engineer on the strength and was commanded by a Superintendent. It was agreed that the planned cost of all this expansion was to be kept within £50,000 per year, but right from the start Shaw's plans were handicapped by a lack of funds and of the constant parsimonious attitude of his political masters.

As if to underline the dramatic and unpredictable nature of fire, on the very first morning of the new brigade's existence, it was tested to the extreme by another huge Thameside fire that broke out in St. Katherine's Dock, close by Tower Bridge. The fire originated in a jute store and was soon spreading right along the wharf frontage and its warehouses packed full of flammable goods. Massey Shaw dashed to the scene to take command and within a short time had committed most of his manual pumps to fighting the blaze. Inevitably, the Hodges brigade got in on the action with one of their powerful new steam pumps as did several brigades from the outer suburbs not under Shaw's command. Fortunately, the fire was finally contained after several hours but some £200,000 of damage was recorded to the affected riverside warehouses and their stocks.

It is likely that the St. Katherine's Dock fire convinced Massey Shaw that he should replace the MFB's front line manual pumps with steam power. The first steam fire engine appeared on the scene in 1829 and by the 1850s steamers were becoming more common. Shaw's predecessor, Braidwood, had for over ten years continually failed to utilise the superior pumping power and reliability of the steam fire engines, fearing that their high pressure water jets would damage the fabric of London's buildings. However, in a change of mind in 1860, Braidwood did finally order two steam pumps from Shand Mason Ltd of Blackfriars, although these were particularly heavy machines and took three horses to pull to fires.

When Shaw placed the first large orders for steamers for the MFB they were divided between the two most prominent suppliers, Merryweather and Sons of Greenwich; and Shand Mason Ltd of Blackfriars. Interestingly, the MFB orders were for compact sized models with moderate outputs of 350 gallons per minute, even though more powerful models were

London's Fire Horses

During Braidwood's years in the London Fire Engine Establishment, horses for pulling the fire engines had been hired from various livery stables in the central London area. However, as the fire engine 'fleet' increased when the Metropolitan Fire Brigade was born in 1866, Massey Shaw negotiated a contract with Thomas Tilling and Sons, a London horse bus company, for the supply of specially bred horses for fire service use. Bred from a stock of sturdy greys of about 15 to 16 hands in height, the MFB horses needed to be strong, for the newly introduced steam pumps weighed some three tons with a six-man crew and all equipment up. At one stage the MFB horse strength numbered some 300 steeds.

Before being handed over to the Brigade, Tilling's staff schooled the young MFB horses in being quick to respond to rein commands, and part of this training included three months spent as a lead horse in a four horse Tilling's bus plying its trade through some of the most densely populated and busy traffic of London town. The route from Peckham in south London to Oxford Circus was a favourite.

Once posted to a fire station, the horses were in the care of an MFB coachman, who normally drove the fire engine pulled by a pair of greys. The animals were extremely well cared for and were probably some of the best turned out animals in London. They enjoyed good feeding, regular veterinary care — Tilling's had their own horse hospital at Peckham — and lots of care and attention from the firemen and the families of those who lived on the fire station. MFB stations were normally allocated five pairs of horses, with two being 'on call'. The horses were stabled in stalls immediately behind the fire engines and could be quickly moved into position between the shafts when the fire bell was rung. Shaw had introduced a clip-on style harness that he had seen during an American trip and this greatly speeded up the hitching-up time, although it helped the crews when the more experienced horses would move of their own volition into position for shackling up.

Once at a working incident, the coachman would unclip the horses and take them to a quiet area away from the smoke, sparks and noise. Here they would be fed buns, sweets and other treats by an admiring crowd whilst the firemen went about their work.

available and already in use in northern brigades including Liverpool's. Nevertheless, the new London steamers were a great success, each pulled by two of the Brigade's new breed of horses giving Shaw's firemen far greater firefighting muscle than they could have dreamed of. No longer did London's fire brigade have to rely upon a small army of volunteer pumpers drawn from the inevitable crowd of onlookers to work the manual pumps. And it was also the end of Shaw's crews having to suffer the professional indignity of watching the two new Hodges private brigade steamers acquired in 1862, at work alongside the LFEE manuals.

Shaw continued to absorb himself in his work in the building up of the new brigade, supervising the building of the fire stations, recruiting new firemen, setting out harsh training routines for his existing crews, visiting various premises including theatres across central London to assess their

> 66 *With these hardy sailors came their language and terminology from the seagoing days.* 99

fire hazards, and of course, attending the regular outbreak of fires at all hours of the day and night. He had no deputy and although assisted by his small team of senior officers, Shaw's daily routine and that of his officers was a punishing one for the MFB had no proper administrative staff structure.

Faced with the challenge of virtually doubling the number of professional firemen for the new brigade, Shaw recruited exclusively from the ranks of sailors. Despite some criticism, Shaw knew from his own Irish seagoing experiences in his youth that sailors were strong, capable of working at heights, able to work under pressure, accept discipline and take orders without question. Needless to say, the new former seagoing recruits to the MFB proved their mettle almost as soon as they were placed into the expanding front line of London's fire force. With these hardy sailors came their language and terminology from the seagoing days. Very soon orders in the new brigade reflected those given and understood on board ship, such as 'Aloft', 'Avast', 'Below' and terms such as 'the deck' (the floor) becoming commonplace.

Shaw also spent some time talking to various manufacturers and one result was the introduction of a new firefighting uniform for the MFB. In 1833 the dark tunics introduced for the firemen of the new London Fire Engine Establishment were replaced by a navy blue double-breasted version with brass buttons. The tunic was lined with wool, with a stand up collar faced with scarlet. Each tunic had a red 'MFB' badge with the fireman's service number; the lower the number the more junior the fireman. Other new uniform items included heavy navy serge trousers, fine double-fronted leather boots, axe in pouch, belt, and a top coat for cold weather. A working overalls rig was also provided along with a seaman's round cap.

But the crowning glory of the new uniform was the issue of the MFB's own style of brass helmet. Shaw had given much consideration to the design of these during various overseas visits to both Europe and America. After inspecting the various styles in use he decided on a more compact version of the French 'pompiers' without any projections but with a

small front peak and larger neck curtain to protect the neck and ears from falling hot debris, together with a comb top section. The bold letters 'MFB' sat within a dragon embellishment and Shaw's much-copied new brass helmets became a Victorian symbol of British firefighters that was to last until the mid 1930s when the brass helmets were replaced by cork head-gear. Shaw, as befitted the leader of the London brigade, had a silver helmet of similar style to the brass version.

In 1867 came an important addition to the operational strength of the MFB when Shaw agreed to take over the life-saving work of the Royal Society for the Protection of Life from Fire. This entailed absorbing the 100 street corner wheeled fire escape stations from then on manned at night by MFB firemen. The firemen had a sentry box alongside the escape ladder and during the daytime hours the escape ladders would be pushed back to a daytime resting place.

The following years were full not just of operational action at the grow-ing number of fires attended, but with the steady growth of the capital's fire brigade, despite the constant struggle that Shaw had with the

All potential recruits to the Metropolitan Fire Brigade had to pass this stringent strength test that involved pulling on a block and tackle to raise a wheeled escape ladder into a vertical postition. Some 120 ft of rope was involved and the pull required to be exerted at the start of the test was 240 lbs.

❝ Shaw's much-copied new brass helmets became a Victorian symbol of British firefighters... ❞

Metropolitan Board of Works to fund the MFB at a level commensurate with its needs. In the late 1870s, the Brigade's headquarters in Watling Street were becoming totally inadequate, both as a large central fire station and as a training base for the MFB. The Board eventually gave way to Shaw and agreed to build a new headquarters on a $1\frac{3}{4}$ acre site at Southwark. Shaw's wife Anna, bore him four sons and two daughters and during the planning for the new headquarters Shaw demanded that the Chief Officers house should have no fewer than sixteen bedrooms. In the end, he had to relent, for his new residence known as Winchester House was built with slightly fewer rooms, although still a very imposing residence with a fine frontage. The whole new Southwark headquarters complex was opened in 1878 and its fire station and training school remain in use on the site today.

By now Shaw was travelling widely to propound his views on the need for greater fire safety, especially in places of public entertainment such as theatres. Paris was a favourite trip, but he also visited brigades in America, where at a fire engineers convention in Cincinatti he raised the question of tackling fires and their problems in the ever-growing number of high rise buildings. Shaw also visited brigades in Spain and Austria at this time. In 1871, the Foreign Office had asked Shaw to visit Egypt to advise on fire protection in Cairo, Alexandria and other centres and he took the opportunity of drilling some fire crews along the way.

In the early 1870s, Shaw and the activities of the London Brigade had become the regular focus of attention of a number of aristocratic and society gentlemen who regarded themselves as amateur 'fire buffs'. Shaw became increasingly socially involved with this group who included the extremely wealthy Duke of Sutherland, the Earl of Caithness and Lord Richard Grosvenor. Many of these gentlemen had set up their own fire brigades on their country estates. The Earl of Caithness had been a member of the committee that had organised the first fire engine trials at the Crystal Palace in 1863 and through this connection Shaw first met

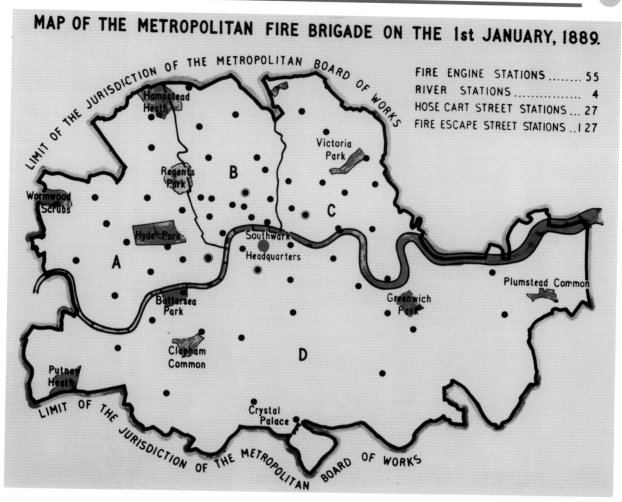

MAP OF THE METROPOLITAN FIRE BRIGADE ON THE 1st JANUARY, 1889.

FIRE ENGINE STATIONS 55
RIVER STATIONS 4
HOSE CART STREET STATIONS ... 27
FIRE ESCAPE STREET STATIONS ..127

A map of the London area covered by the Metropolitan Fire Brigade at January 1889.

Edward, Prince of Wales, or 'Bertie' as he was known to his friends. Like them, the Prince also had a healthy interest in all things to do with firefighting, no doubt sharing their view that the whole firefighting business was something akin to a sport.

However, this was a period of time when the Brigade was losing firemen at an alarming rate through resignation due not just to the long hours of duty and the harsh conditions of the job, but partly through a widespread concern over pensions. The families of married firemen had a particularly rough time. Often living in cramped rooms above the fire station, a wife and children had to contend with the onerous 24 hours a day, all week long routine. Time off to be with families was granted only with the goodwill of the station superintendent.

Whilst the old LFEE had been generous in its financial provision for the widows and families of firemen killed or injured on duty, despite Shaw's entreaties, the Metropolitan Board of Works was not at all benevolent in its attitude towards bereaved families. The example of the treatment

Shaw and the Fireman Prince

Massey Shaw probably first formally met Edward ('Bertie') Prince of Wales in 1863 at the Crystal Palace fire engine pumping trials and through the introduction of the Duke of Sutherland and Lord Richard Grosvenor, then started to move socially within the various activities of this elite circle. By 1865, Bertie and his aristocratic friends were beginning to turn up at fires in central London as spectators, and soon the Prince had a fire uniform kept at Chandos Street fire station, near Covent Garden, to enable the future King to attend fires once Shaw had sent word to him at his residence, Marlborough House. This practice lasted for many years and it was a regular occurrence for the Prince and his friends to spend an evening playing billiards with the duty crew at Chandos Street, literally waiting for a fire call to come in.

The formation of the London Auxiliary Fire Brigade in 1875 consolidated this arrangement for the heir to the throne to go to fires. On a number of occasions, notably the blaze on the icy cold night of 7 December 1882 that destroyed the Alhambra Theatre in Leicester Square, the Prince was in fact extremely close to immense danger. On this night, Shaw had sent a carriage to Marlborough House to collect Bertie and take him on to Leicester Square. The Prince was never left on his own, usually being accompanied by one of Shaw's officers.

About an hour after the first alarm and with twenty steamers hard at work, the Prince was assisting some firemen pull some hose lines further down an alleyway when part of the gable end wall of the theatre fell outwards, burying three firemen under red hot masonry and burning roof beams and striking five others working nearby. The Prince of Wales was unhurt but badly shaken yet quickly lent a hand to assist the rescue operation led by Shaw to frantically release the three buried men. Above them, the fire spewed out angrily in a bright red and orange pyrotechnic display. Another ten pumps were called to the scene and by 2.30 am, the fire had been contained within the theatre block but by then one fireman was dead and seven had been dug out seriously injured. Three of the injured were based at Chandos Street fire station.

Much later that morning, the Prince of Wales, accompanied by Massey Shaw, visited the injured men in Charing Cross Hospital. Both the future King and London's fire chief wore dark morning suits and top hats and Bertie's equerry carried seven boxes of cigars. After a short while, they quietly left the ward and went to the still-smoking ruins of the Alhambra nearby.

The next day, the *Times* duly reported the Prince's visit to the hospital to see the injured firemen and that Shaw had then taken him on to see the fire scene at first hand. The *Times* reporter knew full well that the Prince had been at the fire soon after the first call but, of course, few outside of the Metropolitan Fire Brigade really knew just what a fire buff the future monarch was.

❝ Ford heard the screams of another person and returned up the ladder to rescue a female. ❞

meted out to the widow of Fireman Joseph Ford caused an uproar, both amongst the brigade and the general public.

On the night of 7 October 1871, Ford had been on duty at a street escape station in Holborn and had pushed his heavy wheeled fire escape to a fire in a chemist's shop in Gray's Inn Road. Braving flames, great heat and thick smoke, he extended the ladder and ran up to rescue five persons trapped on floors above the spreading fire. Having got all these people safely down the escape ladder, Ford heard the screams of another person and returned up the ladder to rescue a female. As he dropped her safely into the arms of the crowd below, he became entangled with the wires of the under-slung rescue chute and was literally roasted alive by the ferocity of the flames. The Board of Works agreed to pay Ford's widow a pension of £1 per week but when public subscriptions in recognition of Ford's gallant acts grew to reach £1,000, the pension was promptly withdrawn.

Shaw viewed the growing number of outer London volunteer and parish brigades with some disdain because of their widely differing standards and competence. In 1875 he saw a opportunity to relieve some of the pressure on the MFB manpower haemorrhage by encouraging the formation of a London Auxiliary Fire Brigade. This was set up on the lines of a gentleman's club, with upper class candidates having to be recommended by an MFB Engineer and pay an entry fee of one guinea, together with an annual subscription. Members had to provide their own uniforms which had black instead of the brass buttons of the professional MFB crews, and black painted brass helmets. The auxiliaries trained under and accepted the orders of Shaw's regular MFB officers and were allowed to attend fires.

Shaw's workload continued unabated. He had introduced the newly-invented telegraph to all his fire stations as an improved means of communication. Queen Victoria had, by now, received Shaw on several occasions at Buckingham Palace, and he was invited to visit both Osborne House on the Isle of Wight, and Sandringham in Norfolk to report and advise on fire precautions at the royal palaces.

A later photograph of Captain (later Sir) Eyre Massey Shaw, the first Chief Officer of the Metropolitan Fire Brigade, in his firefighting uniform.

> 66 *At the end of 1878, Shaw was able to report that the Metropolitan Fire Brigade had attended 4,199 outbreaks of fire.* 99

In 1878, Shaw published what was to become one of his most widely read works, *Fire Protection — A Complete Manual of the Organisation, Machinery, Discipline and General Working of the Fire Brigade of London*. The same year he returned to an old theme when he published a further book entitled *Fires in Theatres*, the contents of which caused a sitting Parliamentary Select Committee to add theatre safety to its remit. Eventually this resulted in Shaw being asked to produce a report on the work needed to make all London's theatres safe from fire. Shaw's report to the government ran to 370 pages and was produced in a little over seven months.

Operatic Immortality

Despite his constant attacks on theatre owners and managements to improve fire safety, Massey Shaw was a keen theatre-goer. As the audience assembled for the first night in November 1882 of the new Gilbert and Sullivan comic-opera *Iolanthe* at the Savoy Theatre, W. S. Gilbert, the librettist, saw Shaw take his place in the stalls and immediately amended the libretto. Imagine Shaw's surprise when, instead of singing to the sentry, Private Willis, the Fairy Queen came down from the stage to the stalls and sang directly to Shaw:

'On fire that glows with heat intense
I turn the hose of common sense
And out it goes at small expense.
We must maintain our fairy law
That is the main on which to draw —
In that we gain a Captain Shaw!'

Then followed a chorus that may perhaps have been originally penned by Gilbert with knowledge of Shaw's dalliances with the society lady friends of the Prince of Wales:

Oh, Captain Shaw!
Type of true love kept under!
Could thy Brigade with cold cascade
Quench my great love I wonder?'

By the end of 1897, the Metropolitan Fire Brigade had closed all the street escape stations and replaced them with horse drawn fire engines carrying 50 ft wheeled escape ladders. The purpose of these escapes was purely that of rescue from upper floors and they were usually the first engine away to the scene of a call, closely followed by a steam pump to provide the firefighting water.

At the end of 1878, Shaw was able to report that the Metropolitan Fire Brigade had attended 4,199 outbreaks of fire. Over 2,500 were classified as 'small' being dealt with by hand pumps but there were, of course, a number of major blazes in this twelve month period that taxed the resources of the brigade. Shaw also reported that the force now had 48 operational fire stations across London, some of which ran with both a steam and back-up manual pump. There were now four river stations on the Thames, and 107 street escape posts. He was the driving force behind the installation of London's first street fire alarms in 1880. In 1883, Shaw received one of his more serious injuries whilst commanding an incident when he fell off a ladder. Although not breaking any bones, this accident left him with a permanent limp in his left leg.

Shaw's penchant for socialising with the aristocracy could have cost him his career. In 1886, Shaw, along with several other prominent personalities, was cited as co-respondent in the divorce of Lord and Lady Colin Campbell. The nub of the case was that Lord Campbell had brought the case on the grounds of his wife's adultery with four men,

> 66 *In 1883, Shaw received one of his more serious injuries whilst commanding an incident when he fell off a ladder.* 99

including the Duke of Marlborough and Captain Massey Shaw. The case eventually collapsed when the jury had to consider much conflict of evidence. Shaw was cleared, gaining costs into the bargain.

Amid all this activity, Shaw continued to battle with the Board of Works for sufficient funding to expand the MFB to better serve London's population, even occasionally going so far as to leak the contents of various confidential reports to London's newspapers in advance of Board meetings.

But change was on the way, for on 21 March 1889 came the abolition of the Metropolitan Board of Works and the creation of a new local authority for London — the London County Council (LCC) which, amongst other things, was to be responsible for the fire brigade. Such was the esteem that Shaw and his Brigade were held in that the new LCC decided to stage the very first Annual Parade of the MFB in Horse Guards Parade in 1889. No doubt it was with the Prince of Wales hand that the event soon became a Royal Review at which the Princess of Wales' was to present gallantry and long service medals. But on the day the event was completely overwhelmed by the sheer numbers who flocked to see the gathering and the police could simply not control the exuberance of the crowd. Chaos reigned and the main ceremonies were abruptly curtailed. Shaw was furious as, no doubt, were the members of the Royal Family and the elected members of the LCC.

Shaw had hoped that his relationships with his political masters might improve under the LCC but it was not to be. When Shaw returned from a month long overseas trip surveying various urban fire brigades, members of the LCC suspected that their Chief Fire Officer had been 'on holiday'. It was the final straw for Shaw, who had commanded and led London firefighters and its brigade for almost 30 years, through thick and thin. On 26 June 1891, he gave four months notice of his intention to retire.

Punch magazine published a poem and cartoon under the title of 'The Fire King's Abdication' calling for him to be knighted.

Southwark fire station, part of the new Metropolitan Fire Brigade's headquarters complex in Southwark Bridge Road, c.1897. The three fire engines are (from left): a Merryweather steamer; a 50 ft wheeled escape; and a second steam pump, a Shand Mason.

Shaw's greatest moment came the next week when as the President of the National Fire Brigades Union, he presided over the Union's National Review at the Crystal Palace. Not unsurprisingly Edward, Prince of Wales, attended along with his cousin the Emperor of Germany, the Duke of Clarence and the Duke of Edinburgh. In front of a huge and well-behaved crowd basking in the summer sunshine, 56 galloping fire engines from over 130 British fire brigades and some 1,400 firemen resplendent in their brass helmets paraded past the royal visitors and Captain Massey Shaw.

Punch's earlier public demand was met on 30 October 1891, when a knighthood was duly conferred by Queen Victoria upon 'The Fire King',

> 66 *…Some 1,400 firemen resplendent in their brass helmets paraded past the royal visitors and Captain Massey Shaw.* 99

on the day that Sir Eyre Massey Shaw, KCB, hung his fire uniform up for the very last time. That evening at his Southwark Headquarters there was a full gathering of as many of Shaw's officers and men as could be spared. Amongst his many gifts was a fine engraved clock from Queen Victoria.

In a voice unusually full of emotion, the 61 year old 'Fire King' spoke falteringly to the assembled throng. Afterwards, his message was conveyed to all those men of the brigade who were unable to be present.

A contemporary painting of a Victorian London street fire scene with a steam pump at work.

Captain Sir Eyre Massey Shaw's final words to his beloved Metropolitan Fire Brigade drew strongly on a maritime analogy:

'Shadows may come across your route, mists and fogs may obscure the vision of those in charge, the darkness of night may come down and obscure on every side, yet there is a compass on board and those in charge can continue their course onward, confidently and patiently, until the mists disperse and the day dawns....

You know your duty. Your position is this: The inhabitants of this vast metropolis, numbering some five million persons, desire to be protected from the ravages of fire and have employed you for this purpose....

It is your duty always to be loyal...'

CHAPTER SIX
The Motor Age

Upon his retirement in 1891, Shaw was succeeded by his deputy, James Sexton Simmons. The new Chief had an engineering background within the brigade but he soon found the 'Fire King's' act a most difficult one to follow. At first, all appeared well, but Simmons had none of Shaw's natural leadership charisma that had helped to bond the firemen of the Metropolitan Fire Brigade (MFB) together into a tight and disciplined group of professionals. In addition, the aristocratic group of fire enthusiasts who had for many years supported Shaw and his drive for development during the 1870 and 1880s began to fall apart when the Duke of Sutherland died. The Prince of Wales was now increasingly participating in matters of state and had little time for firefighting matters and the Brigade therefore no longer had the regular royal support it had informally enjoyed for two decades and more.

Edward VII — 1909 Review

One of King Edward VII's last official engagements before his death was on 19 July 1909 when he took the salute at the Annual Parade of the LFB in Hyde Park. After presenting a number of gallantry and long service awards to the very smartly turned out ranks of brass-helmeted firemen paraded in front of their shining motor and horse drawn fire engines, the King recounted his earlier days with Captain Eyre Massey Shaw. Edward VII told the assembled ranks that as a younger amateur fireman, he had liked nothing better that to help the Brigade extinguish fires, and that even now, he still watched the development of firefighting in London with great interest. The Monarch went on to say that he had never seen a finer body of men, and exhorted them to continue to always be zealous and active in their duties. The Annual Parade ended with a most impressive drive and gallop past the King's saluting position.

Soon after this event, it was announced that Edward VII had sanctioned two new medals to be known as the King's Fire Service Medal and the King's Police Medal, and their modern day equivalents are still awarded for conspicuous devotion to duty, not just to London firefighters, but to those from across the British Fire Service.

" The Prince of Wales was now increasingly participating in matters of state and had little time for firefighting... "

In 1902, the Merryweather Fire King self propelled fire engine had arrived but the MFB was not at first convinced of its efficacy, preferring instead to convert an existing Merryweather steamer to self-propulsion in the Brigade workshops. Here this unique conversion is pictured in operational service with its officer and crew outside Whitefriars fire station, just off Fleet Street, c.1903.

MOTOR FIRE ENGINE.
WHITEFRIARS, M.F.B.,

One of the LFB's Merryweather Fire King's self propelled steam fire engines and crew pictured in the yard of Southwark headquarters, c.1908. This was one of a batch of six that the Brigade eventually purchased at this time. Unfortunately, the Fire King's slow road performance and the onset of the petrol engine soon made these magnificent looking fire engines redundant and by 1916, they had all been replaced by motor pumps.

Despite this, the London County Council (LCC) agreed that MFB firemen should for the first time be entitled to an annual week of leave along with a regular day off each week. Widow's annuities were also increased by £5 to £20 per year. But it was still a demanding life for London's fire crews with long working hours. There were now 825 uniformed men in the force and the LCC was not slow in pointing out that the annual cost of the MFB had risen to almost £130,000 per annum: some of this could be attributed to new fire stations, long requested by Massey Shaw during his latter years of command. These included those opened at Brompton, East Dulwich, Hackney, New Cross and Wandsworth.

Unfortunately, Chief Officer Simmons increasingly showed that he was not up to the job. With a clear loss of morale across the Brigade over conditions of service and the still overly long working week, Simmons' days came to an end when he was discovered to have been involved in a commercial deal involving the supply of equipment to the Brigade. After a hearing before the LCC, Simmons was struck off the Brigade strength.

When seeking a replacement, the LCC opted for an 'officer and a gentlemen' as London's fire chief. In the autumn of 1896 they considered a list of over 80 army and naval candidates before appointing Captain Lionel De Latour Wells, a retired Royal Navy officer. Wells immediately set about trying to improve some of the working conditions despised by the

❝ Just before the turn of the century,
the Brigade was on average turning
out to about ten outbreaks of fire
a day. ❞

firemen. One of his early changes was to allow married firemen who lived in accommodation at their fire station to take their meals with their families. Another of his changes was to cease the practice of reducing a fireman's place in the promotion seniority list if found guilty of a minor disciplinary offence.

On the equipment side, more steam pumps continued to be regularly introduced to replace the older and well worn manuals. When the LCC took over responsibility for the Brigade in 1889, manual pumps still out-weighed the newer steamers. However, by 1897 new steamers were being commissioned at a significant rate and by 1899, all of the LFB's 90 front line fire pumps were horse drawn steamers. The old manual pumpers were finally relegated to reserve duties and within two years had finally been disposed of.

Chief Officer Wells was also active in introducing more effective fire-fighting and rescue equipment. In 1897 he introduced a horse-drawn wooden 50 ft wheeled escape ladder, very similar to that in use by the street escape stations. Upon arrival at the fire, the escape ladder could be immediately 'slipped' off the fire engine onto its large carriage wheels and extended into the building to provide both a rescue staircase and an access into the premises for fire crews. The much faster response speed of the new horse drawn escape ladders sounded the death knell of the street escape station that had for so long been part of the London scene. By the end of 1897 they had all been closed, with their firemen transferring to fire stations.

Another significant innovation was the introduction of canvas hose to replace the heavy leather version that was both heavy and unwieldy to use. For the first time, lengths of hose could be carried in the lockers on the pumps in a rolled form, although it was still bulky and even heavier when wet, requiring to be hung up a drying hoist inside the drill towers of the newer fire stations being opened.

Just before the turn of the century, the Brigade was on average turning out to about ten outbreaks of fire a day. In 1898, the number of street corner

This c.1912 view of a public drill demonstration at Southwark headquarters shows plenty of fire engines at work. On the left is a horse drawn wooden turntable ladder extended up to its 85 ft maximum height against one of the tall drill towers. A line of hose has been taken up the ladder. In the centre is a Merryweather motor pump working alongside a Shand Mason steamer whose horses are still somewhat unusually still in the shafts. Both pumps have some impressive hose lines to work, whilst on the right are some parked 50 ft wheeled escape ladders, no doubt used for recruit and ordinary training sessions. This part of the old Southwark headquarters is still in use today as part of the modern LFB's Training School complex.

fire alarms was increased to over 500 and had a simple 'pull handle' arrangement connected to the nearest fire station. When activated, the crew would immediately turn out to the location of the fire alarm from where the caller would, hopefully, inform firemen of the precise address of the outbreak. Unfortunately, the number of false alarm fire calls given at street fire alarms increased so much that in 1895 an Act of Parliament imposed penalties of a fine of £25 and up to three months imprisonment for giving a false alarm of fire.

With the coming of the first internal combustion engine, the early years of the 20th century were a time of continual experimentation and development for both the Metropolitan Fire Brigade, and other brigades around the country as they considered how best to adapt the internal combustion engine for fire service work.

The Sidney Street Seige, Winston Churchill and the London Fire Brigade

The Sidney Street siege began just before midnight on 16 December 1911, when a break-in was reported at a jewellers shop in London's East End. When police arrived in some numbers, they were fired upon wildly and the gunshots wounded five officers. The gang members then fled into the night but not before one of the gunmen was accidentally shot in the back. Three of the policemen died soon after of their wounds.

The gang went to ground in a safe house in the East End but called a doctor to treat the injured criminal. Such was the man's injuries that the doctor left the house to fetch further medicines and dressings, but on his return the criminal was dead and the rest of the gang had gone. A search revealed a girl still burning documents and several weapons and ammunition which indicated that the gang was an anarchist group.

The police then began an extensive manhunt across the East End that was to end during the early morning of 3 January 1911 when they were led to 100 Sidney Street, a four storey lodging house just off the Mile End Road. There the gang had apparently taken refuge. Once the property was surrounded the police attempted to make contact and encourage the gang to surrender, but this appeal was met with a volley of shots from within the house. Another policeman was wounded. More police were then ordered to the scene and the area cordoned off, following which it was decided to request a contingent of the military. By this time a large crowd of onlookers had gathered and within the hour, a company of Scots Guards arrived and took up strategic positions along Sidney Street as the siege continued.

Another arrival later in the morning at Sidney Street was the Home Secretary, Mr Winston Churchill MP, who took charge of proceedings from the senior police officer. Soon after, more shots rang out from the house and these were returned by the Scots Guards. Smoke was then seen coming from an upper window and a street fire alarm was pulled. Within several minutes, a motor pump escape and motor pump from Mile End Road fire station arrived at Sidney Street,

shortly followed by another motor pump from Whitechapel. However, all the LFB crews were instructed by the Home Secretary to stand by and await his further orders. As they did so, the fire on the upper floor of the house continued to develop with flames showing at the front windows of the top floor. Occasional gunfire was still heard from within the house but it was not until all had been quiet for some further time, when the fire had broken out through the roof, that the Home Secretary gave the go ahead for the firemen to begin to tackle the flames.

A 50 ft wheeled escape was pitched to the second floor and a hose line worked into the front room on that level. Another jet was got to work from the rear whilst a third hose line was brought to bear over an adjacent roof. By the time the fire was progressively brought under control, much damage had occurred throughout all floors of 100 Sidney Street. As firemen began to search through the smouldering debris, a heavy hearthstone crashed down from the top floor, fatally injuring a District Officer. Amid the destruction wreaked by the fire, firemen found two badly burnt bodies, one of which had apparently been shot in the head.

At the subsequent inquest, the senior LFB officer present at Sidney Street was asked why he had not taken steps to tackle the fire as soon as the LFB arrived. As a result, the Home Secretary was called to give evidence. Winston Churchill unequivocally told the Coroner that he took full responsibility for preventing the LFB from immediately carrying out their firefighting and humanitarian duties, following which a verdict of Justifiable Homicide was recorded on the two bodies. At the Inquest it was believed that the fire could have been started by the anarchists, perhaps as a diversionary tactic, or that a bullet had punctured a pipe and ignited gas. Either way, the fatal blaze at 100 Sidney Street, London E1 will be remembered as a most unusual event in the Brigade's history and the only occasion when the Home Secretary personally stopped the LFB from going into action.

One of the first true self-propelled fire vehicles of the Brigade was this 10 hp car acquired in 1903. With chassis and bodywork modifications carried out by the Brigade workshops, it had no inbuilt firefighting equipment and ran simply as a general purpose tender before being replaced in 1910.

Even before the end of the 19th century, there had been several attempts to couple a petrol engine to drive a reciprocating fire pump. One of the earliest British examples was that of 1895 for the Hon. Evelyn Ellis' private estate fire brigade in Datchet in Buckinghamshire. This consisted of a trailer mounted Daimler engine that drove a single cylinder pump via a belt drive.

By the turn of the century, the use of motorised vehicles gathered pace. In 1901, Liverpool Fire Brigade converted a 24 hp Daimler chassis to carry a 60 gallon water tank linked to a cylinder of carbonic gas that discharged water through hose reel tubing. In the same year, the Eccles Brigade in Lancashire were the first of several brigades to adapt early car chassis, such as the Bijou, for fire service use. Despite its modest 7 hp engine, the Bijou managed to carry a crew of five plus the driver together with a ladder, some hose and extinguishers.

The London-based Merryweather and Sons Company had been building manual pumps since the 18th century and horse drawn steam pumps since the 1850s for home and overseas fire brigade customers. In 1899, conscious, no doubt, of the growing threat of the petrol engine to their business, Merryweather introduced their first self-propelled steam fire engine. The model was called the 'Fire King' and the rear wheels of the vehicle were chain driven from the 30 hp two cylinder reciprocating steam engine that also powered the fire pump. Capable of delivering up to 500 gallons of water per minute and with the boiler fuelled by either coal or paraffin, the new Merryweather horseless fire engine carried sufficient water and fuel to travel almost ten miles. Although cleverly engineered, the Fire

> ❝ *The MFB had in fact, commissioned its first self-propelled vehicle in 1902.* ❞

King was very heavy, weighing in at $5\frac{1}{2}$ tons. As a result, the braking system left a lot to be desired and although capable with some inducement by the driver of 25 mph on a level road, the hill climbing performance of the Fire King was poor. It certainly did not compare with the overall turnout speed of a two horse escape or pump.

The MFB, therefore, did not immediately take to Merryweather's Fire King, preferring to spend several years adapting one of the company's existing horse drawn steamers in the MFB fleet to self-propulsion. In trials and operational use, this MFB conversion also suffered from being

Delivering the Water

Leather hose had been invented for firefighting use during the 17th century and consisted of a strip of leather riveted into a circular section by copper rivets and it was a great advance when several lengths of hose could be joined together to form a longer line of hose. Unfortunately, these were hardly watertight and even under very moderate pressure from manual pumps would leak like the proverbial sieve. Another drawback of leather hose was its propensity to crack very easily and to combat this, leather hose was regularly and liberally anointed with a concoction of tallow and cod oil. Then in the late 1790s came a loom that could weave flax yarn to produce a pipe without a seam and although much lighter than the leather hose lengths, the flax hose also let water through its outer jacket and was not widely adopted. However, in the early 19th century came the first attempt to line the internal surface of flax firefighting hose with a rubber solution to prevent percolation. Once this technique had been perfected, flax delivery hose in lengths up to 100 ft became commonplace. Carried in rolls in the lockers of London's fire engines, each length of hose was joined together by round-thread screw couplings and every fireman carried a hose spanner for this purpose on his leather belt. Towards the end of the 19th century, few other British fire brigades had adopted the London round-thread coupling, preferring vee-thread, gas pipe thread or several types of bayonet connection. This was to prove a serious difficulty both during enemy raids in both World War I and particularly World War II when fire brigades reinforced each other, only to find that their respective hoses would not join up without special adaptors. Right up until after the Second World War, generations of London firemen proudly called themselves 'The Round Threads'.

> ❝ *...It was soon evident that these early cars were simply not sturdy or powerful enough to serve as proper fire engines.* ❞

unable to provide sufficient steam on rising gradients to maintain a good road speed and was converted back to a horse drawn status in 1905. However, in that same year, the Brigade must have seen some merit in the self-propelled steamers for they ordered six Fire Kings from Merryweather & Sons for delivery over a three year period.

The MFB had in fact, commissioned its first self-propelled vehicle in 1902. This was a Stanley steam car for the use of Chief Officer Wells. With these first moves to harness the petrol engine for fire engine use, later on that same year, the Brigade took delivery from Merryweather of what was to become their last horsedrawn steam pump. Perhaps more significantly, in the autumn of 1902 the Brigade purchased two small 12 hp two cylinder car chassis and converted them into tenders fitted with a tank carrying 50 gallons of water that was expelled through pressure from carbon dioxide gas. These fire engines did not carry ladders and did not last in operational service very long as it was soon evident that these early cars were simply not sturdy or powerful enough to serve as proper fire engines.

This was a Merryweather 'Greenwich Gem' model having a two-cylinder compound steam pump rated at 500 gallons per minute. Its cost was £500.

But it was not the MFB that was to enter the record books for being responsible for the first truly bespoke motorised fire engine. Surprisingly, this honour went to the small Tottenham Fire Brigade who protected the residents of their small borough in north London. In early 1902, Tottenham's Superintendent Eddington produced an outline design for a bespoke motorised fire engine. This specification called for a petrol engine vehicle able to carry a 50 ft wheeled wooden escape ladder and have an inbuilt 60 gallon chemical extinguisher fed through hose reel tubing on a rotating drum.

An order was placed with Merryweathers to build the vehicle and in 1903 Tottenham Fire Brigade proudly took delivery of the first British motor propelled fire engine. The historic Merryweather was powered by

One of the Brigade's early Dennis fire engines was this emergency tender. Based at Clerkenwell fire station, this vehicle's primary purpose was to provide breathing apparatus sets for use at serious fires. This view c.1914 shows some of the early one hour duration oxygen sets in use, together with a petrol generator carried on board to power some basic floodlighting at incidents.

a 4 cylinder 30 hp Aster engine and was housed in a new fire station at Tottenham specifically designed with the motor age in mind, rather than the stabling and other needs of horse drawn fire engines.

Not to be outdone, Chief Officer Sly of the nearby Finchley Borough Brigade also had plans for a motorised pump and in 1904 his brigade took delivery of a similar Merryweather/Aster. Like the Tottenham vehicle, Finchley's Merryweather also carried a wooden wheeled escape ladder and chemical extinguisher. However, the true significance of Finchley's new fire engine was that it was the first to have its inbuilt fire pump driven by a power take off from the road engine. The pump delivered 500 gallons per minute and it also carried 180 ft of canvas delivery hose. The Finchley Merryweather was the world's first truly self-contained motorised pumping fire engine and is today part of the vehicle collection in London's Science Museum.

Whilst all this pioneering motor fire engine activity was going on in two small local brigades in north London, the MFB itself was about to undergo a major change. The body responsible for the Brigade, the London County Council (LCC) felt that with the increasing number of London organisations having the word 'Metropolitan' in their titles, the

❝ Over 100 years on, this title is still today proudly borne on London's fire engines, firefighters' uniforms and much else besides... ❞

Brigade should be formally renamed 'The London Fire Brigade (LFB)'. As the MFB had been created by Act of Parliament, it required further Parliamentary legislation for the change and once this had been enacted in April 1904, the MFB became the London Fire Brigade. In practice the firefighting force of the capital had been known by this unofficial title for some time. Over 100 years on, this title is still today proudly borne on London's fire engines, firefighters' uniforms and much else besides, and the mention of the London Fire Brigade commands respect and admiration amongst fellow firefighters around the world.

In 1905, the London Fire Brigade ordered its first turntable ladder (TL). This was still drawn by two horses and had three individual telescoped wooden ladder sections that could be extended by hand winding mechanisms up to full working height of 85 ft. London's first TL was also rotated by hand and appeared successful in its operational and training use. Within six months, the Brigade ordered a second model, although this had its ladder sections extended by compressed air stored in cylinders on board.

It is also interesting to record that during these early years of the 20th century, the London Brigade had a brief flirtation with battery electric driven pumps. These were the product of the Cedes Electric Traction Company, by then makers of early electric trolleybuses, and in 1906, the LFB ordered eleven Cedes battery electric fire engines for use as escape vans. Merryweather & Sons also produced a similar electric model. In the event, at a time when the increasing number of new motor pumps were showing themselves to be increasingly reliable and powerful, the two ton deadweight of lead/acid batteries under the bonnet of the electric pumps together with problems of battery maintenance soon resulted in their obsolescence.

In 1906 the London Fire Brigade (LFB) took delivery of its first true factory built motorised fire engine. This was built by John Morris Ltd on a Belsize chassis and carried a 50 ft wheeled escape and was known as an escape van. The Brigade then committed itself to the full adoption of

> 66 *In 1906 the London Fire Brigade*
> *took delivery of its first true factory*
> *built motorised fire engine.* 99

This petrol Merryweather/ Hatfield pump was one of six ordered by the LFB in 1907. These were the first Brigade's motor pumps to have a fire pump driven off the road engine. These Merryweathers were chain driven and could reach 30 mph, and when working at fires were able to deliver up to 500 gallons per minute of firefighting water.

motorised fire engines, both escape vans and pumps. Turning to its long association with Merryweather & Sons, the LFB ordered six Hatfield model motorised pumps from the Greenwich concern. Three new fire stations opened during 1906 were all designed to accommodate motor fire engines. The new stations concerned were those at Wapping, Lee Green and Tooley Street, near Tower Bridge.

One emerging fire engine company of this time was soon to become a major player on the British scene. The Dennis Brothers company started life in a small shop at Guildford in Surrey in 1895, firstly manufacturing bicycles before expanding into motor powered tricycles and then cars. The two founding Dennis brothers, John and Raymond, built their first fire

engine in 1908. This was a pump for the City of Bradford Fire Brigade and cost the princely sum of £900. Powered by a White & Poppe 60 hp engine with a four-speed gearbox, it had a power take-off that drove a Gwynne-Sargent centrifugal pump.

The Bradford Dennis naturally attracted a lot of attention from other fire brigades at a time when motorised fire engines were increasingly replacing steam and horse drawn pumps. In 1910, the London Brigade placed an order for ten of the same Dennis model as Bradfords, thus beginning a long lasting relationship between the company and the capital's fire brigade that was to last for 80 years. The early London Dennis motor pumps had solid rubber tyres with steel studded fabric gaiters to combat the risk of skidding on wet tramlines.

Not unsurprisingly, in the face of the increasing reliability and power of the motor fire engine, the attraction of the Merryweather 'Fire King' steam self-propelled model began to fade. By 1916, Merryweathers took a sensible commercial decision to move exclusively into the motorised market as an increasing number of enquiries were received from city and urban fire brigades who, like the LFB, wanted to dispense with steam

From 1910, the London Fire Brigade took delivery of its first Dennis fire engines, and over the next seventy years it became a regular customer of fire engines built at the Company's factory at Guildford. This first batch of ten were all in operational service by 1914 and included this pump escape attached to Tooting fire station. These were some of the first LFB machines to have a single 'first aid' firefighting hosereel mounted centrally and fed from an inbuilt 50 gallon water tank, although the provision for the crew hanging on each side of the Dennis was still pretty spartan.

" The early London Dennis motor
pumps had solid rubber tyres with
steel studded fabric gaiters to
combat the risk of skidding..."

and adopt motor power across their fire engine fleets. Interestingly, Merryweather's major 19th century British steam competitor, Shand Mason, resisted the temptation to move into complete motorisation. The LFB had purchased a number of Shand Mason steamers in the second half of the 19th century and as late as 1913, Shand Mason was still experimenting with fitting one of their steam pumps onto the rear of a Daimler motor chassis. The Shand Mason Company was finally acquired by Merryweather & Sons in 1922.

In Captain Wells' last years of service he introduced two motor canteen vans able to serve hot drinks and basic refreshments at the scene of major fires. This was much welcomed by LFB firemen who were still working very long hours and could often be detained 'damping down' for some considerable time in all weathers at a protracted incident. Other new motorised fire engines included six new 85 ft turntable ladders to replace the older horsedrawn models. Four of these were mounted on Tilling-Stevens petrol electric chassis, whilst the other two were on Cedes battery electric chassis. All six turntable ladders had their ladder movements (extension, elevation angle and turntable rotation) powered by the chassis motors. This was yet another first for the Brigade as the motor fire engine progressively replaced horse power across the front line of the LFB. The end of horse drawn fire engines in London was in sight.

CHAPTER SEVEN

The First World War and Beyond

When Great Britain declared war on Germany on 4 August 1914, the London Fire Brigade had 38 motor escapes, 38 motor pumps and 11 electric turntable ladders in operational use. In addition, there were still a number of reserve horse drawn fire engines. The total uniformed strength of the LFB was 1,251 uniformed officers and firemen.

It was, of course, a time of great concern, not just because of the international situation between the great powers. Within days of the outbreak some 280 London firemen who were army and navy reservists were called up. In addition, a further 120 volunteered for military service with the result that by the autumn of 1914, the LFB was seriously under strength. Another issue was that just before the outbreak of war there had been some optimism amongst the Brigade that the London County Council (LCC) might increase the pay scales for all ranks and consider an increase in the leave entitlement to one day off in seven. In the gloomy circumstances, the LCC deferred any consideration of this 'for at least six months or the end of the war' whichever might be the earlier.

Interestingly, the government did not seem to consider London to be vulnerable to aerial attack by the enemy despite the fact that there were some major raids in April 1915 by Zeppelin airships which started major fires in towns in Eastern England. However, there were a few minor raids on the London area and on 8 September 1915 a single Zeppelin high explosive and incendiary attack caused 29 separate fires in the Wood Street and Cheapside areas of the City of London. Twenty-two motor pumps dealt with the outbreaks and one fireman was killed during the bombing.

66 *...The government did not seem to consider London to be vulnerable to aerial attack by the enemy...* 99

The aftermath of a Zeppelin bombing raid on the City of London, 8 September 1915. This is some of the damage caused in Little Britain, EC, near St. Paul's. One fireman was killed during the raid. Three of the London firemen pictured damping down are wearing additional waterproof topcoats and their branch has a hand-controlled valve, probably one of the first examples of its kind.

When in 1916 conscription into the armed forces was introduced, professional firemen such as all those in the LFB were exempted, although volunteer and rural 'retained' firefighters throughout the country were not. To bolster the diminished numbers of firemen in the Brigade, the War Office allocated several hundred men from the London Rifle Volunteers, a sort of early form of 'Home Guard', whilst The Royal Engineers placed some lorries and drivers at the disposal of the LFB. In addition the London Salvage Corps, a uniformed body set up by the insurance companies to attend fires and mitigate damage by water and

> ❝ *The depleted Brigade struggled on and often had to reduce crew numbers...* ❞

smoke to the fabric and contents of buildings, also offered to assist the LFB at major fires. Salvage corps were also established in Glasgow and Liverpool.

The depleted Brigade struggled on and often had to reduce crew numbers until August 1917, when the City of London suffered the first of three daylight raids caused by German Gotha bombers. Circling unchallenged over St. Paul's Cathedral, the enemy aircraft and their incendiary bombs lit many fires in the buildings below, including the main General Post Office headquarters. Over three days, some 219 Londoners

The Brigade Says Farewell to its Last Horses

A significant event in the history of the Brigade took place at Kensington fire station, Old Court Place, in late 1921. The rapid adoption of motor power in the LFB since the end of the World War I had slowly seen the horse-drawn fleet steadily diminish, until Kensington's turntable ladder was the last horse drawn London fire engine remaining 'on the run'. Chief Officer Dyer decided that this important event should be properly marked and on 21 November 1921 quite a large gathering of Brigade senior officers and personnel assembled in Old Court Place to say farewell to the last horses of the LFB. A correspondent for the Daily Telegraph reported:

'Punctually at two o'clock in the afternoon, a gentleman undistinguished from the well-dressed passers-by in Kensington High Street approached the fire station and pulled the fire bell. A daring thing to do, but the police officers in attendance looked on and never interfered. The double doors of the fire station were thrown open and with that alacrity which the London Fire Brigade never fails to display, there tumbled out in succession, all fully manned, a fire escape on a motor carriage, two motor pumps, and — finest sight of all — the horsed turntable ladder, drawn by Lucy and Nora, two perfectly-conditioned and groomed bay horses. Both knew the meaning of the alarm quite as well as the firemen and had ears as acute.

'"Hi-Hi! Hi-Hi!" How good to hear the cry again as the horsed fire engine dashed into the traffic of Kensington's busiest street. Four brass helmeted comrades rode with Coachman George Cox and they gave the great London fireman's cry with lusty vigour for the very last time. Those who heard the cry distantly fade away realised that something had gone out of London's life. The London Fire Brigade had had its last horsed turnout.'

The camera catches an historic event in Brigade history when on 21 November 1921, the very last horse drawn fire engine was withdrawn from service. This was a turntable ladder based at Kensington fire station in Old Court Place. Saying farewell to the last horses of the London Fire Brigade is Chief Officer Dyer with some of his senior officers.

died in these attacks and the Cabinet lost no time in recalling from the colours all the LFB men who had been called up or had joined as volunteers. By the end of 1917, the Brigade was back up to full strength.

However, it was not just the air raids that posed great risks during this wartime period. Many temporary munitions factories had been set up in various parts of the country and a number of these were in operation in the Greater London area. In January 1917, a small fire broke out in a large riverside armaments factory in Silvertown, east London. This area was within the Borough of West Ham and one of their motor pumps was called to the outbreak. As the West Ham crew were dealing with the fire, there was a huge explosion that wrecked the entire building. Two of the West Ham firemen were killed instantly and their motor pumps blown to bits. Sixty-nine residents in nearby houses died and the massive explosion set fire to a nearby gas holder. Huge embers were sucked up into the updraft and drifted across the river to set fire to a tar works and other properties in Greenwich. Houses several miles away in Blackheath, on the south side of the Thames, had their windows blown in. To further add to the general panic, the blast had set off many street fire alarms in the LFB's area of east London, and those that had not actuated were pulled by residents who had heard the blast and could

" Huge embers were sucked up into the updraft and drifted across the river to set fire to a tar works..."

A twin turntable ladder attack on a major fire in a dockside warehouse in Wapping, east London. The view is probably taken about an hour into firefighting operations and it appears that for safety reasons, all crews have been withdrawn from close-quarters firefighting within the building and are containing the fire to the affected building. March 1929. (*Daily Mirror*)

> 66 *Many persons were trapped in a
> basement being used as an air raid
> shelter...* 99

now see the distant orange glow and black pall of smoke rising up into
the sky. Amid all this frantic activity, the LFB despatched 29 motor
pumps and two fireboats to assist the overwhelmed remains of the
West Ham Brigade deal with the disaster and its aftermath, remaining
in attendance for ten days.

Another outcome of the 1917 air raids on the City of London was
that the Home Secretary required a better co-ordination of all the
local fire and industrial works fire brigades across the 750 square mile
Greater London area. This was aimed at providing a more effective
reinforcement scheme and although a large number of these brigades
in the outer suburbs only had a single motor or horse drawn pump
to protect a small borough or parish, it was felt that they could all
contribute to a more collective effort. The Chief Officer of the LFB,

Three firemen who have
suffered burn injuries are
taken to hospital in a senior
officer's car following a fire
in Commercial Road, E1, in
November 1930.

Lieutenant-Commander Sladen, was designated in overall charge of this regional fire force if it was needed. In addition, all LFB fire stations were linked by special telephones to give early warning of enemy attack and fire off maroons as a form of public alert.

Only weeks later the new schemes were tested when in December 1917 six German aircraft dropped 276 incendiary bombs across a wide area of London and started 52 separate serious fires. Under the new re-inforcement arrangements, motor fire engines from Twickenham and Wembley in Middlesex came into central London to assist LFB firemen in the Shoreditch district and conversely, London pumps were sent to help out at a number of fires in the outer suburbs. The last major raid of the war was on 28 January 1918 when high explosives and incendiaries fell on an area of the West End. Forty-one people were killed with the worst incident occurring at the Odhams Press printing works in Long Acre, Covent Garden. Many persons were trapped in a basement being used as an air raid shelter and LFB teams were able to tunnel into the compacted debris and bring all those trapped out to safety.

The scene of devastation following a 20 pump fire involving the People's Palace, a popular music hall in the Mile End Road, Stepney, E1, on 25 February 1931. The probable cause was recorded as a carelessly discarded cigarette end starting a small smouldering fire in one of the seats as the theatre was shut down for the night. (*Planet News*)

Over the years firefighters have had to be prepared to work in all weathers, and this view shows operations during a serious fire in a large warehouse on Butlers Wharf, Southwark, SE1, on 9 March 1931 during a spell of sub-zero weather. There is plenty of ice formed by the firefighting water run-off and the three firemen in this crew are also pretty well iced up.

When peace was finally declared in November 1918, some 567 bombs containing 75 tons of high explosive and 355 incendiary bombs had been dropped on the Greater London area, causing the deaths of 524 people and injuring 1,264. Between 1915 and 1918 there had been 24 major air raid attacks. Few firemen of the LFB would have thought that this was but a taste of what was to come during the 1940–41 Blitz.

One immediate issue that had been festering during the last year of the war was the growing pressure from LFB ranks for better pay and conditions of service. After some protracted discussions and arbitration, London's firemen won the right to be represented by a trade union. This led to the formation of the London Fire Brigade Representative Body and its first secretary, James Bradley, was later to hold the same post in the Fire Brigades Union which was subsequently set up to represent firemen's interests nationally. In late 1918, the new body won a wage increase of five shillings a week together with an entitlement to one day's leave in ten. Perhaps more significantly, in 1919 the LCC agreed to rates of pay parity with the police service and the introduction of a two shift duty system. This latter improvement to LFB firemen's

❝ In late 1918, the new body won a wage increase of five shillings a week. . . ❞

This London fireman is seen testing one of the Brigade's updated new street fire alarms introduced in 1931. The new fire alarms used numerical coding circuits and replaced the existing 1,650 pull-handle manual alarms that were very prone to malicious false alarm calls, especially when children were around. The new system also incorporated a telephone link to a district control room for the use of fire crews. Pocock Street, Southwark, 5 May 1931 (*Sport & General*)

An unusual view of a street scene during a large fire in the Royal London Insurance building, High Holborn, EC, on 16 June 1932 with the soldier on the war memorial looking on.

working conditions meant almost a doubling of the Brigade strength. Another hard fought concession won by the Representative Body was that for the first time, all ranks up to that of station officer were not required to live on a London fire station. Station officers and above continued to work very long hours, often many days and nights of continuous duty.

These improvements to a London fireman's lot also coincided with the government appointment of a committee under Sir William Middlebrook to consider improvements to the fire service. The committee duly reported in May 1920, recommending amongst other things, national rates of pay, a standardisation of ranks and uniforms, and superannuation. When no action was taken on the Middlebrook recommendations, various fire service associations demanded some progress and the government agreed in 1921 to set up a Royal Commission of Fire Brigades and Fire Prevention. The outcome of this enquiry was to endorse the earlier findings such as the need for improved training standards and hose couplings, but in addition called for proper means of escape in factories, the safer conveyance of

Chief Fire Officer Morris escorts the Chairman of the London County Council, Lord Snell, through the ranks of assembled fire engines and firemen during the Brigade's Annual Review held in Victoria Park, east London, July 1934. The line of firemen in the foreground is rigged in one hour duration oxygen breathing sets.

> ❝ *Members of the Brigade took no part
> in the General Strike of 1926...* ❞

petrol, and better safety in the storage and use of celluloid products. Interestingly, the Commission also found the case clearly made for a move towards larger brigade units, probably administered at county level.

Unfortunately, little progress was made on any of these headings for this was a time of growing economic downturn. In 1922, as part of a national belt-tightening exercise, personnel of the LFB reluctantly accepted a $2\frac{1}{2}\%$ pay cut. This was achieved through acceptance of a contributory pension scheme, but in June 1923 the personnel of the LFB were again asked to agree to a further reduction. This time after arbitration, it was judged that this was not the moment to disturb police parity. Members of the Brigade took no part in the General Strike of 1926, for in comparison to other workers of that time, men in the LFB had an enviable position and there was a long waiting list for vacancies.

Folding jumping sheets were carried on LFB pumps as a last-resort rescue device right up until the outbreak of the Second World War. Crews underwent a weekly drill that involved one of the crew acting as 'jumper' and this view shows a 'jumper' in mid air having come out of the second floor window of the Lambeth drill tower.

❝ Before long, two other emergency tenders joined the LFB fleet and carried the first primitive rescue tools... ❞

On the equipment front there continued to be considerable improvement and development taking place. As far back as 1912, the Brigade had commissioned its first emergency tender (ET). This was a semi-enclosed van-style Dennis, whose role was primarily to provide oxygen breathing apparatus at serious fires where penetration into a smoke filled building was needed. Apart from breathing sets, this first ET had an inbuilt generator to provide floodlighting at night time incidents. Before long, two other motor ETs joined the LFB fleet and carried the first primitive rescue tools such as jacks, other lifting gear and flame cutting equipment needed at the growing number of non-fire accidents and emergencies. In 1925, to meet the increasing risk of a large scale oil or petrol fire, the LFB introduced its first specialist foam tender capable of producing 5,000 gallons of foam at such an incident.

With a full-scale motorised fire engine fleet, the LCC area of London was well covered and as a result, in the early 1930s, the authority was able to close 15 fire stations leaving a total of 59 land stations and three river stations. Even then, the Brigade was able to be in attendance at the scene of an emergency call within five minutes of an alarm, and could muster a minimum force of 20 pumps with 100 firemen within 15 minutes. Most London fire stations now had at least two fire engines, one with a wheeled escape ladder and the other with the pumping capacity. A number of inner London stations were also allocated a turntable ladder, able to reach up to 85 ft.

1934 saw the introduction of the Brigade's first new 'dual purpose' pumping fire engines with 100 gallon water tanks feeding hose reel on rotating drums. Built by Dennis, these were still open machines but equipped with mountings to carry either a 50 ft wheeled escape (when they were termed a pump escape or PE) or a 35 ft extension ladder (then known as a pump or P). The new fire engines enabled the disposal of a number of old motor escape vans, that could only carry a wheeled escape and had no pumping capability whatsoever.

66 Even then, the Brigade was able to be in attendance at the scene of an emergency call within five minutes... 99

The First Non Fire Rescues and Emergencies

In the early 1920s, the LFB found itself being called to a modest number of non-fire emergencies where the speedy response and teamwork skills of the Brigade were able to save life and restore some normality to a situation. These early non-fire calls are nowadays termed 'special services'. Examples of 'special services' attended by the LFB some 80 years ago include the protracted rescue of 16 workmen on 26 October 1923 when a five storey building under reconstruction in Edgware Road, near Marble Arch, collapsed. Although the LFB was only attending about 50 special service calls a year at this time, they could be challenging and dangerous incidents. On 8 April 1926, the LFB rescued two sewermen who had been overcome by fumes whilst working underground in Marlborough Lane, Charlton. Led by Sub Officer Armstrong, a crew rigged in breathing apparatus were lowered 140 ft down a vertical shaft and then had to work their way some half a mile along the sewer workings to locate the overcome men. Using a transfer of oxygen technique from their own breathing sets to keep the casualties alive, the LFB successfully got the sewermen to the surface where they eventually recovered. The crew were commended by the Chief Officer for their fine work.

In 1928, it was the weather that created a major difficult situation for the men of the LFB to deal with. On this particular day, the banks of the Thames were progressively breached by a combination of very heavy rain together with a extremely high tide. A total of 113 separate operations were undertaken in an 24 hour period and at its peak, the emergency saw 51 pumping fire engines at work manned by over 300 firemen. Millions of gallons of water were pumped from riverside hospitals, power stations and underground railway stations. Firemen rescued ten people in immediate danger in the first hour of the emergency alone, and many horses still in commercial use in London were led to safety from their stables. The LFB also recovered the bodies of seven adults who drowned in Pimlico.

These shiny Dennis fire engines also sported an important new body-work feature. For the first time, the LFB technical specification called for inboard tranverse seating behind the driver and officer in charge for the three-man crew. Up to now, most motor pumps still had a body-work style called the Braidwood body on which the crew sat facing outwards down each side of the fire engine. This old arrangement went

back almost 100 years to the days of horse drawn manual pumps of the 19th century, and meant that firemen had to rig in their uniforms en route to a fire, clinging on to a handrail and trying to defy centrifugal forces at corners. Not surprisingly, there were accidents up and down the land, often fatal, where firemen were simply flung off at speed.

The next logical stage of fire engine development in London was the introduction of the Brigade's first fully enclosed, or limousine type, dual purpose pumping fire engines and the first of these were built and delivered by Dennis in 1935. They were allocated to strategic stations as they carried three breathing sets inside the rear crew compartment. It was to be another forty years before every London fireman had a personal breathing set on every front line fire engine. Another major benefit of the new all-enclosed pumps was that crews did not freeze or arrive soaking wet at the scene of the fire. As a matter of course, a few of the 'old hands' in the LFB moaned about 'mollycoddling' but the majority of firemen much appreciated the new found protection from the weather afforded by the new limousine fire engines. Four years later, Leyland also built a number of similar limousine pumps for the LFB and these were notable

Accompanied by Chief Officer Morris, King George VI moves off to inspect a range of the Brigade's fire engines and their crews. Queen Elizabeth can be seen some way behind in the right background. 21 July 1937 (*Topical Press*)

> 66 *As a matter of course, a few of the
> 'old hands' in the LFB moaned
> about 'mollycoddling'...* 99

as the first diesel-engined fire vehicles in the London fleet. All of the new batch of new 1930s open bodied fire engines remained in service right through the Blitz years and up until the late 1950s.

A further new specialist fire engine introduced to London in 1936 was the Brigade's first high-speed hose laying lorry. This was built on a Dennis chassis and was designed for use at large fires where it was necessary to relay large quantities of water from remote water mains. The new hose layer had its hose compliment ready flaked out in its rear compartment and could run out two lines of hose at speeds up to 30 mph over a distance of half a mile.

Another pioneering development instituted by Chief Officer Morris in 1935 was the setting up at of a 'command post' at major London fires from where the proper coordination of firefighting operations, liaison

King George VI and Queen Elizabeth pause at the Brigade's canteen van whilst inspecting some of London's fire engines during the opening of the new Headquarters at Lambeth, 21 July 1937. (*Topical Press*)

> *In the 1930s, the LFB's River Thames section operated three fireboats...*

with the police and ambulance service, various other local agencies and the press could take place. At first, this facility was simply set up in a doorway or suitable area close to the fire scene, but by the time of the London Blitz, mobile control vans were part of the LFB scene, forerunners of today's sophisticated mobile command units in use by the British fire service and indeed across the world's fire brigades.

In the 1930s, the LFB's River Thames section operated three fire-boats which were based at Battersea, Blackfriars, and Cherry Garden Pier, Bermondsey. In 1935, the Brigade placed an order for a new fireboat to replace one of the older vessels. Built at Cowes on the Isle of Wight, the new fireboat was named 'Massey Shaw' after the redoubtable Victorian Chief Officer. Designed specifically for working in shallow water, the new fireboat only drew 3 ft 9 inches in draft and could pump an impressive 3,000 gallons of water ashore or onto a burning riverside warehouse or ship.

For some time during the early 1930s, there had been a scheme to consider a new headquarters for the Brigade. The existing Southwark HQ opened by Massey Shaw in Southwark Bridge Road in 1878 was becoming increasingly cramped and lacking in the full command and administrative accommodation necessary for a Brigade the size of the LFB.

A Fateful Site for the Brigade's New Headquarters

When in late 1934, the site was finally chosen for the new Headquarters for the London Fire Brigade on Albert Embankment, SE1, there were more than a few officers and firemen who saw the tragic irony of the riverside location at Lambeth. Back on 30 January 1918, the Brigade had been called to a fire at the same site, then occupied by a complex of buildings including a large warehouse, pottery, shops and a boatyard. Amid the winter fog of that morning, the fire developed rapidly into a 15 pump affair, and just as firefighting efforts were gaining an upper hand, a front wall of the warehouse fell outwards, instantly killing two Sub Officers and five firemen. This sad loss still remains the worst peacetime loss suffered by the London Fire Brigade or its forebears.

King George VI and Queen Elizabeth opened the new Lambeth Headquarters of the London Fire Brigade on 21 July 1937. In this view the King, escorted by Chief Officer Morris, reviews some 100 firemen drawn from fire stations across London. Crews based at the Headquarters fire station parade in front of their various fire engines. (*Associated Press*)

Accordingly, a suitable two-and-a-half acre site on the Albert Embankment by Lambeth Bridge was acquired by the LCC. The new ten storey building had a 210 ft frontage with seven turnout bays for the various fire engines attached to the HQ fire station, and a fine view of the Palace of Westminster across the Thames. Above the engine house was fire station accommodation, administrative offices and quarters for the Chief Officer Morris and his family, together with similar flats for ten other officers. In a rear block was a five storey building housing the Brigade's motor repair workshops and stores for hose, ladders and a host of operational equipment. The large drill yard featured a 100 ft high tower at one end and a bandstand at the other, soon to be regularly occupied by the LFB Band during regular public displays.

The new Lambeth Headquarters were opened on 21 July 1937 by HM King George VI and Queen Elizabeth. Lined up for the royal inspection were 150 highly polished and immaculately turned out brass helmeted officers and firemen of the LFB. When the inspection was over, the King and Queen watched a one hour spectacular and well-choreographed

*❝ It was a most scintillating occasion
in the Brigade's history...❞*

Brass Helmets are Finally Retired

The brass helmet first introduced specifically for the Metropolitan Fire Brigade by Captain Eyre Massey Shaw in the 1860s quickly became an iconic symbol of London firefighters which lasted well into the 20th century. However, the growing use of electricity and the conductivity risks to firemen during firefighting situations where live cables and wires were often prevalent, made the much-loved brass helmet an unacceptable hazard. Consequently, in 1935, a new four-ply cork helmet manufactured by Merryweather's was trialled by firemen at Shoreditch fire station for a full year. The new helmets had a built-up comb and a corrugated sponge rubber headband and weighed only 22 ozs, against the old brass helmet's 36 ozs. The cork helmets could withstand high impact forces and were waterproof and electrically safe. At the end of the trial period, the Shoreditch crews gave a strong approval to the new helmets and by the end of 1936, the traditional London firemen's brass helmets were phased out in favour of the cork version. It was indeed the end of a firefighting era in London.

display of firefighting expertise and equipment, culminating in four turntable ladders breaking out Union flags at 100 ft above the royal visitors. It was a most scintillating occasion in the Brigade's history and an event that Massey Shaw would have been proud to have been associated with.

Sadly, this happy time was soon diminished not only by the growing shadow of war over Europe, but also by a return of pressure from the now established Fire Brigades' Union upon the LCC to reduce the working week for firemen to 48 hours. The belief of the Union was that the now majority Labour-held LCC would consider such a demand favourably, but this was not to be. It was only after long and acrimonious arguments between the new Leader of the LCC, Herbert Morrison, and Percy Kingdom, the secretary of the Fire Brigades' Union, that a 60 hour week was finally agreed and a new two shift system was promised for implementation in early 1940.

Three fine looking Leyland fire engines pictured outside Shoreditch fire station, Tabernacle Street, EC2, c.1924. On the right is a 50 ft pump escape, whilst on the left are two pumps, all still on solid tyres. Shoreditch was a station with a particularly high risk area, hence the allocation of three pumping fire engines.

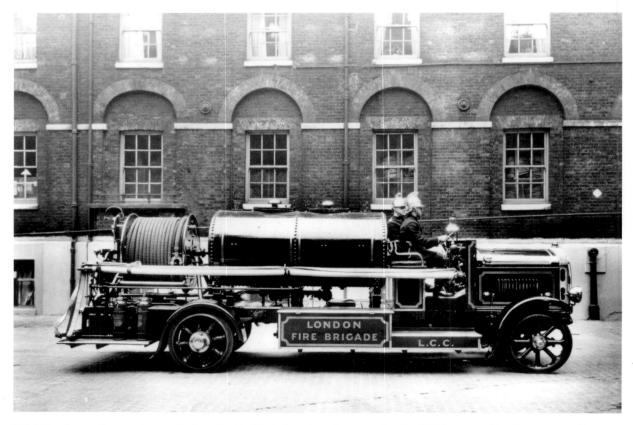

This Tilling Stevens foam tender was the first of its kind in the Brigade and was introduced in 1925. It was capable of producing 5,000 gallons of foam for use at fires involving flammable fuels.

A bird's eye view of one of the Brigade's new 100 ft all steel power operated turntable ladders during a training session at Southwark Headquarters, August 1935. These high rise fire engines were used for both rescue and for projecting a powerful water jet into the upper floors of a burning building. This model used a Morris Commercial chassis and a German Magirus ladder.

Introduced in 1936, this Dennis was the Brigade's first hose laying lorry capable of laying out half a mile of twin lines of large diameter hose at speeds of up to 30 mph to bring extra water to the scene of major fires. Note the method of stowing the joined up hose lengths to ensure that it runs out freely.

> 66 *Sadly, this happy time was soon diminished not only by the growing shadow of war over Europe...* 99

CHAPTER EIGHT

Prelude to War

The incendiary bombing by the Luftwaffe of the civilian population during the Spanish Civil War brought home the horrors of aerial fire attacks. A particular sharp and shocking focus was the 2,000 civilian casualties inflicted on the defenceless Spanish town of Guernica in 1937.

As the conflict developed abroad, many London firemen must have wondered just how the capital would cope with aerial fire raids. In fact, several British fire service conferences had been held during the early 1930s to consider the strategy and preparations that would be necessary to meet the likely effects of such warfare.

In August 1935, the government had set up a committee under Lord Riverdale whose brief was 'to review fire brigade services in England and Wales and to advise whether any steps are needed to improve organisation and co-operation for the purpose of meeting danger from fire'. Reporting one year later, the Riverdale Committee's principal recommendations were that fire brigade law should be consolidated into one Act; each borough and district council should be required to provide a 'public' fire brigade with clearly defined responsibilites; and that there should be moves towards a standardisation of equipment. Another significant point was that the Committee felt that a firefighting reserve of men and equipment should also be provided for use in event of war.

This latter Riverdale recommendation clearly had resonance with the senior officers of the LFB; London presented a vast and highly vulnerable target for any aerial aggressor. The massed riverside warehouses alone were huge fire risks, as had been regularly demonstrated by a number of conflagrations over three centuries and more. In the 1930s, the River

66 *...Many London firemen must have wondered just how the capital would cope with aerial fire raids.* 99

On the run up to war the Brigade continued to deal with 'normal' peacetime fires. This dramatic photograph captures the rescue of two office workers who have been trapped by a developing fire on the top floor of this building in Peters Hill, EC4, near St. Paul's. Two wheeled escapes are in action and, no doubt, a firefighting team are ascending the internal staircase to extinguish the outbreak in some pretty hot and smoky conditions.
8 March 1938 (*Fox Photos*)

Thames was one of the nation's major trade gateways and the warehouses floors were always stacked with highly flammable contents including fats, oils, grain, fabrics, and timber. Many of London's riverside commercial buildings were crammed together in narrow Dickensian streets where fire easily jumped from one building to another, creating a fireman's nightmare. Few firemen serving in the inner London area of the LFB in the late 1930s had not experienced at first hand the drama and dangers of a major Thames side warehouse fire.

The financial centre of the City of London had many buildings packed with workers and the prospect of incendiary attack on the fine structures of London including palaces, cathedrals, museums and other public

> *London presented a vast and highly vulnerable target for any aerial aggressor.*

buildings was too horrific to contemplate. Then there was the civilian population of London, many of whom lived in the slum areas in cramped conditions where rapid fire spread was all too often illustrated by peace-time outbreaks caused by carelessness or accidents involving coal fires, paraffin heaters, gas and electricity, the use of candles, and cigarette smokers.

Two separate Acts of Parliament followed the Riverdale findings, both serving to meet the need for the fire service to be ready to meet the threat of war. The first was the Air Raid Precautions Act of 1937

The camera catches a poignant moment as the funeral cortege of Fireman Charles Sweetlove passes his fire station in Redcross Street in the Barbican. He had been killed in action at a fire in Camomile Street, off Fleet Street, one week earlier. 11 April 1938.

> " *Recruiting into the London AFS*
> *began in March 1938 but the initial*
> *flow of recruits was disappointingly*
> *poor.* "

which took effect on 1 January 1938. This provided a central government grant to finance improvements in firefighting services, including the cost of recruitment and training of a volunteer force to be known as the Auxiliary Fire Service (AFS). Later in 1938 came the Fire Brigade Act to formalise many of the Riverdale recommendations, including the duty of local authorities to provide an *efficient* fire brigade. This Act did not materially affect the LFB and its original constitution under the 1865 Act.

Recruiting into the London Auxiliary Fire Service began in March 1938 but the initial flow of recruits was disappointingly poor. In June, the appropriately named Chief Officer of the LFB, Commander (later Sir) Aylmer Firebrace, CBE, RN, took part in a BBC broadcast along with the Leader of the London County Council, Herbert Morrison, in which an urgent appeal was made for men and women AFS recruits. Firebrace had joined the LFB in 1919 as an officer from the Royal Navy and later in his memoirs recalled that it took the Munich crisis later in 1938 to produce the strong recruiting response that had been hoped for.

There were also AFS recruitment meetings at the large London department stores such as Harrods and the John Lewis chain, and even at the Stock Exchange.

From the outset, there were two types of recruits to the AFS — those who agreed on outbreak of war to give up their peacetime job to join on a paid permanent basis, or those who simply volunteered on an unpaid basis to be available during times of enemy raiding. The lowest age for joining the AFS was 17 whilst in reality, like the Home Guard, there was no upper age limit. Youths of 16 were welcomed to act as messengers and general administrative helpers.

Upon their initial recruitment into the AFS, men and women were streamed into several categories. Apart from the primary one of general firefighting duties, there was a 'modified' firefighting category for older men in which they were not expected to work above the ground floor,

and one for recruits for the River Thames section: these were men who had experience of boats or perhaps worked in London's dockland. There were two grades for women recruits, one for those who were undertaking driving duties and one for those suited to telephone or office work. The initial training courses for AFS firemen recruits covered a period of 60 hours spread over sessions held once or twice a week. Training started in April 1938 at Kensington, Bishopsgate, New Cross, Southwark, Clapham, West Norwood, Brixton and Streatham fire stations. The syllabus included a variety of practical hose, ladder work and pump operation drills, and training for female AFS recruits began soon after. All the AFS instruction was being given by experienced LFB junior officers.

In January 1939 Chief Fire Officer Firebrace, along with several of his senior LFB officers, was seconded to the Home Office to organise an overall co-ordination scheme for all the fire brigades in the Greater London area, to come into effect in event of war. Excluding the LFB, there were 66 other small brigades spread across the outer boroughs of the larger London geographical region, although many of these only ran one or two pumping fire engines to protect a relatively modest low-risk area.

The outcome of the 1939 scheme devised by Firebrace was to leave the 117 square miles of the LFB undivided. This, of course, made great sense, as apart from being the largest fire brigade in the land, it was entirely manned by professional firefighters, who regularly dealt with major fires

Water drawn from the River Thames had been invaluable in organised peacetime firefighting for over 100 years and in this work the crews of London's fireboats had a critical role to play. Here on 11 July 1939, firemen manning London's newest fireboat *Massey Shaw* laying off in the background are using a skiff to get twin high capacity hose lines ashore across the mud just below Cannon Street railway station to supply crews at work tackling a serious fire in a nearby warehouse. Within a year, the *Massey Shaw* was to begin the London fireman's war when in May 1940 she successfully made three return trips to the Dunkirk beaches as part of the small ships flotilla.

The recruitment campaign for Auxiliary Fire Service volunteers embraced many activities and one of these was to use posters on some of the Brigade's front line red fire engines. Here the LFB's Dennis hose layer is plastered with AFS recruiting posters before taking to the streets with its message.

and was consequently extremely well organised as regards operational strategies, communications, and training.

Firebrace divided the remaining 66 outer London fire brigades and their AFS contingents into five operational districts based to cover this 500 square mile area with district HQ at Ealing, Tottenham, West Ham, Croydon and Beckenham. A clear wartime command structure would allow for the senior district officer to mobilise re-inforcements as necessary under the overall command of a Regional Fire Officer based at the Home Office.

As war clouds continued to gather, recruitment into the AFS still progressed rather more slowly than was hoped. There is no doubt that a long delay within the Home Office in announcing what the full-time rate of pay would be for AFS personnel must have contributed to the poor response. Eventually, the AFS pay scales were finally confirmed in February 1939. These gave a weekly rate of £3 for men, £2 for women and 25 shillings to a youth age 17–18, and £1 for a 16 year old.

> 66 *The initial training courses for AFS firemen recruits covered a period of 60 hours...* 99

Precious New Firefighting Water Supplies

An important move agreed by the government in the summer of 1938 emphasised that plenty of water was going to be the key to successful wartime firefighting. The London County Council was allocated an initial sum of £500,000 to provide new large capacity 24 inch diameter steel firefighting water mains across the high risk areas of the capital. Commencing in the summer of 1938, the new mains ran from Dowgate Dock near Southwark Bridge through to the City business district and out to City Road; from the Regent's Canal through Regent's Park down through Oxford Street to Soho; from the Strand to Trafalgar Square; and from the City Road to London Docks. New spur mains were also laid in the City area bounded by St. Paul's, Aldersgate Street, Chiswell Street and Moorgate.

In addition to all this work, the Home Office also provided a large quantity of six inch steel piping to be laid by firemen along the road edges against the kerbstones. However, this work was labour intensive, took much time and LFB senior officers preferred the use of hose laying lorries that could lay out hose at speeds of up to 30 mph. Prior to the outbreak of war plans were laid to commission 40 hose laying lorries for the LFB area. Another improvement in water supplies was quickly achieved by the construction of canvas dams containing up to 20,000 gallons of water and these were installed on suitable plots of land on street corners across London to provide sufficient water for an immediate attack on a fire. From 1939, these dams were increasingly constructed using steel panels. Unfortunately, as soon as the dams were filled with water, they attracted children who during the warm weather treated them as swimming pools and there were a number of fatal drowning tragedies.

Although much of London's old water mains were laid in cast-iron pipes which were extremely vulnerable to the shattering impact of high explosive bombs, firefighting water was readily available from the River Thames. The drawback, however, was that at very low tide it took the efforts of many firemen to manhandle hose lines ashore from a fireboat across the mudbanks that lined both banks of the river, to a shore based fire engine. With an eye also on the fire risk within the many inner dockland wharfs, mid-1939 saw the LFB's peacetime complement of three fireboats increased by ten additional AFS crewed vessels based at six new river stations. In addition, a number of dumb barges were moored at strategic positions alongside Thames bridges, to act as floating platforms on to which portable pumps could readily lift precious extra firefighting water from London's river.

Much work was carried out in 1939 to provide emergency water supplies across London at various strategic sites. To the fire service these were known as 'dams' and some of the earliest were portable and of metal framed canvas construction. These were soon replaced by steel panelled versions together with some permanent brick structures, such as pictured here. Prominently marked EWS (Emergency Water Supply), this one in Great Suffolk Street, Southwark, SE1, contained 50,000 gallons. The signage also indicated to fire crews where the next nearest EWS is located. Unfortunately, these water supplies were a great attraction to London's children especially during the warmer weather, and there were a number of drowning tragedies.
(*The Wardell Collection*)

The overall plan for the LFB area was to provide a minimum of 360 sub stations manned by AFS firefighters to reinforce the 59 regular 'red' fire stations of the peacetime LFB. There were to be six AFS stations attached to each parent LFB station's area. The sub stations were virtually all to be sited in requisitioned premises with suitable accommodation to serve as a wartime fire station, such as garages, schools and small factories. By September 1938, the first London AFS fire stations had been opened: three were in the City at Moreland Street, Bunhill Row and Gravel Lane. Other early AFS stations were in the high-risk areas of the Surrey Docks with their immense stock of imported timber, West India Docks, and in London Docks close by Tower Bridge.

The intention was that each London AFS station would be allocated two pumping units, provided from the stock of government fire engines now beginning to be delivered in significant numbers to London and other large city brigades where the fire risk was thought to be highest. There were three types of government fire engines for AFS use. The first was the heavy pumping unit, usually on a Fordson or Austin commercial lorry chassis with a mounted 900 gallons per minute fire pump, a short extension ladder, hose and other general equipment. The second type of unit was the trailer pump of various manufacture including Coventry-Climax, Dennis, and Scammell. These usually had a capacity of around 350 gallons per minute and were designed to be towed behind a fire engine or van. In 1939, the government had also ordered a number of 100 ft turntable ladders (TL) to supplement those 'red' TLs already in

> *❝ By September 1938, the first London AFS fire stations had been opened...❞*

service in the LFB. All these additional fire engines destined for the AFS were finished in battleship grey, with no unnecessary frills whatsoever, in comparison with the shining red livery and brass of the LFB's regular 'red' fire engine fleet.

Other emergency firefighting equipment was also issued to the AFS from late 1938 onwards. This included hundreds of rolls of $2\frac{1}{2}$ inch hose, much of which was of American origin and came in 50 ft lengths rather than the standard LFB 75 ft long versions. An immediate problem with the American hose was that each length had instantaneous snap-together couplings rather than the screw-type couplings that had been

Throughout the spring and summer of 1939 the training of volunteers for the AFS intensified as they were drilled in pump and ladder work during their 60 hours basic recruits course. Here, under the watchful eye of their London Fire Brigade instructor two AFS fireman are in the early stages of learning the basic yet important skill of running out hose: they are joining two lengths together using the new instantaneous push-together couplings of the hose provided for AFS use. At this time the long established screw-together hose of the regular 'red' London Fire Brigade was also being replaced by the instantaneous type.

The principal self-propelled fire engine provided by the government for the AFS was the heavy unit built upon either a Fordson, Austin or Bedford chassis. These utility firefighting vehicles had high capacity fire pumps able to deliver up to 900 gallons of water per minute, a 30 ft extension ladder, extinguishers, lines and other small gear. The heavy units were finished in battleship grey and unlike the regular fire engines of the LFB fleet were unadorned with brass and chromium fittings. This view taken in Bethnal Green Road, E1 in March 1939 shows a Fordson 7V heavy unit. Note the rear facing crew compartment and, somewhat unusually, the two hook ladders mounted above the main ladder.

in use in the LFB since the early 20th century. A whole series of adapters had to be produced to allow the US hose to marry to existing London hose.

By the summer of 1939 preparations for war on the Home Front were reaching a new pitch. The combined force of the 2,300 professional officers and men of the London Fire Brigade had now been joined by 23,000 Auxiliary Fire Service trained recruits. Some of these AFS recruits came from a professional background, although the majority were from the working classes. At this stage, the two organisations were kept completely separate, with the 'red' crews still attending and dealing with the many daily fire calls, whilst the firefighting volunteers continued to train, equip and prepare for war if it came. However, the two combined forces soon became collectively known simply as the London Fire Service.

As war in Europe looked increasingly inevitable in August 1939, events in the London Fire Service rapidly accelerated. The last week of peace saw

The smaller and more numerous AFS unit was the trailer pump and with a serious shortage of suitable towing vehicles in the summer of 1939, arrangements were made for the use of some 2,000 London Austin taxicabs. These Austins were ideal for this purpose being sturdy and well able to carry a crew and some equipment. This view shows three Austin taxicabs in London AFS service with their crews looking very purposeful. The taxis still have their 'For Hire' meters in place and are hitched up to their trailer pumps ready to go to war. September 1939.

over 570 trailer pumps now ready in place on AFS sub stations and taxi cabs were being fitted with towing attachments. The General Post Office finished installing telephone lines to the 103 empty schools now being used as AFS fire stations — their children having been evacuated. By the end of the month, all 59 LFB regular land fire stations were connected to each of their six AFS sub stations by telephone. The 25 August was the final day for 'passing out' the floods of recruits into the AFS. Five days later, steel helmets were issued to all personnel, both men and women, together with respirators worn in a canvas bag on the chest, and sand bag protection of London fire stations was well in hand.

The 1 September 1939 saw Hitler's troops crossing the Polish border and the final moves to put the combined London Fire Service on a full wartime footing. All regular LFB personnel were recalled from leave and instructed to remain on duty at their stations. All designated vehicles and river vessels were placed in commission and further earmarked premises quickly requisitioned as AFS stations. Then at 17.20 hrs came

Taxicabs Go to War

One early problem for Chief Officer Firebrace's officers during the hectic period of 1938–39 was the very serious shortage of suitable towing vehicles for the hundreds of trailer pumps now being issued to London's AFS crews. Although the LFB fleet had a number of small general purpose vans and small lorries suitable for this purpose, the difficulty was one of the sheer numbers of vehicles needed. Firebrace was reluctant to requisition many different types of van from various sources but the issue was finally resolved when the London Taxicab Committee of the Transport and General Workers Union suggested that the humble London taxi might offer a solution. The Austin taxis were robust, had a tight turning circle, accommodation for a four man crew and driver, and could carry some hose and equipment. The Home Office moved quickly to set up an agreement to lease 2,000 London taxis to join the AFS fleet and many of their drivers also joined the AFS for good measure.

an historic message from the Home Office to Commander Firebrace at Lambeth Headquarters: 'Emergency Fire Brigade measures. Call out the AFS and proceed as in Home Office Circular 23/3/39.'

With the receipt of this message regular London Fire Brigade was symbolically joined together with the London Auxiliary Fire Service to face the as yet unknown intentions of the enemy. When Prime Minister Neville Chamberlain broadcast to the nation two days later at 11.15 hrs and announced that a state of war now existed between Great Britain and Germany, the London Fire Service immediately went to a state of immediate readiness and braced itself for an onslaught of fire from the sky. Rather dramatically, just as Chamberlain finished speaking, the first air raid warning of the Second World War sounded out across London. After several minutes of sheer panic, the 'all clear' was sounded. It transpired that some rather jittery observers at Croydon Airport had mistaken a French aircraft coming in to land for a Luftwaffe bomber.

That first stomach-turning wailing of the air raid warning sirens on 3 September 1939 marked the beginning of the war for the men and women of the London Fire Service. History would tell that for London's army of firefighters, it was going to be an unprecedented and arduous human struggle against some very great odds.

CHAPTER NINE

The London Blitz Begins

As the men and women of the London Fire Service absorbed the reality of a war situation, there was still much to prepare to bring London's fire defence to a state of complete readiness. This was especially true in getting the final auxiliary sub stations in place in hastily requisitioned premises. One of the first major effects of the declaration of war was that Commander Firebrace, London's Chief Officer, was immediately seconded to the Home Office to take up the post of London Regional Fire Officer. This put him in overall strategic command of all of the 67 fire brigades of the Greater London district.

Commander Firebrace was most reluctant to leave his Headquarters at Lambeth to take up this wartime post, and even went as far as appealing directly to Sir John Anderson, the Home Secretary, to be allowed to

The London Fire Brigade's newest fireboat *Massey Shaw* returning up the Thames to Lambeth Headquarters following its foray to the Dunkirk beaches during which it made three return trips rescuing some 700 troops. Note the knotted climbing lines still tied to the side of the vessel and the crew, both regular and AFS firemen brandishing their .303 rifles. 3 June 1940

> **6 6** *Some were downright unsanitary places as the arriving crews quickly discovered.* **9 9**

remain in command of the London Brigade. But the Secretary of State stood firm, Firebrace moved to the Home Office on the other side of the Thames and the Deputy Chief Officer. Major Frank Jackson, took command of the LFB and its Auxiliary Fire Service (AFS).

In that first wartime week of September all LFB regular personnel were placed on a continuous duty system, day and night. Across the several hundred AFS sub stations, men and women reported for duty. Some sub stations had been established for almost a year and were well set up with facilities. However, a very large number were located in schools now abandoned by the evacuation of children to country areas, and quite a few were requisitioned garages and workshops, quite unfit as a base for a round-the-clock fire station, often without proper sleeping and toilet accommodation.

Some were downright unsanitary places as the arriving crews quickly discovered. Auxiliary Fireman 'Mac' Young was posted to Winsland Street sub station located in a Great Western Railway staff recreation hall near Paddington railway station. He and his 24 AFS colleagues found that the hall was not yet ready for occupation and they were ordered to camp out in the adjoining railway delivery stables. Young said:

'*Besides about 200 restless GWR horses, we weren't the only stable occupants that night. There must have been thousands of horse flies hovering around. There was no food and no washing facilities and it was several days before the two taxis and trailer pumps turned up and we could begin to commission the station properly. We even had to scrounge some timber locally to knock up some primitive bunks. All the time we looked anxiously at the sky.*'

Another AFS fireman, Vic Flint, kept a diary during his wartime service and recalled his first few days on his sub station at Whitechapel in east London:

'*No bombs — and no fires! Which after all is surprising to say the least. The sound of the siren yesterday (3 September soon after the declaration) put the fear of God into us. I must say, I've never been so frightened in all my life. This is a miserable place....*'

Some female members of the AFS also had a little difficulty as Auxiliary Firewoman Owtram recounted:

'We had reported for duty at our sub station which was located in a public garage. We had been told that the accommodation was in a large loft above. Only three of the 15 women in the group had uniforms, the others having joined in the last days before the outbreak of war. The AFS firemen had yet to turn up with their pumps. By the wall of the garage was a pile of sandbags. They were symbolic only. We found the loft door locked but then the men arrived, forceful and efficient. The company officer ran up the ladder, used his axe to smash the broken balustrade of the gallery and unlocked the door. We all filed up, some with our belongings and after a short while there was a roll call in the garage below.'

At the outbreak of war, the front line of the London Fire Service consisted of 120 pumps and specialist 'red' fire engines of the LFB together with almost 2,000 AFS motor and trailer pumps scattered across 300 sub stations in the London County Council area.

After tying up on the Lambeth Pontoon, the crew of the *Massey Shaw* paraded before Chief Officer Jackson and their families. This view captures the on-duty land based crews of Lambeth fire station paying a hearty 'hats off' tribute to the fine work of their river colleagues during the Dunkirk evacuation. 3 June 1940 (*Planet News*)

❝ Many AFS firemen only had one tunic and pair of rubber boots... ❞

Recruiting into the London AFS had markedly increased in the run up to war, and from 3 September 1939, recruits were sent to six district training schools to undertake their 60 hours basic training rather than undergoing this at a selected number of LFB regular stations.

During that first week of war, the London AFS undertook some heavy tasks. They filled thousands of sandbags, not just for fire stations but for hospitals, ambulance stations and other critical buildings. Firewomen checked telephone links to LFB district stations and Headquarters, packed first aid kits and rehearsed air raid mobilising procedures. At the end of the first week it was becoming evident that the threatened early strike by the Luftwaffe was not going to materialise. Against a feeling of uneasy anticlimax, Major Jackson after consultation with Firebrace at the Home Office, stood down the continuous duty system in favour of shifts, with 48 hours on, and 24 hours off. Certain other operational

AFS crews were adept at self-sufficiency wherever possible and some firemen took this to extremes. In this photograph AFS personnel at Daniel Street school sub station in Shoreditch, E1, are parading a pig, chickens, duck, rabbits and a guinea pig. (*Frank Reader*)

> ❝ *As the 1939 autumn turned to winter,*
> *the first cold spell saw the street*
> *emergency water dams freezing*
> *over...* ❞

changes were made, including reducing the front line AFS availability to 1,500 pumps, although these were manned and ready to be turned out on an 'immediate' basis.

Since 3 September, one AFS trailer pump and crew had been stationed alongside almost every LFB street fire alarm but on the change to shifts, this practice ceased. This caused some concern in the community and led to complaints from businessman and householders alike, who no doubt, had felt comforted by the visible presence of a fire crew in the street, even though they probably did not appreciate that the AFS crews as yet had no real firefighting experience to call upon. Whilst the 'red' crews of the LFB continued to respond to domestic fire calls and emergencies almost as normal, concentrating the AFS on their sub stations gave a much-needed opportunity to sort out proper messing and sleeping arrangements and to issue the many uniform items that were still arriving from central stores depots. Many AFS firemen only had one tunic and pair of rubber boots and quite a few of these were of the wrong size. It also enabled more training to take place, especially for those recruits who had joined just before the declaration of war and immediately after. By the end of September 1939, 2,700 additional men and women had been enrolled into the AFS since the declaration of war, and the training programme was under great pressure.

As the 1939 autumn turned to winter, the first cold spell saw the street emergency water dams freezing over and with antifreeze in short supply for the AFS, routines were set up through the long cold nights to run all engines to keep them warm. Uniform supplies remained slow in coming through and many AFS firemen still did not possess a complete set of fire-fighting kit and in some parts of London, the auxiliaries were extremely short of bedding.

The days and months went by and during New Year 1940, the AFS daily routines continued unaltered with plenty of pump drill both at fire stations and out in the streets, where the crews could pitch their ladders and use hoses on imaginary fires. There were also a number of major

AFS firewomen were recruited to primarily undertake communication and car and van driving duties. Although it was never envisaged that they would serve in the front line in London, some female AFS recruits were given several hours training in basic hose handling drill. Here the camera catches such a group as they resist the powerful jet reaction of a firefighting water jet. Lambeth Headquarters, 12 June 1940

exercises involving hundreds of AFS pumps getting to work in London's parks, open spaces and in dockland. Nor was there a shortage of spit and polish, although in reality there was little brass and shiny paintwork on the AFS heavy units and trailer pumps and their equipment.

As the 'Phoney War' period continued, Major Jackson decided that in order to alleviate the increasing boredom and repeated training periods being endured by the London AFS, certain auxiliary crews should be allowed to attend peacetime fires alongside and under the tutelage of regular LFB firefighters. The outcome was not surprising, bearing in mind that all in the AFS were still virgin firefighters as yet unbloodied by fire. In sub zero temperatures during the early hours of 24 January 1940, the Brigade was called to an incident at a large general warehouse of seven floors in Oval Road, Camden Town. The fire rapidly took hold of the rambling Victorian structure full of flammable goods and soon brought some 460 officers and firemen to Camden Town. Under the new mobilising arrangements 300 of these were totally inexperienced AFS personnel drawn from sub stations across the area. Records show that the blaze did not come under control until well into the following morning by which

> *Before very long various nicknames started to hurt those in the AFS, such as '£3 per week army dodgers'...*

time 12 officers and firemen had been seriously injured by falling burning debris and smoke inhalation. Five of these casualties were AFS men. A total of 29 LFB pumps, six AFS heavy units and 37 trailer pumps attended the blaze.

The early spring of 1940 still brought no enemy air raids and with London's auxiliaries largely confined to drills, exercises and waiting for the Luftwaffe to arrive, the public's regard for the AFS started to diminish. Before very long various nicknames started to hurt those in the AFS, such as '£3 per week army dodgers' and 'the darts brigade' and even sections of the national press began to vilify the reserve firefighting force. However, if those men who joined the AFS hoped to avoid conscription into the armed forces, this was not to be. From early 1940 AFS firemen between 20 and 25 years of age found themselves called up, as were a significant number of regular LFB firemen who were army and navy reservists.

Incensed by the growing public antipathy towards the reserve London firefighters, AFS fireman Michael Wassey wrote an article that spoke for itself:

'The AFS was deeply hurt, alas, by unkind innuendoes in the national press. The newspapers, on the whole, were being far from understanding. We appealed to their sense of fair play. It is the firm conviction of every AFS man that the press has failed to give the AFS a square deal. What is it that has caused the enthusiasm and patriotic fervour of the AFS in the early days of mobilisation, to degenerate in some cases into what almost constitutes surly acquiescence or, at the best, indifference to their job in the fire-soldiers' front line?

'The national firefighting scheme as a whole is efficient, and there is no question as to the firefighting abilities of the AFS section. Nor have the AFS any quarrel with their professional brothers and leaders. When intensive air-raids begin, the percentage of casualties expected to occur among the personnel of the AFS is likely to be amazingly high — far higher than those expected in any other section of the Air Raid Precautions. We know the risks we take, and we accept them.'

> 66 *The master put the burning vessel*
> *into the Thames Estuary...* 99

Many buildings requisitioned for use by the AFS were quite unsuitable as fire stations, often lacking basic facilities, either for the firemen or their fire engines. Bath Street sub station near Moorfields Eye Hospital, Shoreditch, EC1, was a good example and this view shows the general lack of covered accommodation. From the left are a heavy unit, a former LFB van with trailer pump, another heavy unit, and two officers' staff cars. June 1940 (*Frank Reader*)

The manpower losses combined with the sinking AFS morale began to have an effect on London's overall firefighting force, and by April 1940 resignations from the AFS increased alarmingly. Jackson and his officers were powerless to stop this exodus of firefighters until the government hurried through a statutory order to stop the flow of those leaving. This still did not address the increasing amount of antipathy felt in some parts by members of the regular LFB. Hundreds of temporary wartime promotions from the ranks had been made and a particular problem appeared to be a number of AFS recruits from professional backgrounds who had been rapidly elevated to AFS officer rank over the heads of experienced regular LFB officers.

Then, in May 1940 with the British Expeditionary Force (BEF) being pushed increasingly back by the German advance to the Belgian and French coast, it all began to change for the London Fire Service. A Dutch vessel, the SS *Prins Wilhelm Van Orange* was attacked off the

66 *Small fires were started in the south east suburbs...* 99

Belgian coast and a single incendiary penetrated the ship's hold and started a deep-seated cargo fire. The master put the burning vessel into the Thames Estuary off Gravesend and six London fireboats including the *Massey Shaw,* the Brigade's newest, were despatched to deal with the burning ship. Despite a major firefighting effort, the Dutch boat was seriously damaged.

Only two weeks after this first home front skirmish of the Second World War for the London Fire Service, it was the fireboat *Massey Shaw* and her crew that were in direct wartime action. On Sunday 26 May 1940, the full evacuation of the BEF began from the beaches of Dunkirk and by the following Wednesday, the operation was in full swing with an armada of small boats involved in the action of lifting exhausted troops off the beaches.

On Thursday 30 May, the Admiralty urgently requested that the Brigade provide a fireboat to proceed to Ramsgate to act as a fire safety measure there amongst the hundreds of petrol engined small boats milling around before their crossing of the Channel. Stationed at Blackfriars Bridge and named after the Brigade's famous Victorian Chief Officer, the *Massey Shaw* had been commissioned in 1935. She was twin screw vessel, 78 ft long and with a shallow draught of only 3 ft 9 inches designed for working in close at ship and riverside fires where she could pump up to four tons of water a minute. After hurriedly loading extra stores and compass, *Massey Shaw* and her crew left her moorings in the Thames supplemented by some AFS firemen as extra hands. Arriving at Ramsgate at midday amid hundreds of small boats, it appeared that the situation on the Dunkirk beaches had deteriorated and the London fireboat was now going across the Channel to assist the evacuation effort.

Over the next three days and nights and armed with no more than .303 rifles, *Massey Shaw* made three return trips to the Dunkirk beaches and rescued a total of some 700 weary British troops from uncertain fate. The London fireboat and her crew finally returned to the fireboat station at Lambeth Headquarters some days later to a hero's welcome provided by the families of the crew and a large gathering of London firefighters.

The personnel of Auxiliary Fire Service sub station 73X, in Euston, NW1, pose for the camera in the month before the beginning of the London Blitz. The station appears to be located within the premises of a linoleum factory. The three attached London Fire Brigade officers are seated in the centre of the front row and wear sailor type caps. A few of the AFS firemen have still not been issued with full uniform. August 1940 (*Brightman*)

There then followed another short lull during which the following London Fire Brigade General Order No. 310 dated 8 May 1940 was issued. It makes interesting reading:

'Dress for immediate duty at night — With the exception of riders of red appliances, despatch riders detailed to follow red appliances, the crew of the "duty" machine at each sub station and night duty men on river craft, personnel of LFB and AFS need not sleep in their clothes between 10 pm and 6.45 am.'

However, it was not long before the fury of war finally broke over south east England, and subsequently, the capital. Throughout late May, enemy bombs fell in open countryside in Kent and on 8 June at Addington in Surrey, close to the London County Council border. The evening of 17 August saw the first recorded incendiaries falling in the London Fire Brigade area. Small fires were started in the south east suburbs of Eltham and Woolwich that were quickly dealt with by regular crews. AFS fireman Michael Wassey was moved to record in his diary:

'On the eve of a new and decisive phase of this bitter war and to every man, woman and boy in the service — Stand by your pumps, God be with you and let your courage, determination and bravery merit your place at the head of the Civil Defence Services.'

> 66 *Within the hour, some 1,500 London*
> *firemen were committed to this first*
> *proper Blitz raid…* 99

From August 1940, during the Battle of Britain, air raid warnings in the capital were beginning to be a regular occurrence but on the night of 24 August 1940, the Luftwaffe bombed and set fire to several tanks at the fuel farm at the Thameshaven installation on the Essex shore of the Thames Estuary. The fires there soon overwhelmed the resources of the local fire brigade and support was required from surrounding brigades. The LFB was soon to go in some force to assist with the Thameshaven firefighting.

Worse was to follow, as several German bombers continued up the line of the Thames and discharged their incendiaries and high explosives over the City of London and parts of dockland. Within 20 minutes of the raid starting, 200 pumps had been mobilised to the Barbican area of the City, whilst in the West India Docks and surrounding east London streets, 150 pumps were soon at work. Within the hour, some 1,500 London firemen were committed to this first proper Blitz raid, many of them AFS crews, all gaining their first real exposure to scorching flames and thick swirling black smoke. By the early morning of 25 August, the London Fire Service had also been called out to deal with 48 minor fires, mostly on rooftops, caused by large burning brands from the major fires blowing downwind and settling upon unaffected roofs and ledges. For Chief Officer Jackson and his senior officers, the stark reality of this first raid by only a few aircraft was that major fires had caused a huge workload. Although this raid had helped to bond together the regular LFB and hundreds of untried auxiliaries, what was going to be the effect of a focused and intense air raid?

The answer was not long in coming. At about 4 pm on the afternoon of Saturday 7 September, the first German aircraft were sweeping over the Channel and heading for a new strategic target — London. With the Battle of Britain lost, the clear directive of Marshal Hermann Goering was simple: his Luftwaffe crews were to flatten the capital city.

The air raid sirens wailed out over London at 4.33 pm sending many thousands down into the air raid shelters. Within minutes the first high

> *Even as the first fire engines were being despatched during the first minutes of the raid, hundreds of fires were started...*

Thameshaven

James Gordon had been a journalist on *The Daily Telegraph* and he joined the London AFS the day before war was declared. He was one of several hundred LFS firefighters who formed a convoy to go to Thameshaven on 5 September 1940 to support the local Essex fire crews. He wrote:

'*We bumped slowly over the broken roads, quietened by the horror of destruction. The burning tanks flung up dense, black oily smoke that looked almost solid and effectively obscured all signs of flame. Past tanks battered, squashed and melted into fantastic shapes, past men unrecognisable in squelching veils of oil. Oil oozed into the soil and over the roads like black blight.*

'*The officer-in-charge, his brass epaulettes smeared and deadened, gave them their orders and directions in a voice made hoarse by bawling over the mêlée. All were dismayed, even Tommy and Ginger. Their tunics were new, their boots and leggings well blacked. Now they were ordered to get to work on a burning tank which stood in a concrete pit which was deep with oil.*

'*They set our Heavy Unit to work under some scaffolding bridgework and unrolled their clean hose and saw it submerge into the oil. They started to get a foam generator to work in an oil pond. One by one they reluctantly jumped over the parapet and, wading knee deep into warm oil, began to capture empty drums which floated in the viscid current. These they opened and held under the oil until they filled and sank. Then they piled one on top of the other until they made a slippery platform on which they set up their foam generator.*

'*Hervey shouted timid orders from outside the pit until they indignantly demanded that he come in with them. He walked towards them gingerly, holding up his arms like a tight-rope walker. Suddenly he disappeared into the oil with a horrified glug. He had stepped into a bomb crater. They pulled him out and laughed, then went on with their work.*

'*The order was sent back to Mac for water, and the long, awkward branch became alive as, pointing upwards like a gun, it delivered its ammunition of foam into the oil tank which boiled and belched like a volcano. The top was red-hot, and as the fire took hold lower and lower in the oil, steel melted and drooped inwards into the seething fire. The sides were pierced with machine-gun holes and hot oil spurted into the pit in steady streams.*

'*Paul guided the thick jet, his mind recoiling on itself at the horror and nearness of danger. He kept wetting his lips with his tongue. Whenever he lowered his eyes he was confronted with the nightmarish landscape. It was unreal. It couldn't exist. Yet here he was inches from an awful death. His mind burrowed back frantically at the memory of quiet, sunlit streets and level lawns, but his body struggled with the weight of the branch and the heat and smell of oil.*

'"*Do you realise that if some of that burning oil falls into this pit we shall be fried?*" *he asked quietly.* "*I s'pose so*", *said Fred miserably. The bag of sweets in his pocket was saturated with oil, and his palate longed for the tartness of an acid drop. He was a mug to have volunteered for this job. If anything happened to him, his wife and kid would suffer. He felt the oil creeping up his leggings and wondered what his wife would say about his ruined pants.*

'*The way back to London was a triumph. The road threaded through towns and suburbs where people turned and saw the grey AFS and red LFB appliances with their loads of oily men and hose. They cheered them as they passed. Ginger stood on the suction hose and took the cheers as though he was a prince and waved his arm in royal salute. The others grinned at him and borrowed cigarettes from each other. As they passed through Romford, the sirens howled another warning. What were sirens now?*'

Two views of the effects of the repeated enemy bombing of the fuel tanks at Thameshaven, on the Thames estuary in Essex. London Fire Service convoys, including one of 50 pumps, were sent to support the local firefighters in extinguishing these huge and intense fuel tank fires. Apart from the danger of the burning fuel boiling over, fire crews also came under enemy fire from the Luftwaffe. (*The Wardell Collection*)

> ❝ *Over two thirds of London's fire engines were already committed.* ❞

explosive and incendiary bombs were crashing down on the streets of West and East Ham boroughs, the Royal Docks, Canning Town and across the river at Woolwich. Further waves of aircraft hit the Surrey Dock complex whose quays and warehouses were full with over a million tons of imported timber. Even as the fire engines were being despatched during the first minutes of the raid, hundreds of fires were started in stacks of timber, ships unloading, dock offices and factories and houses in the surrounding streets.

Within half an hour, the situation in West Ham, just outside the LCC area, was desperate and with all their firefighting resources committed, West Ham was urgently asking London Regional Control at Lambeth for

Under Fire

The lethal hazards to which London's firefighters were exposed to throughout the Blitz period was well illustrated during the initial major raid of 7 September 1940. One of the areas in south London on the edge of the badly bombed sectors was Peckham. At the height of the raid at about 6.45 pm, the AFS driver of a four ton Bedford hose laying lorry was parking his fire engine in Bonar Road having just completed the task of running out twin lines of hose to bring in urgently-needed additional firefighting water to four pumps at work nearby. As the Bedford was being parked, a high explosive bomb fell on a row of terraced houses right alongside causing some civilian casualties and considerable blast damage right along Bonar Road. The Bedford hose lorry literally disappeared and it was assumed that it been blown apart by the bomb.

However, several days later when salvage and repair teams were at work, they discovered some hose visible under bricks and masonry and informed Peckham fire station. When a fire crew returned to the still devastated Bonar Road, they began to retrieve the hose, only to discover the still largely intact AFS Bedford hose layer vertically embedded tailboard-down within the upper shell of a terraced house, barely visible from the street below. It appeared that the Bedford hose layer had been blown about 100 ft up into the air to fall back down into the partially collapsed house. No trace was ever found of the hose layer's AFS driver.

Recollections — 7 September 1940

During the early evening of 7 September, a convoy of six fireboats was returning back up the Thames from the Thameshaven oil fires and was ordered to the Surrey Docks. As they came up Woolwich Reach their crews saw an extraordinary spectacle. The LFB officer in charge of this small flotilla wrote:

'We kept close formation until we reached Woolwich and from there on there was nothing but fire ahead, apparently stretching from one bank of the river to the other.... We seemed to be entering a tunnel of fire with burning barges drifting past.... The whole front of a riverside warehouse collapsed into the water and bags of beans poured into the river making a sound like a tropical rainstorm...

'Eventually we arrived at the wharf where we were to spend that endless night. Everything seemed to be on fire in every direction, even some barrage balloons in the sky were exploding. The cinder-laden smoke which drifted all around us made one think of the destruction of Pompeii.' Auxiliary Fireman Peter Blackmore.

Whole street areas right across the centre area of the capital were lit up by the flames as if daytime. One AFS fireman recalled:

'Occasionally, we would glance up and then see a strange sight, for a flock of pigeons kept circling round overhead almost all night. They seemed lost, unable to understand the unnatural dawn. The birds seemed white in the glare, birds of peace making a strange contrast to the scene below'.

500 pumps. Surprisingly, the final phase of this first concentrated raid of the Blitz only lasted for $1\frac{1}{2}$ hours but by 6.30 pm, the large wall map at Lambeth's underground control showing the availability of London's fire pumps looked distinctly bare, with few reserves in hand. It already showed nine 'conflagrations', a fire service term for a blaze actually out of physical control. Amongst these was the huge fire covering 250 acres in the Surrey Docks and another in London Docks nearby. Dockside cranes wilted and buckled in the heat and even the roadways were burning. Around 60 ships were sunk in the docks and the mooring ropes of many barges tied up at wharves burned through, allowing them to drift out into the Thames like flaming Viking funeral ships. By 6 pm Lambeth's disposition board showed nineteen 30 pump fires, forty 10 pump fires and over 1,000 smaller incidents being attended by a single pump and crew. The arithmetic was frightening. Over two thirds of London's fire engines were already committed. Around 8 pm a second wave of 200 Luftwaffe bombers were flying up the Thames towards the capital and guided by the many fires, unleashed more high explosives and incendiaries.

The thousands of warehouses in dockland and in the streets around the Pool of London had an enormous potential fire loading of stored goods, merchandise and raw materials and posed particular problems. As hundreds of incendiaries fell on these premises, they started paint fires that coated both firemen and their pumps in a sticky varnish that took

> *" A network of hoses ran from the pumps in all directions. "*

The London Blitz begins as wharves and warehouses in the Surrey Docks take fire following intense incendiary and high explosive attacks. These docks housed over a million tons of softwood which was soon involved in fire causing the first officer at the scene to urgently call for 200 additional pumps. 7 September 1940.

days to clean off. Hundreds of tons of sugar in sacks caught fire, and soon burned in a liquid form. There were fires involving leather hides, sacks of soya beans, tea chests, and in bales of cotton and wool. When grain sacks became involved in fire, rats were soon running around under the feet of firemen. In Bermondsey, the air was heavy with pungent spices, and when fire spread to drums of pepper in one warehouse, fire crews had to retreat overcome by fits of sneezing. Burning rubber gave off a particularly nasty black smoke so toxic that AFS crews had difficulty in breathing and had to fight this fire from a distance. At one riverside bonded store, rum in barrels spilt out onto the water and the surface of the Thames was on fire.

Whole street areas right across the centre area of the capital were lit up by the flames as if daytime. One AFS fireman recalled:

'Firemen are busy everywhere, and the place is a bedlam of roaring pumps, hissing water and falling roofs and walls. And past it all the Thames flows on uncaring, its murky surface like burnished copper.

Four AFS sub stations had to be abandoned due to fire spread and as the night wore on, the regular LFB station at Pageants Wharf served as both a command and control centre as well as a casualty clearing station for the many injured firefighters. AFS firewomen did sterling first aid work here under some very difficult and dangerous conditions, especially during the early stage of the raid as the first firemen casualties began to arrive, and they were also called to deal with a number of burning incendiaries around the perimeter of Pageants Wharf fire station

When dawn finally rose over London, it revealed devastation on an immense scale. Smoke still hung low everywhere and a pungent and acrid smell pervaded the air. Red LFB pumps and AFS heavy units and trailer pumps seemed to be on every street corner, many with their exhaust manifolds glowing red hot from their long hours at work. A network

Another view of the Surrey Docks about an hour after the first incendiaries fell during the first major raid of the continuous London Blitz. By this time over 200 pumps and 1,000 firemen were engaged in firefighting operations.

A typical street scene in the early hours of 8 September 1940. Although the enemy bombing has ceased, there are still huge fires to be conquered. Heat from the blazing building on the right is threatening to ignite the frontage of the premises opposite and fire crews can be seen directing cooling water to prevent this happening. Borough High Street, SE1.

of hoses ran from the pumps in all directions. Bomb craters marked the fall of high explosives and damaged gas mains were allowed to burn with hose lines protecting nearby undamaged buildings from radiated heat until the gas supply could be isolated. In the docks and other areas worst hit by the bombing, the gutted and charred shells of collapsed buildings still smouldered as firemen wearily worked their cooling water jets over the debris. Piles of masonry, brickwork and timber beams lay in roadways and shards of glass were everywhere along with chunks of razor sharp shrapnel from the bomb casings. Water from burst and punctured hoses gurgled down the gutters and, with many drains blocked, minor floods created large pools of dirty water from the night's battles.

During that first major air raid of 7 September 1940, 430 men, women and children were killed and seven firemen died in action. Over 100 were seriously injured with countless men suffering minor cuts, abrasions, and deafness through the explosions.

A group of weary London firemen take a brief pause from firefighting in this atmospheric image taken on 7 September 1940 at the beginning of the continuous Blitz. (*Fox Photos*)

Another fine character study of two London AFS firemen taking a break at a canteen van. They are, no doubt, reflecting upon the dangers they have faced during the past hours amid the smoke, sparks and falling ash of the air raid.

On the morning after this first major air raid, a greatly understated and cryptic entry in the Brigade's official war diary hardly told the full story of the night's danger, physical efforts and heroism of London's firefighters. It read:

'*September 7/8 1940:*

A big raid caused great fires at Surrey Docks, East and West India Docks, and the Royal Arsenal, which taxed the whole of the London Fire Service.'

Nobody, of course, could foretell the future for London's firefighters, but they were about to enter a period of 56 unrelenting and continuous nights of pyrotechnic hell and firefighting operations on an unprecedented scale.

CHAPTER TEN
The Relentless Raids and the National Fire Service

Mindful that fresh enemy raids were likely at any time, Chief Officer Jackson called an urgent meeting with his senior officers at Lambeth Headquarters on the morning of 8 September 1940 to take stock of the previous night's action. The principal problems during the previous night's raid included a poor level of communication between the various fire areas, a severe shortage of water in some districts exacerbated by bomb damage to water mains and a lack of a clear working chain of command between regular and AFS crews.

There was little radio equipment available for the fire service and with bombing already causing considerable damage and disruption to the telephone and street fire alarm network, most urgent messages between the scenes of major fires and Lambeth Control were carried by London Fire Service despatch riders. This small corps of riders, all AFS firemen, had been formed to provide a back-up messaging service, but after 8 September it was evident that their work was going to be critical to firefighting operations. The despatch riders had to get through the streets in the darkness even as the bombs were falling and try to avoid the many bomb craters and piles of rubble cascading into the streets from collapsed buildings. Jackson wisely decided that a strengthening of the despatch riders numbers was a priority and firewomen volunteers underwent suitable training for despatch rider duties almost immediately.

Another concern for Jackson and his command team was the need to evolve a new firefighting strategy for Blitz firefighting. It was very clear that the high standards of peacetime firefighting would have to be abandoned; the peacetime LFB had always prided itself on a minimum use of water at most domestic fires, together with prompt salvage

> 66 *The despatch riders had to get through the streets in the darkness even as the bombs were falling...* 99

The London Fire Brigade at war. From the declaration of war armed guards were mounted at fire stations and here an LFB sentry stands ready in the engine house at Lambeth Headquarters between a pump escape on the right and a 100 ft turntable ladder on the left.

operations to clear up and hand back a property with as little trauma as was possible. During the early stages of the 7 September raid, LFB crews attempted to carry out some salvage work as they would at a peacetime fire, before becoming overwhelmed with the scale of the overall situation. At his meeting, Jackson decreed that salvage work would not in future take place. Jackson also decided that close quarters firefighting LFB-style, inside a building, would rarely be an option open to a local commander. The 7 September and the Surrey Docks in particular, had shown that Blitz fires of such a large size needed water on a grand scale, and it was fortunate that many of the conflagrations of the previous night had been close to the Thames which had been at a reasonable tidal level. Hose relays from the river had been put in place early on during the raid. The new firefighting strategy was to try to concentrate available firefighting water to prevent fire spread down entire streets and to protect protected unaffected buildings by massed curtains of cooling water.

During the afternoon of 8 September, damping down and hose recovery was still going on at many locations and those crews who were allowed to snatch some sleep on fire stations across London first had to dry their

❝ *Major fires burned from the City eastwards through dockland to West Ham...* ❞

sodden uniforms. Many of those AFS recruits who had joined up in the months before the outbreak of war still had no second uniform or great-coat and sometimes had to undertake duties on station in their under-clothes. There were two brief air raid alerts around 5 pm when, as was normal, all crews stood to, rigged, ready to go and expecting the worst. But no Luftwaffe aircraft appeared and with crews stood down it was not until 8 pm that the sirens wailed again and soon after the first high explosive and incendiary bombs started to fall once again on London, dropped by a force of 200 Heinkel and Dornier aircraft.

A view of the London Fire Service Headquarters Control Room at Lambeth showing some of the multiple operator and plotting positions. September 1940.

HM King George VI and Queen Elizabeth paid several visits to Lambeth Headquarters to meet firemen and women during the Blitz, V1 flying bomb and V2 rocket years of the war. Here the King, accompanied by London's Chief Fire Officer Jackson and a fireman, pauses to look at a trailer pump. 16 October 1940.

Almost immediately the areas around St. Paul's in the City and on the south side of the Thames, Woolwich, were badly hit. Within an hour of the raid starting, Jackson was asking Home Office control for urgent re-inforcements from outside the London Region and pumps were ordered to London from Birmingham and East Anglia. Whitechapel fire station received a direct hit with a number of casualties including firewomen. Major fires burned from the City eastwards through dockland to West Ham Borough. Unlike the short concentrated raid of the night before, the bombing continued sporadically right through the night until 5 am on the morning of the 9 September. Jackson found time to get out into the streets before dawn to see some of the night's worst conflagrations and briefly give encouragement to his crews. Water relays on this second night seemed to be better organised and in place far more quickly with the regular service and the AFS crews seemingly working in much greater unison.

Thus the Blitz pattern was set for the next 55 days and nights as the Luftwaffe raided London with regular attacks involving up to 200 aircraft at a time. Such was the intensity of some of these continuous raids through to November 1940 that regular firefighting support was ordered in from fire brigades from the outer London region under the wartime Regional Support Plan.

The Blitz comes to central London. This view shows some of the aftermath of the previous night's bombing in Oxford Street, near New Bond Street, W1, with crews still damping down and no doubt preparing for the return of the Luftwaffe in a few hours time. 17 October 1940. (*Fox Photos*)

> **" An AFS sub station in Plumstead received a direct hit... "**

One positively good development for the men and women of the Auxiliary Fire Service was that since the first Luftwaffe raids on Thameshaven over the previous two weeks, the public view of the auxiliaries changed. National and local London newspapers openly applauded the work of the fire service, both in text and cartoons and almost overnight, the capital's firefighters received a sincere approbation that most found hard to believe. In pubs, shops and in the streets, they were all greeted as London's heroes.

The War Diary of the London Fire Service makes interesting reading as it simply records some of the principal action at the early days of the Blitz:

10th September: A determined attack on St. Katherine's and London Docks. Numerous large fires were started.

11th September: Great anti-aircraft barrage. Eighteen large fires with one in Lambeth involving sixteen separate small factories. Brigade lives again lost by bombing and shrapnel but morale improved by AA fire.

The Birth of the Benevolent Fund

The first fire raids on London were to lead to the foundation of the principal fire service charity — The Fire Services National Benevolent Fund. Right from the first Blitz raid, the number of fire service widows grew, many of these with young families. Incredibly, there was no specific fire service death grant for the widows of AFS firemen killed in action. Even widows of regular London Fire Brigade firemen had to suffer means testing in order to receive state benefits. This situation led to the princely sum of £24 being collected in public donations by the end of the first week of the Blitz in mid September 1940. As further donations came in, a London Fire Service Benevolent Fund was set up as a wartime charity to dispense financial help to a growing number of fire service widows. Then came several significant sums from American and Canadian firefighters that totalled £15,000 and once the National Fire Service was born in 1941, the Fund changed its title to became a national organisation with HM The Queen becoming Patron in 1953. Since those early days the Fund has grown to become a major charity that boasts two recuperation homes, a rehabilitation and therapy centre for injured firefighters and sheltered housing schemes. Nowadays, the Fund supports over 1,400 dependents and undertakes a great deal of other supportive work.

Another view that captures the drama of Blitz firefighting. Illuminated by the flames, this crew struggle to get a powerful jet to work on railway lines alongside Blackfriars Goods Depot, EC4. October 1940.

12th September: Heavy bombing of Belsize, Hampstead and Fulham areas. Fires, although numerous, were small and only two — the Western Fever Hospital in Marylebone and the Church of Our Lady of Victory in Kensington, required twenty pumps each but a thirty pump incident occurred in Westminster Bridge Road. An AFS sub station in Plumstead received a direct hit; two firemen and one firewoman killed and several injured. The Palace of Westminster was hit by an oil bomb but was quickly tackled by London Fire Service crews stationed inside the historic precincts.

13th September: Afternoon raid resulted in a number of small fires, only two (one in Scotland Yard) being serious. During the night ten fires were classed as serious and one as a major incident. AFS sub station at Abbey Choir School, Westminster, suffered direct hit and four firemen injured. An escape ladder unit attached to a Battersea AFS sub station wrecked by bomb blast. A delayed action bomb exploded outside Buckingham Palace.

14th September: High explosive bombing of St. Thomas's Hospital necessitated a twenty pump attendance. North and east blocks of Southwark fire station hit by bombs but no serious casualties. Brixton, Clapham and Balham received the worst bombing. 230 small fires reported in those areas as well as five serious incidents. Later in the night came major fires at Shadwell and in the Old Kent Road.

15th September: A Luftwaffe bomber shot down by an RAF fighter crashed into the forecourt of Victoria Station causing some casualties.

> **" For most London fire crews day merged into night... "**

16th September: Nearly 700 fires logged during the night. Bombing very severe in the City, Northern, Eastern and South Eastern districts. Sixteen serious and three major fires in these areas.

And so it went on. Until 28 September the raids continued during both day and night. From the 29 September, heavy raids occurred almost mostly during the dark hours. By the end of September 1940, 50 firemen had been killed in action and almost 500 injured so seriously that they would be invalided out of the service. The continuous raids continued into the first week of November by which time most London firefighters were utterly exhausted, both mentally and physically.

The famous *Daily Mirror* cartoon by Donald Zec that captured the public's feelings towards the fire and civil defence services during the phoney war period and after the London Blitz raids began.

A Poetic Tribute

Thank you, firefighters, harnessing your hoses,
Busy at your pumps, or patiently at play,
Once upon a time we used to throw you roses:
You don't see quite such a cloud of them today.

Some of us remember the blitz and the burning,
The black-faced force in the red and the blue,
St Paul's in peril and the Hun returning,
The tanks all dry and the night half through.

When they sound the sirens, some of us are sleeping,
Some of us turn over, some of us complain,
But you are on the job still, we are in your keeping,
And one fine night we'll be glad of you again.

(*A. P. Herbert*)

AFS fireman Vic Flint recalled in his diary:

'*It is strange when you are exhausted as I am these days how little the opposite sex can mean to you. I came up the night before my leave ended, but when I got to London there was a heavy raid on. So I reported to Westminster and they gave me a blanket on the floor of their watchroom. I went to sleep and when I woke up I found myself lying next to a very lovely blonde. She was one of the watchroom girls, and in our sleep we had moved into each other's arms for warmth. So we stayed like that for the rest of the night, but as far as I was concerned it didn't mean a thing. I must be getting old, or something.*'

For most London fire crews day merged into night, not just because of the firefighting work during the raids but in the tiresome and wearying tasks of clearing up hose after a fire was finally extinguished. AFS fireman Charles Poulson had been a pre-war cab driver with the London Taxicab Company and had joined the AFS when the taxi cabs were assigned to pull trailer pumps. He recalled the tiredness that everyone felt even after the first week of continuous raids in September. Arriving as a relief crew with others in London Docks he wrote:

'*A policeman and the Home Guard appear like magic in our headlights and wave us in... Outside, everything is dead and deserted, a lifeless city wrapped up in fear and darkness. But here, within these shattered walls, is bustle and activity. Huge ruddy piles glow everywhere. All the docks and their storehouses are burning ... Hammet's Wharf. And before it on the Thames river bank stands the pump we have come to relieve, roaring like an aeroplane. The operator leans against it, black and grimy from head to foot. We pull up and dismount.*'

The Home Secretary, the Rt. Hon. Herbert Morrison, MP, takes a personal aerial look from the head of a London Fire Brigade 100 ft turntable ladder to see the fire damage caused during the previous night's raid on the City of London. The turntable ladder is working close to the Bank of England and the Royal Exchange and below in the streets are fire pumps and hose relays still in use following the night's battles. 30 December 1940 (*Daily Mirror*)

'"24Z?" (a sub station of Brunswick Road fire station) asks Jim, as he's in charge.

'The other, a tall brawny young man, nods wearily, as though past interest. The whites of his eyes shine out of his filthy smoke-blackened face. Then he smiles politely, and his teeth show a white flash.

'"We're 38W" (a sub station of Kingsland Road fire station) says Jim, "We're relieving you."

'"It's about time."

'He seems to have had a hard time. That does not augur well for us.

'"Been here long?" I ask.

'"Well", he replies with delicate sarcasm, "what day is it?"'

66 *Then on 29 December came a very intense three hour raid on the City of London.* 99

Another view looking down on Whitecross Street, EC1, on the morning after the intense incendiary attack on the City. Some of the burnt out abandoned fire engines are testimony to the flames that have engulfed the street from both ends.

" *Everywhere there seemed to be a shortage of water.* "

Many of Sir Christopher
Wren's fine churches were
wrecked during the Blitz.
Here on the night of
29 December 1940 the tower
of St. Bride's, Fleet Street,
burns fiercely.

> *The first incendiaries fell in Queen Victoria Street, then around the Guildhall.*

From 8 November the enemy temporarily switched its attacks from London to the provincial cities. Birmingham, Bristol, Coventry, Liverpool and Southampton were all bombed and in December it was the turn of Sheffield, Liverpool (again) and Manchester to suffer the force of the Luftwaffe's aircraft. During this period the London Fire Service sent firefighting convoys out of it's area, including one to Coventry and one to Southampton. In both cases, the firefighting resources in those cities were near to collapse. The London convoy to Southampton was formed of a force of 400 officers and firemen, 20 pumps, four water units, four lorries loaded with spare hose and supplies, four canteen vans manned by AFS fire-women, and six despatch riders.

During the Blitz raids dressing stations were kept busy with fire service casualties, many of whom suffered from eye injuries caused by the sparks, ash and dust which were constantly swirling around the fire-fighting action in the streets. (*The Wardell Collection*)

This photograph, taken solely by the light of the flames, shows a typical firefighting scene during the London Blitz. On this occasion there appears to be a good supply of water from the pumps. Note the water jet on the far left being trained on the building opposite to that on fire to prevent it igniting due to the radiated heat. The expressions of the crew in the right foreground show the tension of the moment. Tabernacle Street, Shoreditch, EC2. 11 January 1941.

Despite all this attention to the provinces, the Luftwaffe returned to London with some particular venom during December 1940. On 8 December, a widespread attack over a wide area of the capital led the Brigade's war diary to record that in 24 hours, almost 2,000 separate fire incidents had been attended. Then came a very intense three hour raid on the City of London on 29 December. On this night, all of the City's largest water mains were damaged in the early stages of the raid. Nor did it help that the Thames was at a very low ebb and fireboats had to lay off in the middle of the river. Getting firefighting water from there to the shore was a time consuming and difficult task. Hose lorries laid water relays from the Elephant and Castle area, almost two miles away.

The first incendiaries fell in Queen Victoria Street, then around the Guildhall. A serious fire in the City Road was soon spreading out of control and a similar situation was developing south of the Thames in the Borough, Southwark. Fires were started as far westwards as Trafalgar Square and in the east, London Docks were also taking another hammering. St. Paul's was ringed by fire. Everywhere there seemed to be a shortage of water. Redcross Street fire station had been acting as a control point although its pumps and crews had long since disappeared amid the

> **❝** *Fourteen firemen were killed in action during the night…* **❞**

smoke and sparks: soon surrounded by fire, its AFS firewomen had to abandon their posts and flee. Cannon Street fire station, too, had to be evacuated and several conflagrations were declared — whole areas of streets burning out of control.

The worst of these was Whitecross Street in the Barbican district. Here, increasingly hemmed in on all sides by spreading flames and collapsing buildings, 15 pumps had to be abandoned when their crews were ordered to abandon their positions. The firefighters were lucky to make their escape beneath the inferno via the Underground railway. Once again, AFS firewomen played an invaluable role during the raid. They drove petrol carriers loaded with jerrycans into the heart of the danger zones taking precious fuel supplies to keep the roaring pumps at work. They also manned canteen vans, brewing hundreds of gallons of tea and cocoa,

During the unrelenting Blitz raids of 1940–41, the mobile canteen vans manned by AFS firewomen were much appreciated by London's weary and often dehydrated firefighters. Here, with the previous night's fires coming under control, this crew can be briefly spared to enjoy a cuppa and a cigarette. Note the AFS firewoman in the canteen van in the background. Borough High Street, SE1. February 1941. (*London News*)

On the night of 16 April 1941 Cannon Street fire station in Queen Victoria Street, EC4, suffered bomb damage including this parked Vauxhall staff car which has a hole in its roof caused by falling masonry. The damaged Vauxhall is pictured the morning after the raid with its female AFS driver and Cannon Street's LFB station officer. (*Westminster Press*)

whilst all across historic square mile of the City of London, fine white particles of ash fell covering the streets, fire engines and blinding many firefighters like some benign snowstorm.

Of the 1,500 serious fires logged on the night of 29 December, only 28 were located outside of the City of London. Afterwards, Marshal Herman Goering boasted that his Luftwaffe crews had dropped 100,000 incendiaries on the square mile in the three hour raid. For once, most London firemen believed him to be telling the truth. By the time the 'all clear' sounded at 9.45 am the next morning, eight of Christopher Wren's churches, the Guildhall and many livery halls, offices and warehouses had burnt like torches. The Tower of London and the Law Courts had also been hit. Fourteen firemen were killed in action during the night and four AFS firewomen were subsequently awarded gallantry awards for driving petrol carriers through the bombs of that dreadful night. Records showed that some 13,000 Londoners had died in the Blitz between 7 September and the raid of 29 December, with over 20,000 others seriously wounded.

The devastating City raid served to underline the need for occupiers to provide a reliable firewatching vigil to try and deal with incendiaries as soon as they fell. The German incendiaries weighed one kilogramme and ignited upon impact, but if confidently and promptly tackled with sand they would burn out and be contained. That St. Paul's had survived the night's fiery onslaught was attributed to the cathedral firewatchers on

> 66 *The Tower of London and the Law*
> *Courts had also been hit.* 99

Blitz Diary Recollections

'*Returning to the station we find that seven of our men are missing... Later we hear that four of them are so badly burned as to hardly recognisable... The next morning I saw the wife of one of them sitting with a white blank face in the station officer's room. We tried not to notice her as we went about our daily routine...*'
(Auxiliary Fireman Philip Henderson)

'*I can well remember the sight of Fireman McAwley (from Fulham) lying in the gutter with one of his legs off and water running over his face... Somehow the sight of a man you've known lying there and nobody being able to do anything puts the wind up you... And then the sub officer told me to get up the ladder and put some water into the warehouse...*' (Auxiliary Fireman Vic Flint)

'*At seven o'clock as I went home no pump had yet returned... The darkness of the streets after the glare of the control room seemed, for a moment, like a wall... I felt the wind that cut at my face and hands. I felt the longing for sleep, to which, so soon I could yield... and to which the men at the pumps could not — perhaps for hours... And most of all, I felt — as I still feel — pride at being connected, however slightly, with so proud a service.*' (Auxiliary Firewoman Grace Owtram)

duty. Winston Churchill thought so too. Despite the heroic work performed by London's firefighters, the Premier was apparently furious that the City had suffered so much damage and that property owners had not provided sufficient fire watchers. As a result of a war cabinet meeting later that day, a Fire Precautions Order was rushed through Parliament making it an immediate statutory requirement to provide fire watchers in high risk areas of the capital and elsewhere.

Further heavy raids in early 1941 continued to hit London targets on 11/12 January, 8/9 March, 19/20 March, and on 19/20 April. In addition, firefighting convoys from London were also despatched to support the fire brigades in several cities. Fortunately, February 1941 was a month of prolonged poor weather with rain, low clouds, mist and fog that grounded the Luftwaffe bombers. This welcome respite was a godsend for the London Fire Service to regroup, restock and replace its equipment where necessary, and await fresh calls to arms.

One of the many fine wartime paintings produced by fireman artists of the AFS is this study by Leslie Carr of the smouldering ruins of St. Bride's Church, Fleet Street. 30 December 1940.

The final raid of this Blitz period of the war came on the cold night of 10 May, Cup Final night after Arsenal had taken on Preston North End at Wembley. At London Regional Control it was soon clear that this was a very heavy raid. The West Ham area was first to be hit and within 15 minutes bombs fell and started fires in Bethnal Green, Whitechapel, Shoreditch, Clerkenwell, the City, the West End, Paddington, Marylebone, Battersea, Bermondsey, Blackfriars and Southwark. The roof of the British Museum in Bloomsbury was fired by incendiaries high up on its dome, whilst the sweeping roof and platforms of St. Pancras railway station took a direct high explosive hit, exposing the Metropolitan Underground lines below. Mobilising telephone lines between Lambeth Regional Control and the District control rooms were lost for several hours and with all its 72 pumps already long-since despatched to fires,

The fireman artists of the London AFS produced some fine work that was exhibited in London, the provinces and America. This wartime painting is by AFS fireman Stanley Flegg, and is entitled *Came the Dawn*.

'B' District Control at Clerkenwell had no idea where to send the re-inforcing pumps that were beginning to arrive from outer London fire brigades. Every link over the Thames from London Bridge to Lambeth was at some stage affected and not for the first time, fire service despatch riders, many of them firewomen, truly earned their keep.

As many huge blazes came under some control in the chilly first light of dawn, the damage reports started to come in; 700 acres of London had been damaged by fire. Most of London's main line railway stations had been hit. There were fires in historic buildings including Westminster Hall, Westminster Abbey, the Temple, St. Thomas's Hospital, and Lambeth Palace. At the other end of the scale, hundreds of terraced dwellings around the Elephant and Castle, Walworth Road and Kennington were areas of severe fire and bomb damage.

> ❝ *Most of London's main line railway
> stations had been hit.* ❞

During the early afternoon of 11 May there were still many fires not under control and several thousand pumps still committed. There had been 2,200 fires recorded including nine official conflagrations (fires burning out of control) in addition to 20 major fires each needing 30 pumps and 37 requiring 20 units. Home Office Commander Firebrace and Chief Officer Jackson both agreed and briefed the War Cabinet that even more supporting pumps from the outer regions should be mobilised into central London to meet the expected raiding of that coming night. Expecting the worst, the Regional Fire Control ordered over 1,000 extra firefighters into London ready for the night's action.

A dramatic view of Blitz firefighting operations in Queen Victoria Street in the heart of the City of London, April 1941.

During one of her visits to Lambeth Headquarters Queen Elizabeth talks to two AFS firewomen dispatch riders, who as a group performed sterling work during the Blitz raids in maintaining essential communications.

But the raids were not to be. On the darkened evening of 12 May 1941, many of the weary firefighters of the London Fire Service 'stood to' ready to turn out from their various fire stations alongside pumps from towns such as Chipping Ongar, Slough and Wimbledon, but London's network of air raid sirens stayed eerily silent. The Luftwaffe did not return and after two successive peaceful nights, it was clear from intelligence reports that Goering's Air Fleet Two were moving on from their airfields in France and Belguim to be redeployed on the Russian Front. For utterly exhausted firefighters, both regular and AFS, together with a war-weary population, the silence of the night of 12 May 1941 marked the end of the London Blitz. The real threat of another Great Fire of London had been averted, thanks largely to the unrelenting sweat, toil and bravery of its firemen and women.

*** The real threat of another Great
Fire of London had been
averted... ***

Fire Service Casualties

Two of the worst fatal Blitz incidents involving the loss of London's wartime firefighters occurred near the Elephant and Castle, South London and at Poplar in the East End. The most serious fire service loss of life during the Blitz occurred when a high explosive bomb fell on The Old Palace School, Poplar, on 19 April 1941 when it was being used as an AFS sub station. On this day, AFS crew from Beckenham, Kent, had arrived to relieve hard-pressed London firemen. The bomb killed 13 London firemen and firewomen, and a further 21 Beckenham firefighters. The Old Palace School fatalities still represent the largest single loss of life of fire service personnel in British history and today a plaque on the wall of the school erected on the site after the war records the wartime sacrifice of all those years ago.

The second of these incidents took place during the huge raid of 10 May 1941 that afterwards marked the end of the intense Blitz period. There was a severe water shortage in the Elephant and Castle, Southwark and Blackfriars districts and as crews worked to set up water relays and booster pumps, a land mine fell near the site of the Surrey Music Hall in Blackfriars Road, instantly killing 17 firemen.

Since November 1940 the heavy air raids upon the provincial cities had shown many local firefighting resources to be insufficient to cope with the demands of wartime fire situations. Indeed, for some time both within and outside the uniformed service, there were growing calls for a stronger central co-ordination of the nation's fire brigades and even before the final London Blitz raid of 11 May 1941, events moved towards this objective. In fact it was a meeting on the evening of 18 April between Home Secretary Herbert Morrison, Commander Firebrace and Sir Arthur Dixon, then head of the fire service division of the Home Office, and others that first put in place the concept of the National Fire Service (NFS). A parliamentary Bill soon followed and the NFS formally came into being on 18 August 1941, with the aim of concentrating firefighting forces wherever they might be needed.

The country was at first divided into 11 regions, subdivided into 33 (later 43) fire force areas. The London region was designated No. 5 Region made up of five (later four) fire forces embracing all the personnel,

This Bedford heavy unit sustained serious blast damage whilst pumping in Alderney Street, Pimlico on 11 April 1941 and is pretty typical of the effects of sustained bombing upon a number of London Fire Service fire engines during the Blitz years.

fire stations and fire engines of the regular London Fire Brigade, the London Auxiliary Fire Service, together with the other 66 outer London brigades and their AFS sections.

Commander Firebrace was appointed Chief of Staff at the Home Office whilst a number of London's senior officers were appointed to command other regions of the NFS. In a hectic three month period the allocation of personnel, fire engines and equipment had to be finalised, along with the chain of national operational command. In addition came NFS badges and insignia, the first unified rank structure and a standard pay scale. New training manuals and regimes were also instituted. All this was achieved under wartime conditions where fresh air raids were expected although in late 1942, never materialised.

In fact, the NFS was never really tested by fire and by April 1942, the strength of the NFS London region was put at 42,000 firemen and firewomen. In 1942 and 1943, there were only 23 minor air raids over the London region although the 'Baedeker' caused considerable casualties and damage during raids on other historic cities during 1942. During these bombing attacks, London firemen and their pumps formed convoys and re-inforced cities from Exeter to Norwich, and from Birmingham to Bath. January 1943 saw the resignation of Major Jackson as Chief Commander of the NFS London Region in order to take up a non-uniformed government post in the Department of Scientific and Industrial Research. Jackson's place was taken by Frederick Delve, the former Chief Fire Officer of the Croydon Fire Brigade.

*" In fact, the NFS was never really
tested by fire..."*

Wartime Firemen Artists

People from all walks of life, including the world of literature and the arts, joined the AFS during the war and the firemen artists went on to record images of the Blitz in a unique and personal way. Encouraged by Commander Firebrace at the Home Office and Chief Officer Jackson, the firemen artists soon became a high profile group and arrangements were put in hand to display their works. Exhibitions were held in aid of the Fire Service Benevolent Fund and many prominent people purchased paintings.

In March 1941 the Central School of Arts and Crafts saw the first exhibition by the fireman artists which then toured the United States. In August 1941 the artists held their first and highly acclaimed exhibition at the Royal Academy which attracted over 64,000 visitors in one month alone: some paintings were bought for the Nation and some were also later exhibited in America.

However, it was not only in the capital that exhibitions were staged. In May 1942 the fire service paintings were displayed at the Cooling Gallery in Bond Street before touring the provinces, being seen in many of the principal town and cities of the United Kingdom.

Over 76,000 people visited a second exhibition held at the Royal Academy in August 1942, when not only the Government purchased paintings, but also the High Commissioner of Canada who bought one for the second year running. The following year other prestigious exhibitions were mounted, opened by such well known personalities as Herbert Morrison and Lady Louis Mountbatten and supported by the Prime Minister's wife, Clementine Churchill, whose Red Cross Fund greatly benefited from the sums of money raised.

Although 1942–43 were relatively quiet periods for the much enlarged personnel of the London region of the NFS, there was still plenty to do. With new allocations of pumps and turntable ladders, there was plenty of training to get on with. Many firemen in the service had special skills as motor mechanics, bricklayers and plumbers; these were used to the full and properly rewarded in their pay scales. In their stand down time firemen were also engaged in fabricating small components for industry and

> **"** *Many firemen in the service had*
> *special skills...* **"**

toy making schemes, often using timber from bomb damaged premises. In preparation for the D-Day landings an overseas NFS column was formed to give fire cover on the beaches and to follow up the infantry's advance in case of a scorched earth policy. And when the first Mulberry Harbour cassions were built on the Thames, 400 firemen worked for a period of six months providing high pressure jets to clear the mud from under these huge constructions in order to get them launched, often spending hours up their waists in mud. The last sporadic air raid on London by piloted aircraft was recorded on 19 April 1944.

Almost two thirds of London's fire stations were damaged during the Second World War and this view is of a devastated AFS sub station and its various towing vehicles and trailer pumps following a direct hit. Eltham, south London. April 1941.

> 66 *...the real test for the NFS came with the final phase of the London firemen's war.* 99

This poignant view shows a simple lying-in state prior to their funeral of two firemen killed in action during a Blitz raid. April 1941.

A view taken from the dome of St. Paul's on the morning after the last major Blitz raid of 10 May 1941 looking down Ludgate Hill towards Fleet Street. Many fires are still burning and fire crews and pumps are still at work.

However, with the D-Day landings making significant progress into the enemy's territory, the real test for the NFS came with the final phase of the London firemen's war. This began on 13 June 1944 when the first of Hitler's new terror weapons fell on open ground near Barking. At first it was believed to be an enemy aircraft but when a second and a third alert sounded and further crashes and fires were reported, it slowly became clear that these were pilotless explosive projectiles being fired at London. The V1 Flying Bomb had arrived.

The V1s carried 1,000 kg of high explosive and were powered by a rather noisy petrol-injection ram jet engine that propelled the weapon at 350 mph towards its target. The engine would then cut out and the V1 would fall silently to earth with a huge explosion, the blast from which would easily demolish several properties. Quickly dubbed 'doodle bugs' by Londoners, the V1 kept coming both through the day and during the night. The NFS attended every incident even though fire did not always result. In these cases, the fire service would assist the civil defence rescue units and ambulance service to cope with the large number of civilian casualties. Massed V1 attacks took place on the London area from June 1944 with

> *" The public continued to praise the changing work of the fire service. "*

A contingent of firemen of No. 5 Region (London) of the National Fire Service march smartly through Admiralty Arch and into The Mall during a parade of the armed forces, fire service and civil defence personnel. 14 June 1942.

a total of 638 V1s in that month alone. With a 'normal' average of 12 to 18 V1 incidents per day, the peak days were on 2 July 1944 when 80 fell and on 3 August when 97 crashed to earth. RAF fighters managed to down a daily number but the V1s still kept coming, causing death and destruction in their wake and there were many large incidents. A tar works in Bermondsey received a direct hit causing a massive blaze; another V1 hit a gasometer in Kennington, also setting fire to 10,000 gallons of paraffin nearby; a bus garage at Elmers End received a direct hit badly damaging 53 buses.

SEEING IT THROUGH

Thank you, fire fighters, harnessing your hoses,
   Busy at your pumps, or patiently at play.
Once upon a time we used to throw you roses:
   You don't see quite such a cloud of them today.

Some of us remember the blitz and the burning,
   The black-faced force in the red and the blue,
St. Paul's in peril and the Hun returning,
   The tanks all dry and the night half through.

When they sound the sirens, some of us are sleeping,
   Some of us turn over, some of us complain,
But you are on the job still, we are in your keeping,
   And one fine night we'll be glad of you again.
                        A. P. Herbert

Artist E.H. Kennington First Published 1944 Ref. No. 1611

One of a series of wartime Underground posters depicting the Home Front. The poster, by E. H. Kennington is entitled *Seeing it Through*, and shows a firewoman driver of the National Fire Service and a poem by A. P. Herbert, reproduced elsewhere in this chapter. (*London Transport*)

The arrival of the VI flying bombs brought new rescue challenges to the fire and civil defence services due to the widespread and compacted blast damage to buildings. This is a typical scene after a VI has fallen. Middlesex Street, Stepney, E1. 10 November 1944.

Firefighters had many narrow escapes and here during a 1944 VI incident, a crew is rapidly evacuating down a turntable ladder from a building in which the fire has developed out of control. (*The Wardell Collection*)

In 1944 Queen Elizabeth paid another visit to Lambeth Headquarters, now the No. 5 Region Headquarters of the National Fire Service. The Queen is talking to Assistant Fire Force Commander Ronnie Greene who, in 1940, was personally responsible for setting up the London Fire Service Benevolent Fund that became a national organisation three years later, benefiting all wartime fire service widows and orphans. Today the Fire Services National Benevolent Fund is the principal charity of the fire service and Ronnie Greene's name is commemorated in a modern recuperative home run by the Fund at Littlehampton, Sussex.

Manned observation towers were set up on the top of the tall drill towers on regular fire stations and those manning the posts were able to accurately report the fall of the V1s. Working with the civil defence teams, the fire service became adept at carrying out rescues of persons under the compacted debris of collapsed buildings, although fires caused by fractured gas mains were always a problem.

The public continued to praise the changing work of the fire service. A baker who lost his shop in Crayford wrote:

'I would like to put on record my admiration for the firemen who rescued my manageress alive and immediately went back down into the wreckage to rescue an elderly woman...'

Some idea of the scale of the damage caused by the V1 flying bombs and V2 rockets can be gauged by this late 1944 view of Balham High Road, south London following an attack. The rear end of the double-decker bus is barely visible buried in a deep bomb crater. Many casualties resulted, together with quite a few dangerous ladder rescues for the fire service to perform from high up on the frontage of the damaged buildings.

The action in this photograph suggests that it was taken not long after the fall of the V1 in the Aldwych at its junction with the Strand. The fire service is still dealing with a number of fires whilst the search and rescue operation goes ahead. November 1944.

> 66 *On 9 September, a huge explosion occurred in Chiswick High Road...* 99

Another man whose business was hit by a flying bomb in Millwall testified to:

'*the courage and energy displayed by members of the National Fire Service.*'

A family at Streatham recalled:

'*In the rescue work, the fire service is keeping up its tradition and is as usual doing wonderful work. My mother, sister and I were buried under debris and were rescue by firemen. We shall never forget the speed and efficiency with which they worked, but also their kindness. Their cheerfulness and an encouragement did much to alleviate this dreadful experience.*'

A total 531 V1s fell in the London area during August 1944 and the last day of the sustained flying bomb attack was 1 September. After several

There were some remarkable rescues of Londoners during the flying bomb and rocket attacks. This woman was buried alive by a V1 in Whitta Road, Manor Park, east London in November 1944 but was successfully dug out, conscious and largely uninjured.

During the latter years of the war command and control was well organised through a network of mobile control units and dispatch riders. Here, in early 1945, a control unit and its fire service crew, together with dispatch rider check their equipment in preparation for the next turnout.
(*The Wardell Collection*)

days of relative peace in the skies, Londoners might have thought that the Allied forces push into Europe would mark the end of the terror weapons. Alas, it was not to be. On 9 September, a huge explosion occurred in Chiswick High Road that was heard many miles away — the first V2 rocket had arrived. Unlike their V1 counterparts, the giant V2 rockets were one of the first ballistic missiles and gave no warning of their approach, simply falling out of the skies on an unsuspecting civilian population, their one ton warheads exploding on contact.

Although only 16 V2s fell during September they each caused death and destruction on an unprecedented scale, flattening whole rows of properties in a street every time they fell. For the fire service and civil defence teams, the rescue challenges and difficulties of the V1 era were magnified. V2 rockets continued to fall on London right through the Christmas period, reaching a monthly peak of 116 in February 1945 and 115 in March. Generally, more people were killed with many others trapped under rubble and debris after each V2 explosion and the sheer scale of each incident was considerable. The carnage caused was truly awful. On 25 November 1944 a V2 fell in New Cross killing 268 men, women and children. In February 1945 another V2 exploded near Smithfield Meat Market causing 233 fatalities.

The very last recorded V2 rocket fell near Orpington during the late afternoon of 27 March 1945 and it signalled the end of the final phase of

“ *On 25 November 1944 a V2 fell in New Cross killing 268 men, women and children.* ”

A scene in February 1945 that typifies the work of the fire service during 1944–45 throughout the flying bomb and rocket attacks. This London fireman carefully carries an apparently uninjured young child to safety across the piles of brickwork rubble caused by a V2 rocket.

> **Wartime Honours and Awards**
>
> Throughout the war, the bravery of the men and women of the capital's firefighting forces was regularly recognised and an impressive number of gallantry awards were won. A George Cross was awarded to Auxiliary Fireman Harry Errington who, despite being badly burned, rescued two injured fellow firemen when their sub station in Rathbone Street, W1, off Oxford Street, received a direct hit. Other wartime fire service gallantry awards included 38 George Medals, one of which was awarded to Auxiliary Firewoman Bobby Tanner for her coolness and courage under intensive bombardment on the night of 20 September 1940 when she volunteered to drive a petrol van into a major central London fire zone to allow the many pumps at work to be refuelled. The regional senior fire officer also commended 152 members of the LFB, AFS and latterly, the NFS, for outstanding acts of bravery; 17 of these awards went to firewomen. Other wartime recognition for London firemen included one CBE, three OBEs, 13 MBEs and 118 BEMs, plus 11 King's Police and Fire Service Medals for Distinguished Conduct.

the war for the men and women who formed the London region of the NFS. A total of 2,381 V1 flying bombs and 511 V2 rockets had fallen on the Greater London area in nine months since June 1944, causing over 900 major incidents involving protracted rescues and casualty recovery. In the old London County Council area, 30,000 dwellings had been destroyed and almost $1\frac{1}{4}$ million damaged. Wandsworth, Lewisham, Woolwich and Silvertown were all badly hit by V1s and V2s but the worst affected borough was Croydon which suffered 139 individual attacks.

When peace in Europe was finally declared on 8 May 1945, 327 men and women of London's fire service had been killed in action and over 3,000 seriously injured. At some stage or other during the war years, 662 of London's 875 fire stations had been damaged by fire or bomb blast and firefighters had attended over 50,000 separate major fires and emergencies. World War Two on the Home Front was a period of fire and explosion without parallel in British history and the men and women of the fire service could feel proud of their sustained part in the front line.

CHAPTER ELEVEN

Post War: Back to Local Authority Control

When Home Secretary Herbert Morrison commenced the legal process to nationalise the fire service in 1941, he made a promise to local authorities that when peace eventually came the service would be returned to local control. Thus, once hostilities were finally over in 1945, the National Fire Service began to prepare itself for a new peacetime role. In London and elsewhere, the AFS was slowly dis-established. Old AFS sub stations in requisitioned buildings were pro-gressively closed and many firemen were able to return to their pre-war jobs or seek fresh employment as the overall numbers of firemen across the country was reduced to that suited to peacetime fire brigades.

The Fire Services Act of 1947 came into effect on 1 April 1948 and placed the post-war responsibility for maintaining efficient fire brigades

During his time as Chief Officer, Frederick Delve invited a string of well known personalities to Lambeth Headquarters either as his guests at the regular organised displays or for an informal visit. Here, Chief Officer Delve introduces Viscount Montgomery of Alamein to an audience of LFB officers in 1959.

Even though the war was over, firemen still faced danger in their work. This painting entitled *Night Rescue* is by wartime AFS fireman artist Reginald Mills and depicts the heroic rescue of a child by fireman Frederick Davies. He was the first crew member up the wheeled escape ladder and into the burning room where he found a child and staggering back to the window, managed to hand over the infant to another fireman on the ladder. By then, Davies was himself on fire and hardly had the child left his arms when he collapsed back into the inferno where he died. Fireman Davies was posthumously awarded the George Cross for his actions. Harlesden High Street, NW10. 5 February 1946.

on county councils and county boroughs. From that date the London Fire Brigade (LFB) re-emerged under the administration of the London County Council (LCC), whilst the Croydon, East Ham and West Ham Brigades returned under their county borough councils. In a new move by the government, small town brigades that had been part of the outer London region during NFS days reformed to create the larger new county brigades of the Middlesex, Hertfordshire, Essex, Surrey, and Kent county councils. The new Act also for the first time introduced a number of national standards on fire brigades including the measuring of fire risks, the attendance of fire engines to calls, the number of fire stations, and the manpower and fire engine strength of a brigade. In addition, there were new National Joint Councils to negotiate rates of pay and conditions of service, as well as a Council to advise the Secretary of State on matters such as promotion, fire engine and equipment specifications, uniform and other topics.

On 1 April 1948, Frederick Delve, the wartime commander of the London Region NFS, took up his new post as Chief Fire Officer of the London Fire Brigade at the head of almost 2,500 firemen. London was still the largest

A photograph that well encapsulates the post war London Fire Brigade. Here the camera captures some of the Red Watch at D61 Lambeth posing in front of a very clean and well polished AEC Merryweather dual purpose pump.

A view of the funeral cortege of three London firemen killed in action when a wall fell in during a major blaze at Broad Street Goods Depot, Eldon Street, EC2 on 21 December 1951. Here the flower decked fire engines bear the three coffins along the Victoria Embankment, past a guard of honour from nearby Whitefriars Fire Station where all three men were stationed. 29 December 1951. (*Sport & General*)

fire brigade in the country, although the Middlesex Brigade had an establishment strength of over 1,400 and those of Essex, Surrey and Kent were between 1,200 and 1,400, even though quite a number of these served either as regulars, or in the retained service of more rural areas. The post National Fire Service LFB consisted of 58 fire stations and two river stations, organised into four divisions. One of Delve's stated objectives was to restore the London Fire Brigade to its highly efficient pre-war condition that had made it famous throughout the world for its firefighting prowess.

Unfortunately, five and more years of war had left their mark and one of the immediate problems was that many older London fire stations had been damaged by wartime bombing and some were in a parlous state. It was not possible to fund a new station building programme until the mid-1950s but work was put in hand to improve the existing messing arrangements, washing facilities, lighting, and drill yards. The London fire engine fleet had also received tremendous usage during the war

years, with many clocking several thousand pumping hours during the Blitz period of 1940–41 and were very well worn. Although a number of the government pumps and tenders provided new for AFS use in 1939 found their way into the London reserve fleet, Chief Officer Delve moved forward a fire engine replacement that, by the early 1960s, meant that most of the regular Brigade's pre-war Leyland and Dennis open pumps, all veterans of the street battles of 1940–41, were finally pensioned off.

From 1954, all new fire engines coming into the LFB fleet were diesel powered and in 1959 came the first of a new generation of hydraulically operated 100 ft turntable ladders in a programme to replace 23 pre-war mechanically operated versions, all of which had given valiant service during the war years. The crew cabs of the new fire engines were more spacious, allowing for three oxygen breathing sets on selected pumps, and generally better stowage of the increasing amount of other equipment being carried, with a wider use of light alloys. Every new pump had a 100 gallon water tank feeding two hose reels capable of dealing with most small fires. The machines were all dual purpose, capable of running with a 50 ft wheeled escape or simply as a pump with a 35 ft extension ladder. On the River Thames, a new fireboat, the *Firebrace* was commissioned in 1962.

With the growing tension caused by the Cold War, regular large scale exercises were held to test the readiness of the Auxiliary Fire Service. This remarkable photograph taken during such an exercise shows 50 of London's Green Goddess AFS fire engine fleet at work pumping water from the Serpentine in Hyde Park. 27 October 1957.

> 66 *Unfortunately, five and more years of war had left their mark...* 99

This 1958 view shows a typical London Fire Brigade medium sized fire, known by firemen as a 'four pumper' after the number of fire engines attending. The building is a general warehouse of three floors in Tooley Street, near Tower Bridge and the fire appears to have started on the first floor. Two 50 ft wheeled escapes are in use to provide access into the warehouse: a crew in Proto oxygen breathing apparatus is going into the first floor whilst the crew on the escape at the top of the picture are trying to release some of the heat and smoke from the top floor. The well polished fire engine in the foreground is an AEC Regent pump escape based at station 63 Dockhead.

Communications were also radically improved and since the end of the war most London fire engines were beginning to have radio fitted, and telephones were becoming increasingly widespread. As a result, Chief Officer Delve made an important recommendation to the LCC fire authority when he advised the abolition of all London street fire alarms. These still went directly into local fire stations. At first there was great public concern but Delve pointed out that street alarms required testing every week and were increasingly the target of malicious false alarms. The LCC approved their Chief's recommendation and the last street fire alarm was removed in January 1958. Until that same year, all '999' telephone calls were routed into the five district Headquarters stations but with a new central control room at Lambeth Headquarters, it was now possible to mobilise all LFB fire engines and operations from this one location.

Another growing and important area of the Brigade's work was that of preventing fire from occurring in the first place through advice and recommendation. Under the 1947 Fire Services Act, all brigades had a duty to give advice to owners and occupiers on fire safety and prevention. With a number of officers seconded specially for fire prevention duties, many historic buildings across the capital, including the British

By the late 1950s the Brigade was increasingly responding to 'special service calls' — emergencies of a non-fire nature. Fifty years ago these were mainly to road accidents where the Brigade's breakdown lorry was frequently used for the recovery of vehicles involved in road crashes. Here, the LFB breakdown lorry pulls a van out of a basement area at the junction of Gloucester Street and Winchester Street, Pimlico, SW1. 19 January 1959.

Hook ladders had been a valuable part of the rescue equipment of the London Fire Brigade since 1902 and they were occasionally used for successful rescues right up to their withdrawal in the early 1980s. This view shows a recruits squad in training on the drill tower at Lambeth c.1960. In progress is a two man, two hook ladder drill. The fireman on the lower ladder is passing the second ladder up to his colleague out of sight one floor above. The fireman on the lower ladder is hooked on using a special belt that allows him to have his hands free. Using hook ladders called for a fine balance and co-ordination, not to mention upper body strength and by end of the fifth week of the recruits' course, hook ladders had certainly exorcised any fear of heights.

Museum, Westminster Abbey, the Palace of Westminster and St. Paul's were inspected and improvements to advice on fire safety was provided. Similar advice on a goodwill basis followed inspections of the London Underground system, all the major hospitals, large offices and hotels. In addition, the Brigade on behalf of the LCC continued to exercise statutory control over large and tall new buildings to ensure a high level of fire safety. Requirements might include a sprinkler system, fitted hose reels, fire alarms and extinguishers. Specialist LFB officers also inspected theatres, cinemas and other large places of public entertainment on a regular basis, as well as all LCC schools.

Special records began to be kept of premises where there existed particular risks such as radioactive substances, new chemicals and other items likely to be hazardous to both firefighters and members of

the public in event of fire. Another new post-war duty allowed operational crews to spend some on duty time visiting premises within their fire station grounds to familiarise themselves with access, layout and water supplies.

Another post war development was, perhaps, a surprising one. The Auxiliary Fire Service had been absorbed into the National Fire Service in 1941 and was quickly stood down as the fire service was returned to local authority control after the war. However, due to the increasingly uncertain international political direction of the Soviet Union, the AFS was reconstituted nationally in 1948, and this gave a particular problem to the LFB. Recruiting sufficient part-time volunteers to join the London AFS and finding them suitable accommodation was another task for hard pressed administrators, although quite a few of those men and women who had served in the wartime AFS readily rejoined once again.

However, in 1949 the regular Brigade was 400 men under its strength and recruitment into the regular Brigade was affected by the higher pay and more sociable hours offered by work in industry. Nor was this situation helped when the police service received a substantial pay

An action picture that shows a typical 'make up' fire where the first crews arriving at the scene have asked for urgent assistance. This fire in Bradbury Street, Dalston, N16, involved a storage warehouse and dwelling above and required the combined efforts of 50 firemen and eight pumps. 17 August 1967.

> 66 *The depot was a large building of five floors with a complex internal layout...* 99

increase and the Fire Brigades Union (FBU) lodged a similar claim that was referred to an Industrial Court which after due consideration, rejected pay parity with the police. Although firefighters did receive a rent allowance of 11 shilling a week (55p) that was consolidated into their pay, some 18 months later policemen again received an above inflation award, the FBU once again claimed parity. The employers national pay council again rejected this claim and offered a lower figure. This time, the FBU instructed all their members to refuse all duties other than fire and other emergency calls. On 19 and 20 November 1951, over 1,400 London firemen duly followed their union instructions, the first withdrawal of labour in the long history of the fire service. As a result, all those involved were charged under the Discipline Code for refusing lawful orders to work normally.

This fire in a food store in Fulham Road, Chelsea, in March 1969 was dealt with by the crews of four pumps and here the fire is being tackled inside the shop by a crew in Proto oxygen breathing sets. The black toxic smoke is a good example of what London firefighters would call 'a drop of thickers'! (*Tony Jafrato*)

Following the Smithfield Meat Market fire of 1958 in which two London firemen died, breathing apparatus (BA) procedures were strengthened nationally by a number of additional safety features. One of these was the more effective overall control of BA wearers working as teams during firefighting operations. Here a BA Control Officer stands by a special board that records the entry of each BA wearer going into the smoke and his oxygen cylinder contents. From this the working duration of each BA set can be calculated before an alarm sounds to warn of a low oxygen supply. An emergency crew in BA stand by ready for emergencies whilst on the left, a radio link is established with the innermost BA crew.

Several weeks later, even as preparations were being made by Chief Officer Delve to begin to hear this multitude of discipline cases, itself a massive task, the Brigade were called to a fire in a British Railways goods depot in Eldon Street in the City, close to Broad Street and Liverpool Street railway stations. The depot was a large building of five floors with a complex internal layout and the fire quickly spread in all directions to involve all floors requiring the attendance of 20 pumps and five turntable ladders, with Chief Officer Delve taking command. Although flames broke through the roof, the fire was surrounded with good progress being made by firemen working off escape ladders at all floor levels.

Ever since James Braidwood's days, serious fires in buildings always posed a hazard for firemen owing to the building structure weakening in the intense heat. At Eldon Street railway depot, warnings had been given to the crews working around the perimeter of the warehouse to watch for developing cracks in the structure. Suddenly, an outer wall bulged

The Royal Review of 1966 at Lambeth Headquarters in front of HM The Queen and the Duke of Edinburgh saw various drill sequences to illustrate aspects of the LFB's history and operational prowess. Here, in a re-creation of an 18th century fire scene, a crew dressed in period costume are working an early manual pump fed from a bucket supply of water. 11 November 1966.

outwards and despite shouted warnings, crashed down into the street burying a number of firemen fleeing from the danger, together with two turntable ladders and smashed several wheeled escapes on which firemen had been working. Tragically, three firefighters were killed and a dozen were seriously injured, including Deputy Chief Officer C. P. McDuell, OBE., whose injuries necessitated the amputation of his right leg.

Following the Eldon Street tragedy, there was considerable public sympathy towards the Brigade and Delve recommended to the London County Council that all the pending 1,400 disciplinary cases be withdrawn. The LCC quickly agreed and the pay dispute was referred to arbitration, where once again the outcome was a decision not to link fire service pay with those of the police in favour of a detailed consideration of each claim on its merits. This was hardly a satisfactory outcome and one that marked the beginning of a lengthy period of strained industrial relations in the fire service, not just in the London Fire Brigade but across the country.

However, on the vehicle and equipment front good progress was being made in the replacement of pre-war pumps and equipment. As capital

finance became available, it was also possible to begin the long-delayed fire station replacement programme. The duty system for London firemen was reduced to 56 hours per week with the manpower divided between three watches, red, white and blue. Another area of steady improvement was in the levels of training in the Brigade both in working in breathing apparatus and in dealing with the increasing number of non-fire emergencies (or special services as they are called). The latter type of incident had grown very rapidly after the war years with the increase in traffic accidents and incidents involving lifts. This drove research and development of new cutting and lifting equipment being carried out on the Brigade's four emergency tenders and its breakdown lorry.

But it was the smoke from serious fires that again challenged the courage and resources of the LFB on a number of occasions during the post-NFS decade including those at Covent Garden (1949), Goodge Street Underground Station (1956) and Smithfield Meat Market on 23 January 1958. During the early stages of the Smithfield fire, a station officer and a fireman died when their oxygen supply ran out as they searched a smoke filled basement area for the seat of the fire. Sadly, they were both very close to an exit and fresh air and the subsequent inquiry led to national safety improvements for firemen working in breathing

One of the final displays during the 1966 Royal Review involved eight 100 ft turntable ladders undertaking various simultaneous extension, elevation and rotation sequences before finally coming together to break out a Union flag at 100 ft. This view is of the dress rehearsal the day before the Review proper and shows the precision needed by the driver/operators of these aerial fire engines.

> 66 *The new enlarged London Fire Brigade was now one of the largest firefighting forces in the world...* 99

apparatus. The rush hour crash involving two trains in thick fog at Lewisham on 4 December 1957 killed 85 passengers and seriously injured over 130 giving the LFB a huge rescue and recovery task.

Chief Officer Delve was knighted in 1962 and retired in November of that year. He was succeeded by his deputy, Leslie Leete, who was the first officer in the history of the Brigade to have risen through all the ranks having joined the AFS in 1939. One of Leete's first challenges was to steer through a major operational and administrative change when on 1 April 1965, the

Two London firemen from Chelsea Fire Station were badly burned on 8 March 1968 whilst in action at a fire in a restaurant in the King's Road district. Sadly, both died three days later. This view shows their funeral cortege passing Chelsea Fire Station where all three watches were drawn up on the station forecourt to pay their last formal respects to their deceased colleagues.

On 17 July 1969 five London firemen were killed in an explosion whilst dealing with a fire in derelict fuel tanks being demolished at Dudgeon's Wharf on the Isle of Dogs, Millwall, in east London. The full Brigade funeral for the five firemen was a very moving event attended by several thousand London firefighters as well as personnel from fire brigades across the country. Here the first of the five coffins arrives at the memorial service at Stratford Church in east London. 23 July 1969.

London County Council was consigned to history along with Middlesex County Council, the county boroughs of Croydon, East Ham and West Ham, and 83 other boroughs and county districts of parts of Kent, Surrey, Essex and Hertfordshire. This entire enlarged area was covered by 32 new London boroughs (plus the City of London), each with its own elected council. The new overall authority, the Greater London Council (GLC), became the fire authority.

The new powerful GLC brought a mass of difficulties in merging such a large swathe of local government services, and for the fire brigade it was no different. As the new Chief Officer of the enlarged Brigade, Leete had the task of merging the existing LFB 60 fire station force with all of the firemen of four proud neighbouring brigades and some of those from the four others. Right from the beginning there was a feeling that the LFB had 'taken over' Middlesex and the rest. It might have helped to

> *" The communications network had to be capable of handling upwards of 60,000 emergency calls per year... "*

create a cohesive feeling if a new collective badge had been created but instead, the old London Brigade badge was slightly modified and all the other eight brigades had to accept it. Senior officers of the brigades joining London were in some cases demoted and there is no doubt that Chief Officer Leete's tact and diplomatic skills were taxed to the limit as the new Brigade came into being.

The new enlarged London Fire Brigade was now one of the largest fire-fighting forces in the world, with another 1,000 personnel serving in the London Auxiliary Fire Service together with 1,000 administrative, technical and manual civilian support staff. With 122 fire stations and two river stations, the LFB could now muster 360 front line fire engines including 111 pump escapes, 115 pumps, 29 turntable ladders, eight emergency tenders, eight hose layers and six foam tenders. Vehicle workshops were maintained at Lambeth, Ruislip, Barking and Croydon Headquarters.

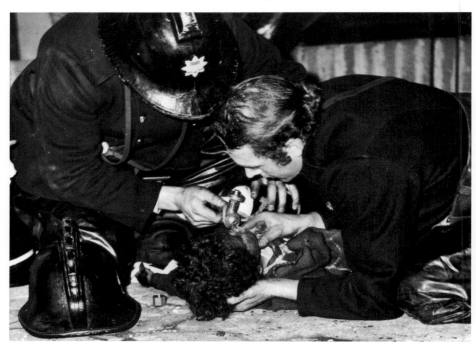

A dramatic photograph of two London firemen attempting to resuscitate a child overcome by smoke in a fire in residential flats near the Elephant and Castle, SE1. 10 December 1971. (*Owen Rowlands*)

The Brigade Headquarters remained at Lambeth but for '999' call mobilising and communications purposes, the Brigade was now organised into four operational command areas, with Lambeth controlling the central London fire stations, Northern Command based at Wembley, Southern at Croydon and Eastern at Stratford. The communications network had to be capable of handling upwards of 60,000 emergency calls per year, with the first use of teleprinter links to mobilise fire stations being introduced and each of the four control areas had its own radio network.

The old LFB Training School remained at Southwark, supplemented by the former Middlesex Training School at Finchley. At these two centres recruits were taught hose, pump, ladder drills and range of other practical skills, along with a theoretical syllabus embracing a number of subjects including hydraulics, building construction, physics and chemistry, and fire service law. However, in 1965 the Brigade was still short of 1,500 firemen and the Brigade instituted a new 100 place Junior Firemen course at a new training college at Swanley in Kent. Here 16 and 17 year olds underwent educational and practical training to prepare them for joining the professional service at 18 years of age but the course failed to produce the numbers required of it and it was closed down in the late 1960s.

A driver's eye view as a London fire engine from Euston Fire Station follows its sister pump escape through the rush hour traffic across traffic lights outside St. Pancras Station, en route to a '999' emergency call in the Kings Cross area. c.1970. (Women's Realm)

The spread of fire can can be frighteningly rapid. The first call to smoke issuing from this empty building on Gardners Corner, Aldgate, EC3, came at midday on a weekday, yet within minutes of the arrival of the first crews from Whitechapel fire station all floors of the structure were fiercely ablaze. Twenty pumps were needed to control the blaze and prevent the flying sparks settling onto remote buildings in scenes reminiscent of the London Blitz. 22 May 1972.

Two events of 1966 that helped to cement the new Brigade together was the tercentenary of the Great Fire of London and the 100th anniversary of the founding of Eyre Massey Shaw's Metropolitan Fire Brigade. One special celebration was a Royal Review of the Brigade staged on 11 November 1966 at Lambeth for HM The Queen and the Duke of Edinburgh.

On the uniform and equipment front, new stronger fire helmets were being trialled and yellow overtrousers to replace the old style black leggings worn since the 1930s were introduced. Compressed air breathing sets began to be phased in alongside the existing oxygen sets to increase the availability of respiratory protection for fire crews against the toxic effect of smoke, now increasingly involved thanks to man made plastic products even in a small domestic fire. Several new fire stations were at last completed, including those at Chelsea and Shoreditch. These were both of a simple and modern design to replace their Victorian counterparts often sited in the back streets, sometimes making for difficult '999' turnouts onto London's new thoroughfares.

As part of the Jubilee celebrations, HM The Queen visited Lambeth Headquarters on 9 June 1977 to meet a representative number of Brigade personnel, both uniformed and civilian. Here the Queen is pictured arriving at Lambeth and being greeted by Chief Officer Peter Darby.

> " *Compressed air breathing sets began to be phased in alongside the existing oxygen sets...* "

Parading for the Queen

Two events of 1966 that helped to cement the new enlarged Brigade together were the tercentenary of the Great Fire of London and the 100th anniversary of the founding of Captain Eyre Massey Shaw's Metropolitan Fire Brigade. One special celebration was a Royal Review of the Brigade staged on 11 November 1966 at Lambeth for HM The Queen and the Duke of Edinburgh. After the Queen had met a representative parade of officers, firemen and firewomen, and visited the '999' Control Room, there followed a well-choreographed hour long display as a procession of gleaming fire engines swept into Lambeth's yard as fire crews demonstrated their prowess during a range of drill sequences. These included massed 'rescues' using wheeled escape ladders, and an item where, at its climax, there was a firemen on a hook ladder at every window of the nine floor drill tower. Emergency tender crews released 'trapped' casualties from an overturned car, and a water fire power drill saw 20 jets create a massive water curtain. In an historical tableau to show some aspects of the Brigade's heritage, firemen dressed in Victorian uniforms with brass helmets and others in period costumes used hand squirts, manual pumps and finally a gleaming preserved horse drawn steamer of the Metropolitan Fire Brigade tackled a simulated 19th century building fire. With steam to spare coming from its safety valve, the 100 year old fire engine showed that it could still power a jet of water over the roof of the drill tower. The display concluded when eight turntable ladders broke out the union flag at 100 ft. as all the crews and fire engines that had taken part in the event finally paraded before the royal visitors. It was a stunning show of the Brigade's skills and equipment.

During the late 1960s and early 1970s there was a series of large fires in hotels and hostels in the inner London area and these, in part, brought forth a new fire precautions Act of Parliament to ensure more regulated conditions in these types of premises. By then, operational personnel were also undertaking a wider involvement in fire safety inspections in shops and small offices.

Two notable events of 1968 were the final standing down of the Auxiliary Fire Service with hundreds of their 'Green Goddess' pumps

going into mothballs; and with an uncanny similarity to the events of 9/11, a major accident exercise in which an aircraft was assumed to have crashed into the 33rd floor of Britannic House in the City. Here the new 'Major Accident Procedure' was tested in which fire, police, medical and ambulance staff worked together with lifelike 'casualties'. Just over a year later came a real tragedy for the Brigade, when on the morning of 17 July, a crew from Millwall fire station were called to a fire in some old fuel tanks under demolition at Dudgeon's Wharf, Manchester Road, on the Isle of Dogs. On their arrival, workmen appeared to have extinguished the fire in a 20,000 gallon tank that had contained oil and spirits. As the LFB crew climbed on top to use water to flush out the inside of the tank, there was a huge explosion. Five firemen along with one of the site workers were killed instantly.

Chief Officer Leete retired at the end of 1969 and was succeeded by Joseph Milner, a former British fire officer who had moved to Hong Kong in 1951 and then worked his way up through the ranks to become the Director of the Hong Kong Fire Service. Milner arrived to take command of London at a extremely challenging time. After four years, it seemed that the enlarged LFB had still not properly settled down

One of the groups of firefighters who met the Queen during her Jubilee visit on 9 June 1977 was this immaculately turned out crew from Greenwich fire station pictured here in front of their gleaming pump escape.

> ❝ *Amid all this activity, the LFB continued to deal with some major incidents.* ❞

into one cohesive unit. To many there were still two Brigades — one 'inner' and the other 'outer' London. Added to this the findings of a governmental review of the fire service under Sir Ronald Holroyd was published in June 1970 the outcome of which was to ask Chief Fire Officers to submit their observations on Holroyd's 100 plus recommendations. In view of the continuing disputes not just in London but nationally, the government commissioned yet another inquiry under Sir Charles Cunningham to look specifically into fire service pay and conditions. This inquiry began its work in early 1971 and eventually produced a number of recommendations relating to future pay and hours of firefighters. The fire service unions were not happy with the outcome and when a further committee was suggested, the tone of industrial relations in the fire service progressively worsened.

Despite this, the Brigade pressed on with more organisational and technical improvements. In the '999' control rooms at Lambeth, Wembley, Croydon and Stratford, the first visual display units and keyboards were being introduced to replace operators having to physically write down the details of incoming emergency calls. The system would then offer the operator the nearest fire engines to the incident and mobilising became much more efficient. The first thermal imaging cameras, enabling firefighters to see through smoke, were trialed and a prototype radio communication system was commissioned for use at deep penetration fires to enable breathing apparatus wearers to talk to their control point in fresh air. The somewhat dated oxygen breathing sets began to be replaced with shorter duration compressed air versions that were more comfortable to wear and required less servicing. A pilot scheme evolved by Charles Clisby, an officer with the old Middlesex Brigade, was introduced to instantly identify the growing number of hazardous substances in transit or storage. Through its simple coded sign and up to four numerals and letters it told firefighters the immediate steps they must take to protect both themselves and the public. The 'Hazchem' scheme as it was known was soon to become a nationally adopted one.

A Fireman's Job

During early 1971, the government appointed Sir Charles Cunningham to chair an inquiry into the work of the fire service, especially with regard to pay and conditions of service. Amongst a raft of recommendations in Cunningham's final report was one that broadly said:

'We could find no evidence that a fireman's pay was seriously out of line with that of most comparable workers but the danger and unpleasantness associated with it should be taken into account.'

These findings were naturally a disappointment to officers and men in the service as well as the fire service trade unions and associations, especially as another paragraph from Cunningham' report made the following rather remarkable statement:

'A fireman must have special personal qualities. He must have physical courage. On occasions he must voluntarily face extremities of danger which confronts few other people in time of peace. It is the element of risk and the demand for courage which sets a fireman's job apart from others. But bravery is not the only personal quality needed. A fireman must be able to work as part of a closely integrated team, the watch to which he belongs. He must be prepared to obey orders without question, especially on the fireground. At the same time he must be able to show initiative when working on his own. All of these qualities may be needed in other occupations; but we know of none in which, together with courage in the face of danger, they are needed in combination to such a degree as in the fire service.'

Amid all this activity, the LFB continued to deal with some major incidents. In 1973 came the first IRA bombing incidents in central London that continued sporadically for over a year. During this period, a number of serious hotel fires also taxed the Brigade where a number of heroic rescues were carried out. These included the Leinster Towers Hotel, Bayswater (6 June 1969), Hills Hotel, Bayswater (11 May 1971), and the Worsley Hotel, Maida Vale (13 December 1974). Then in the morning rush hour on 28 February 1975 came a horrific crash on the Underground's Northern Line at Moorgate, when a shuttle service due to terminate at the station ran through the platform at about 40 mph and crashed into the buffers inside a dead end tunnel some 50 ft beyond. The first officer on the scene found the leading three coaches badly compacted and crushed with the impact and many casualties trapped within. Major Accident Procedure was quickly instituted and it was not until ten o'clock in the evening before the last living passenger was freed. It took the Brigade a further five days and four nights before the last of the 42 fatalities were extricated. It was the worst peacetime disaster yet to challenge the LFB and Chief Officer Milner afterwards paid tribute to 'my 1,000 selfless heroes' who collectively attended the Moorgate tragedy during that dreadful week.

" ...Chief Officer Milner afterwards paid tribute to 'my 1,000 selfless heroes'... "

One of the Cunningham Report recommendations was to reduce the basic working week for firemen. In order to achieve this, in 1974 the LFB in common with other large brigades embarked upon an intensive recruiting campaign and later in that year, sufficient recruit firemen had been recruited into the establishment to create a fourth shift (the green watch) and allow a 42 working week to be introduced.

Chief Officer Milner retired from the Brigade in June 1976 and was succeeded by Peter Darby, the Chief Fire Officer of Greater Manchester Fire Service. A very experienced officer, Peter Darby threw himself into the challenge of improving the industrial relations in the Brigade, introducing a corporate management system that was soon to bear fruit at grass roots, even achieving a national award from industry.

By the middle of 1978 the 50 ft wooden wheeled escape ladders so beloved by London firefighters were becoming extremely difficult and expensive to maintain and were progressively replaced by 45 ft three section alloy extension ladders. This view shows one of the new Volvo dual purpose LFB fire engines termed a pump ladder, carrying one of the new alloy ladders.

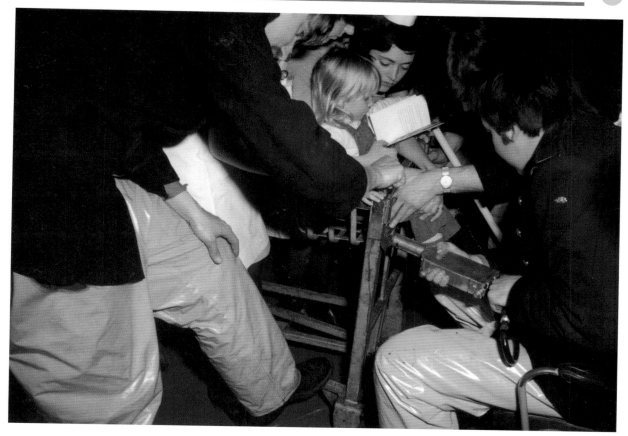

But in the summer of 1977, a national pay dispute was still rumbling on and as the Winter of Discontent approached, on 14 November of that year, some 43,000 members of the Fire Brigades Union (FBU) up and down the country began an official strike that was to last for eleven weeks. In London, all 122 fire stations were closed and fire cover was provided by the military personnel using former AFS Green Goddess pumps with police escorts.

After much deliberation, the strike ended in January 1978 after the employers and the FBU agreed a formula which recognised the value of the firemen's work and awarded them an index-linked pay system which was also to be adopted by the police and armed forces. Many personnel of the London Fire Brigade felt that their image and standing with the population of the capital had been seriously damaged by the protracted strike, but the LFB was back into its stride by the spring of 1978. A rolling programme to replace almost half of the Brigade's turntable ladder fleet with hydraulic platforms was initiated. These more modern high rise fire engines had a more variable operating scope and were able to compliment the work of the existing 100 ft ladders. Another development brought the end of the 50 ft wooden wheeled escape ladders that had been a traditional

On 1 February 1978 firemen from Euston fire station were called to an unusual 'special service' call at Euston railway station. Here a three year old girl had been temporarily put in a luggage trolley by her mother and had promptly got her index finger stuck in the brake mechanism. Having removed the child and trolley to the nearby University College Hospital, it took two crews over an hour to extricate the child using some very careful cutting techniques, whilst the nursing staff of the A and E unit kept the young girl occupied with books and toys.

> ❝ *A serious event in London's history involving the Brigade took place on 6 October 1985...* ❞

part of the LFB since the 19th century. It was becoming difficult and uneconomic to maintain the wheeled escapes and over a period they were replaced by aluminium ladders. Another initiative was one of the first studies into the effect on firemen's health of wearing breathing apparatus and heavy protective uniforms. This was at a time when sport and welfare activities within the Brigade were at an all time high with a wide range of events going on, from the annual AAA (Amateur Athletic Association) top class meeting, to inter service and brigade matches, and plenty of fund raising, especially for the Fire Services National Benevolent Fund.

On the very last day of the existence of the Greater London Council, fire broke out in an apartment at Hampton Court Palace and quickly grew to threaten the entire historic complex. Fortunately, some 100 firefighters battled successfully for several hours to isolate the fire and in some difficult and dangerous conditions, they managed to contain the flames to a residential wing. This is the external scene during the early stages of the fire, with the Headquarters Control Unit being set up to the left of the main Palace entrance as further pumps arrive. Widespread media coverage ensured that details of the Brigade's outstanding firefighting prowess at this major fire was transmitted to an international audience. 31 March 1986.

In 1980, Peter Darby was appointed as HM Chief Inspector of Fire Services at the Home Office and on his retirement from the LFB was knighted. He was succeeded by Ronald Bullers, who had been Peter Darby's deputy in the Greater Manchester Fire Service. He continued much in the mould of his predecessor and dealing with a range of issues including that of equal opportunities, with the Brigade appointing its first female firefighter recruit, Sue Batten, in May 1982. With only ten black firefighters in the LFB, there also began a sustained recruiting effort to attract more recruits from London's ethnic population. Bullers also began to phase out the hook ladder which had been carried on London's fire engines for over 80 years and had been successfully used for rescue, particularly in the LFB's 'A' Division covering the West End on a number of occasions.

A serious event in London's history involving the Brigade took place on 6 October 1985 when fire crews were called to the Broadwater Farm Estate in Tottenham, where rioters swept through the area setting fire to a supermarket as they went. As firefighters from several stations arrived, they were amazed to come under attack and had to be given police protection

After the excitement and drama of the firefighting effort at Hampton Court had subsided, the painstaking work of the fire investigation team of the Brigade began. Here two officers carefully sift through the charred debris close to the seat of the fire in their quest for forensic evidence to help establish the cause of the outbreak. 31 March 1986.

" As firefighters from several stations arrived, they were amazed to come under attack... "

from the crowds. Both police and firefighters soon had to retreat but two policemen fell and were attacked by the mob. Firefighters managed to extricate one of the policemen from the dangerous situation and returned with other policemen to retrieve and resuscitate the second police casualty. Sadly he died from his injuries. Divisional Officer Trevor Stratford was subsequently awarded the Queen's Gallantry Medal for his brave actions.

1986 was the first year that the Brigade responded to an international emergency when it despatched a three man advisory team to Mexico following a devastating earthquake. In later years, similar LFB rescue teams were sent to disasters in El Salvador, Armenia, Afganistan and Northern Iraq. As a result of this activity, an international disaster response team was formed by personnel from all UK brigades and co-ordinated by the Home Office, and this has since performed some sterling work all over the world.

The political wind of change was also felt by the London Fire Brigade in early 1986. During the previous parliamentary year, the strong majority power of the Conservative government had enacted the Local Government Act of 1985. On 1 April 1986 this legislation abolished the Greater London Council and from that date, the fire protection of the capital was vested in the newly created London Fire and Civil Defence Authority (LFCDA).

CHAPTER TWELVE

Towards the New Century

The London Fire Brigade (LFB) was by far the greatest responsibility of the newly formed London Fire and Civil Defence Authority (LFCDA). The new body was composed of one councillor nominated by the majority party from each of the 32 London boroughs and the City of London.

It was a time of continuing change for all personnel in the Brigade, in both uniformed and civilian support teams. A very pertinent illustration of just how busy firefighters had become in London was that during 1965–66, the first year of the now defunct Greater London Council

The London Fire Brigade fireboat *London Phoenix* demonstrates its pumping power with this artistic display underneath Tower Bridge. c.1987.

As the number of non-fire special service 999 calls answered by the Brigade increased, so too did their variety and complexity. This is the aftermath of a crash involving a mobile crane that has collided with several parked cars in Hendon, north London. Fortunately there were no serious injuries. 6 January 1987.

(GLC), the LFB responded to 55,516 separate '999' calls to fires and other emergencies. In 1986, the last year of the GLC authority, this '999' call total had risen to a staggering 148,737 operational incidents.

Concurrent with the arrival of the LFCDA, Chief Officer Bullers and his senior officer team reorganised the LFB's operational structure from its existing three operational commands (North, South and East) into five new Area Command structures. These were: North West (with Area Headquarters at Wembley); North (Paddington); North East (Stratford); South East (Lewisham); and South West (Croydon). These Area Commands were aligned with groups of London boroughs and were radially drawn from the centre of London giving each a mix of inner city centre with its commercial and industrial premises, together with residential and semi-rural districts on the outer edges. Amongst new capital developments under construction were new fire stations at Barnet, Ilford and Islington.

Chief Officer Bullers had agreed to see the Brigade settled into its first year under the LFCDA before taking his retirement and in August 1987, Buller's deputy, Gerald Clarkson took up his appointment as Chief Officer.

> 66 *In 1986, the last year of the GLC,*
> *this '999' call total had risen to a*
> *staggering 148,737 incidents.* 99

Clarkson was the first man to have joined the Brigade as a regular and as such to have risen right through the ranks to the top job. He was a very experienced officer and had a reputation for getting things done, often by unconventional means.

On 18 November 1987, Clarkson was in China as part of an official government overseas mission when news of the Kings Cross Underground fire, in which 30 commuters and LFB Station Officer Colin Townsley were

Domestic pets are sometimes caught up in a fire situation and this rather bedraggled spaniel is now safe in the hands of an LFB sub officer, having been rescued from the smoke during a fire in a public house.

The Brigade were called to the River Lea in east London when this horse fell in and was unable to make its own way out of the water. Using special animal slings, the firefighters were able assist in the successful rescue of the animal. 20 May 1987.

killed came through. Clarkson flew back to London without delay and immediately after the full Brigade funeral, began with preparations for the forthcoming Public Inquiry into the fire. The Kings Cross disaster was an especially bitter tragedy for the LFB: the Brigade had been warning about the fire risks on London's transport systems for some years, but was handicapped due to its lack of statutory powers of fire safety enforcement. The Inquiry undertook a rigorous examination of the events of that fateful evening at Kings Cross and despite some minor criticisms of the fire service, many lessons were learnt on all sides although the Inquiry Chairman, Desmond Fennel, QC, also praised the courage of the LFB firefighters at Kings Cross.

The Kings Cross tragedy showed that improvements were necessary in protective equipment for fire crews, command and control procedures and first aid skills, particularly whilst in a hostile environment. Clarkson wasted no time in addressing these issues and tasked Assistant Chief Officer Ken Knight to lead a searching Research and Development Section charged specifically with implementing the 'Kings Cross' improvements.

Before long, London was the first brigade in the country to introduce a new 42 minute duration lightweight compressed air breathing set on all front line fire engines.

Another post Kings Cross safety innovation was the fitting of a new automatic distress warning unit on the new breathing sets. The older versions of these units needed to be activated manually but the new models were completely automatic in use. When a wearer of a breathing set checked in at the control point and handed in his 'tally' before entering a fire situation, the distress warning unit was armed, and once inside the smoke, if the firefighter remained motionless for 20 seconds, the unit would go into alarm mode and sound a continuous loud note. Firefighters tunics were improved with the introduction of a Nomex material that provided a higher level of protection against both the intense heat of a flashover and from water percolation. The new tunics were followed by new Nomex leggings, together with a new design of helmet constructed of Kevlar.

This view during a training exercise shows the new style helmets and firefighting uniforms introduced following the Kings Cross Underground fire disaster. Both firefighters are wearing the lighter compressed air breathing apparatus sets with the new automatic distress signal units in place. These are coloured blue and marked 'Big Ben'. 10 September 1990.

66 *Another post Kings Cross safety innovation was the fitting of a automatic warning device on breathing sets...* 99

High Rise Fire Safety

In the early 1990s Londoners were seeing some very high and complex building developments coming into use, particularly in Docklands. There, the 50 floor high Canary Wharf Tower was then one of the tallest structures in Europe and both here and on other major new high and low rise developments, the Brigade's officers worked alongside architects and design teams to ensure that the very highest levels of fire safety were achieved. At Canary Wharf the fire protection equipment included electronically supervised automatic sprinkler systems, mechanical smoke extraction, an increased fire resistance in the various protected stairways, phased and planned evacuation, a two-stage fire alarm system and floor wardens whose role was to supervise general safety issues. At the other end of the scale in domestic properties, few could fail to hear the Brigade's constant messages about fire safety and the life saving potential benefit of fitting a simple smoke alarm to give the earliest possible warning of fire.

A little over a year after the Kings Cross disaster came another major accident when on the morning of 12 December 1988, an incoming rush hour train crashed into a stationary one just outside Clapham Junction in south west London. 37 passengers were killed and many were critically injured and trapped in the compacted wreckage. The crash occurred in a deep cutting making the extrication and removal of those trapped a particularly difficult physical task for firefighters, paramedics and medical teams at the scene.

Another gradual change taking place on London's fire engines could hardly be missed by anyone in the streets of the capital. From the time when the first bells replaced the 'Hi! Hi! Hi!' cries of the crews of horse drawn fire engines of the 19th century, warning devices were being regularly improved to give other road users warning of the approach of a speeding fire engine and to make for a safer passage for the emergency vehicle. The first electric sirens and horns had appeared in the late 1960s and, in early 1990, the LFB fitted a new electronic system to all its front line fire engines that gave the officer in charge a choice of sounds from 'two tone', through a 'wailing' note to a very urgent 'yelp'. The latter was only

intended for use in the most congested traffic situations which was fast becoming a increasing problem for London's fire engine drivers charged with the onerous responsibility of getting their crews to the scene of a '999' emergency within a stipulated time.

In 1990, the Brigade placed an order for 34 new fire engines based on a Volvo chassis with bodywork by Saxon Sanbec to replace a number of ageing machines in its 500 strong vehicle fleet. Other orders were for six new hydraulic platforms/aerial ladder platforms and 12 others designed to run as heavy emergency tenders or other demountable equipment systems. In addition, the first of the new vehicle breed called a Fire Rescue Unit, being a combination of a pumping fire engine and an emergency rescue tender, also appeared.

Another major new capital development was the opening of a new Command and Mobilising Centre (CMC) on the site of the old bandstand at Lambeth. This facility brought the LFB fully into the age of the computer and saw the closure of the existing '999' control rooms at Wembley, Croydon and Stratford. The new CMC was thought to be the most advanced fire brigade mobilising centre in the world and in its first year of full operation handled some 250,000 emergency calls for help from across the capital.

On 25 October 1990 a commemorative service was held at St. Paul's to mark the 50th anniversary of the London Blitz. The service was attended by the Prince and Princess of Wales, Princes William and Harry and this view shows Prince Harry trying out the driver's seat of an immaculately preserved 1937 Leyland turntable ladder which served in central London throughout the war years before being retired in 1964.

" The new CMC was thought to be the most advanced fire brigade mobilising centre in the world... "

Sporting Firefighters

Sport has always played a significant part in the off duty activities of the London Fire Brigade and apart from football, rugby, cricket, squash, athletics, road and cross country running, other sections within the Brigade include parachuting, rock climbing, archery, skiing, and deep sea fishing. Fire Service sport took on an inter brigade aspect in the 1960s and nowadays has grown to a truly international nature, with a World Firefighters Games being held on a regular basis. Fund raising by firefighters, not just for the principal fire service charity, the Fire Services National Benevolent Fund, but also for other organisations is another activity that has seen some amazing and unusual initiatives. Such events have included a 45 mile round London rowing marathon via the canals and the Thames; the hauling of a 6 ton fire engine from Westminster to Brighton; a world pumping record using a 19th century manual fire engine and the ascent of Ben Nevis by a team wearing breathing apparatus.

One of Chief Officer Clarkson's important acts in his last year of service was to drive forward the concept of a memorial to mark the courage of Blitz firefighters in London and in the provincial cities. Earlier in 1988 Clarkson, aided by other principal fire officers, had established the Guild of Firefighters and one of his first projects as the Guild's first Master was to raise sufficient funds for the Blitz memorial. It was a very proud moment when, on 4 May 1991, the Queen Mother unveiled the memorial sited in Old Change Court, close to St. Paul's Cathedral and since then an annual service of remembrance is held at St. Paul's to remember all those firemen and firewomen who gave their lives during the Second World War.

However, the dangerous side of the Brigade's work was once again underlined on the 10 July 1991 during a fire in a document store in an old bonded warehouse in Gillender Street, Bow, in east London. Amid the dense smoke and complicated layout of passages, Firefighters David Stokoe and Terence Hunt lost their lives. The inquest into their deaths heard that the cause of the fire was arson and a verdict of unlawful killing was returned.

❝ *The projected cost of the Authority and its services in 1992–93 was £242,000,000.* ❞

Having overseen the Brigade's inquiry into the tragedies of the Gillender Street fire and its lessons, Gerald Clarkson retired in October 1991 and handed over the command of the Brigade to the Deputy Chief Officer, Brian Robinson. Like his predecessor, the new Chief had come through the ranks in the Brigade, and at 44 was the youngest Chief Fire Officer of the London Fire Brigade since the brass helmeted and horse drawn days of Captain Eyre Massey Shaw. Since the inception of the LFCDA in Clarkson's days, the Chief Fire Officer's title also embraced that of the Chief Executive of the Authority. The LFCDA consisted of 40 committees, sub committees, departments and sections with a civilian staff of some 1,000. The projected cost of the Authority and its services in 1992–93 was £242,000,000.

In 1992 a review of the application of the national standards of fire cover to the London area was carried out. The existing nationally agreed standards were linked to the potential fire risk of any particular building. In the capital, there were four risk categories:

'A' Category: This embraced the high risk areas in the centre of London and a '999' call attracted an attendance of three pumping fire engines with ladders, two arriving in five minutes and the third in eight. An aerial ladder was also on the turnout to these districts.

'B' Category: London's most common, involving built up areas with small factories and shopping centres. The required attendance was two pumps with ladders, the first to arrive within five minutes and the second within eight.

'C' Category: This included the less built-up areas and would require the attendance of one pump with ladder to arrive within 8 to 10 minutes.

'D' Category: This included the semi-rural areas on the country edges of London. One pump only required to arrive within 20 minutes.

It should be noted that in 1992, the London Fire Brigade always despatched two pumps to all '999' fire calls from 'C' and 'D' risk areas.

The fire cover review of 1992 closely examined the incidence of fire together with such factors as running times, traffic density and new road

This London firefighter at the head of a turntable ladder has a bird's eye view of a large fire in a Deptford warehouse, south east London. Note that he is wearing a breathing apparatus set to protect him from the fumes from the fire. 9 February 1992.

improvements. The outcome was the closure of Sanderstead fire station and the removal of a further 10 fire engines based elsewhere which were redistributed so that five stations received additional fire engines.

Following the IRA terrorist activity in the mid 1970s, bombers struck again in London at an office block in St. Mary Axe, EC3 on 10 April 1992 when three people died. On 24 August 1993 the target was again a commercial premises in the City at Bishopsgate, EC2. Both bombs caused a huge amount of blast damage and 20 pumps and 100 firefighters were involved in rescues at both incidents and in the subsequent clearing up and making safe operation that went on for several days and nights.

During 1992–93 the Brigade suffered two separate tragedies when firefighters were killed in action. On 30 September 1992, Sub Officer Kevin Power lost his life during firefighting operations at Scrubs Lane, NW10, and Firefighter Michael Hill died on 10 May 1993 during a fire in Villiers Road, Willesden, NW2. For many years going back to the late 19th century, the Brigade has maintained its own chaplains and missionaries able to offer some comfort and solace to the bereaved families on these sad occasions. From the early 1990s, the LFB also provided six trained counsellors able to provide a service for those members of the Brigade suffering from stress as a result of their work experiences.

Since the early 1970s the Brigade has had to deal with the aftermath of occasional terrorist activity in the capital. This is the scene following a huge bomb blast in St. Mary Axe, EC3, in the City of London that killed three office workers and caused extensive damage to buildings all around. The fire still burning in the foreground is a gas main ignited by the explosion and it is being allowed to burn under controlled conditions before the main is isolated. 10 April 1992.

❝ Both bombs caused a huge amount of blast damage and 20 pumps and 100 firefighters were involved in rescues... ❞

Another view of the bomb blast in St. Mary Axe, EC3, showing the extensive damage to a high rise office block and surrounding buildings. 11 April 1992.

In 1994 a fire in a cinema club in Smithfield, EC1, believed to have been started by an arsonist, trapped many patrons on upper floors and led to 11 fatalities. For some time, the working of the Area Command structure had been under review and in 1995, the five operational Area Commands were reduced to three and at the same time a major reorganisation of the Brigade's management structure took effect. Also in 1995 the first Brigade trials began involving the use of helicopters and on the operational front, the LFB had a busy night during civil disturbances in the Brixton area of south London.

Another unusual incident occurred during the afternoon of 17 January 1996 when a tar boiler caught fire on the roof of one of London's tallest buildings, the NatWest Tower in the City. The visible smoke seen drifting out of the top of the tower was spotted by many people at work in other office blocks and quickly led to over 500 separate '999' calls being received within a few minutes at the Brigade's Command and Mobilising Centre. Six pumps and 35 firefighters dealt with the occurrence. A far more serious call to the Brigade came on 19 September 1997 when an Inter City high speed 125 train collided head on with a freight train at Southall in west

Terrorists attacked the City of London again on 24 April 1993 when a bomb exploded in Bishopsgate, EC2. Once more tremendous damage was done to the frontages of a number of buildings, causing glass and metal work to crash down into the surrounding street injuring many office workers and passers by. The Brigade was involved in the rescue of the many casualties before assisting in the task of making safe much hanging debris.

66 *During 1992–93 the Brigade suffered two separate tragedies when firefighters were killed in action.* 99

No doubt conscious of the huge fire in 1834 when most of the Palace of Westminster was destroyed, the protection of London's historic buildings has always had a high priority for the Brigade, with regular exercises being held in conjunction with the Palace authorities and other emergency services. In this view of an exercise held during 1993, two pump ladders squeeze through an archway into a narrow inner courtyard before the commencement of the drill. *(Philip Wright, Serjeant at Arms)*

This 1993 exercise at the Palace of Westminster tested the full command and control facilities of the Brigade. Here, at the beginning of the drill, one of the Brigade's Area Fire Control Units has arrived to commence operations. Note that the Control Unit is a demountable unit and at protracted incidents can be lowered onto the ground to release the Volvo prime mover for other duties. (*Philip Wright, Serjeant at Arms*)

Part of the 1993 exercise at the Palace of Westminster was to test the firefighting water available from the River Thames frontage. In this photograph, the Brigade's fireboat *London Phoenix* lays off the rear terrace of the Palace to provide twin lines of hose ashore. (*Philip Wright, Serjeant at Arms*)

When fire broke out on a lower floor of this flour silo in Canning Town, east London, E16, it spread quickly into the upper storeys. Initial firefighting operations inside the building were hampered due to the unsafe condition of the structure and this situation was made worse by the effect of the intense heat. Eventually, fire crews were withdrawn to control the fire from outside and successfully prevented the fire from spreading to surrounding premises. 20 January 1994.

London. Six passengers were killed and 25 were trapped in the wreckage of the front carriages of the train, requiring several hours of careful cutting and extrication work.

Work was also in hand at this time to trial a number of new types of personal protective uniform incorporating a new helmet, fire resistant tunic and trousers, boots and gloves. One year later and following an extensive period of use of many types of firefighting apparel, Chief Officer Robinson approved the Inferno firefighting uniform which began to be issued to all operational personnel in 1998. The LFB was the first brigade in the United Kingdom to commission a completely new coordinated personal firefighting uniform in this way.

On 5 October 1999 came another horrific London rail crash when a Great Western high speed train collided head on with a suburban diesel unit at Ladbroke Grove, North Kensington, not far from the Paddington terminus. Fire broke out amid the wreckage and with Major Accident Procedure instituted, the Brigade mobilised a large force of firefighters and rescue tenders to begin what was to be a massive rescue operation. The two train drivers and 29 passengers died in the crash and over

London firefighters occasionally get called to animals caught in some predicament or other. This bull got stuck in deep mud and working with a vet, two LFB crews came to the rescue using slings, bales of straw and a hydraulic platform acting as a crane overhead, to carefully lift the heavy animal to firm ground and safety. Sidcup, south east London. 12 February 1994.

> " *The Brigade had a busy night during civil disturbances in the Brixton area of south London.* "

An increasing problem for the emergency services in the age of the mobile phone is the trend towards receiving multiple '999' calls for the same incident. Such was the case on the afternoon of 17 January 1996 when a contractor's tar boiler caught fire on the roof of the Natwest Tower in the City, one of the highest and most prominent buildings in the capital. Clouds of black smoke could be seen from all directions coming from the top of the Tower and within a few minutes, over 500 separate '999' calls had been received at the London Fire Brigade Command and Mobilising Centre at Lambeth.

> *Following the Ladbroke Grove disaster, HM The Queen paid a visit to Headquarters to meet some of the rescue teams...*

Fire in a tower block always poses special difficulties and dangers for firefighters. This serious outbreak in Chillingford House, Blackshaw Road, Tooting, SW17, was successfully tackled by the crews of six pumps using all the special features built into such structures including the dry rising water main and fitted hosereels, smoke lobbies, and the fireman's lift facility. There was, no doubt, plenty of sweat and toil also needed before the fire was brought under control. 5 March 1998.

> " *The LFEPA now had responsibility*
> *for the London Fire Brigade.* "

In recent years the extrication of trapped persons following road traffic accidents has become a major part of the work of the fire service. Nowadays firefighters physically rescue more men, women and children from the aftermath of road crashes than from fire emergencies. Releasing trapped drivers and passengers, often in conjunction with medical teams, is a particular skill using powerful cutting and lifting equipment designed for the purpose. Here firefighters and a medical team are using a host of gear, including air bags and hydraulic jacks to release the driver and passenger of this overturned car. East London. 1 May 1998.

After exhaustive trials involving firefighters at various fire stations, a new firefighting uniform was issued in 1998 that included helmet, tunic, trousers, boots , gloves and other items. Of a completely new design, it provided a very high level of co-ordinated personal protection to London's firefighters and was probably the most advanced of its kind in the world. As the new uniform was coming into use in June 1998, one of the Brigade's photographers recorded for posterity the range of uniforms worn by members of the London Fire Brigade over a century and more. Here (right to left) are the uniforms of: Metropolitan Fire Brigade 1866; London Fire Brigade 1935–39; London Fire Brigade/London Auxiliary Fire Service/National Fire Service 1939–45; London Fire Brigade 1948; 1973, 1985 and finally the new rig on the far left.

400 were injured, many trapped inside the crumpled wreckage of the carriages of both trains, requiring hours of careful and skilled paramedic attention from the medical teams at the accident site, in close cooperation with extrication work being carried out by firefighters. Following the disaster, HM The Queen paid a visit to Lambeth Headquarters to meet some of the rescue teams involved in the Ladbroke Grove tragedy.

The dawn of the new century saw a significant change to the structure of the Brigade's existing governing authority (the LFCDA). On 3 July 2000 the Greater London Authority (GLA) was created consisting of the Mayor and the London Assembly. The new Assembly's principal role was to scrutinise the performance of the Mayor's functions. There were four organisations, called 'functional bodies', one of which, the London

Today the Brigade continues its long history of providing fire and rescue cover on the River Thames with two identical fireboats, *Fire Dart* and *Fire Flash*. Both were commissioned in 1999 to meet the LFB's modern requirements for floating fire engines and here with the London Eye, Big Ben and the Palace of Westminster in the distance, the crew of *Fire Flash* are dealing with a small fire in a floating restaurant on the Embankment.

For many decades the Brigade has had a dedicated photographic section manned by uniformed personnel and since then, these photographers have produced some dramatic action shots taken at fires and other emergencies, as well as recording some fascinating pictorial aspects of the life and events of the LFB since the 1920s. There can surely be few more difficult environments to take good quality photographs in than at the scene of fires. However, because the small team of photographers are drawn from the ranks of firefighters they are able to readily work at '999' incidents and the majority of the images in *In Case of Fire* have been taken by LFB photographers over the years. Here the camera catches one of the duty photographers at work at a serious blaze.

As the new century arrived and the infant London Fire & Emergency Planning Authority got into its stride, a number of new fire safety campaigns were launched. One of these was to promote a greater awareness of the dangers of fires involving chip pans which are responsible for over 17% of all accidental fires in the home. Using a special demonstration unit at a shopping centre on 13 May 2000, this London firefighter is showing the dramatic effect of pouring a small cup of water onto a burning chip pan. He then proceeds to show the correct method of dealing with the fire by turning off the heat and smothering the pan with a fire blanket or damp towel, leaving it to cool completely.

The first draft of the Authority's London Safety Plan was announced in September 2003, and one of its principal thrusts was that *Prevention is better than Cure*. One of the causes of accidental fire in London is the misuse or malfunction of electrical appliances. Here is a good example of such a cause of fire where multiple plugs supplying various equipment, including a hi-fi system have been plugged into a single power socket in a domestic property. The electrical loading on the circuit has caused localised overheating and a fire has resulted.

The London Fire Brigade Museum

The London Fire Brigade Museum is situated in Southwark Bridge Road, Southwark, and is located within the Brigade's Training Centre complex. It is housed in two buildings, including the fire engine bays of the original 1878 fire station and in Winchester House, which up to 1937 was the Headquarters of the Brigade and the residence of the Chief Fire Officer. The Museum has a fascinating collection of exhibits that mirrors the history of firefighting and rescue in London across 300 years. Within the Museum are examples of original fire engines including manual and steam powered pumps, as well as firemen's uniforms and breathing apparatus from across the ages. A section is devoted to Captain Eyre Massey Shaw, the Brigade's famous Victorian Chief Officer and his personal uniform, equipment and mementoes. The London Blitz is also recalled together with a fine display of firefighter paintings from that dramatic time. All visits to the Museum are by guided tour and need to be made by prior appointment on 020-7587-2894. The Museum is open Monday to Friday and a nominal admission fee is charged.

Fire & Emergency Planning Authority, superseded the old LFCDA and now had responsibility for the London Fire Brigade. The other three bodies were charged to look after transport (Transport for London), the police (the Metropolitan Police Authority), and economic development (the London Development Agency). Together with the GLA itself, these four organisations were to be known as the GLA Group. Under the new authority, Chief Fire Officer Brian Robinson's title became the Commissioner for Fire and Emergency Planning.

As the new authority settled down into its tasks, the government published its White Paper *Our Fire and Rescue Service* which set out a vision for the future shape of the British fire service. Many of the points set out in the government White Paper had, in fact, been on the agenda for adoption in the London Fire Brigade for some years. From now on, the target was to make London a safer city by minimising the risks and economic costs of fire and other hazards. In June 2002 the London Fire Brigade published an updated report on its safety plan, including details of the progress being made towards achieving its challenging targets which was to reduce fires, deaths and injuries from fire and false alarms calls by 20 per cent between 2000 and 2005.

In March 2003, Brian Robinson retired after 35 years devoted service in the LFB and the authority appointed the Chief Fire Officer of the West Midlands Fire Service, Ken Knight, to assume the mantle of London's Commissioner. Ken Knight was a widely experienced and respected officer who had previously served in the LFB as an Assistant Chief Officer. A whole new era was about to begin for the London Fire Brigade.

CHAPTER THIRTEEN
Some Significant London Fires of the Past 170 Years

The following listing is not definitive but simply shows a few of the major fires that have been tackled not only by the modern Brigade but by its predecessors, the London Fire Engine Establishment and the Metropolitan Fire Brigade. The listing also highlights some of those fires at which London firemen have lost their lives and the wide range of London premises that have suffered a serious fire during the past 170 years and more.

Date	Location	Incident
16 October 1834	Palace of Westminster	Both Houses of Parliament destroyed but Westminster Hall saved
10 January 1838	Royal Exchange, City	Second building on the same site to be damaged by fire
30 October 1841	The Armoury, Tower of London	Collection of militaria back to James II lost; one fireman killed
14 November 1841	Blackfriars Road, SE1	Two firemen killed
19 August 1843	Toppings Wharf, Southwark, SE1	Riverside warehouse and church
28 July 1848	New Crane Wharf, Wapping, E1	Riverside warehouses; two firemen killed
22 June 1861	Cotton's Wharf, Tooley Street, near Tower Bridge	11 acres of riverside warehouse burnt out; £2 million damage; Superintendent James Braidwood killed
7 December 1882	Alhambra Theatre, Leicester Square, W1	Two fireman killed; Edward VII, Prince of Wales attended and was working close to the fatal collapse of building
10 August 1887	Whiteley's, Bayswater, W2	Department store; £500,000 loss
22 December 1891	Tottenham Court Road, WC1	Department store; 25 steam pumps in use
16 February 1896	Church Street, Soho, W1	Tenement dwellings; nine residents died
19 November 1897	Wells Street, Cripplegate, Barbican, City	Fire spread to 100 factories and warehouses; 51 steam pumps in attendance with 230 firemen. 4,000 workers made unemployed

Date	Location	Incident
9 June 1902	General Electric Company, Queen Victoria Street, City, EC4	10 office workers perished on upper floors; public concern led to first turntable and hook ladders
18 December 1909	Arding & Hobbs, Clapham Junction, SW11	Fire in department store window spread to main shop; nine customers and shop workers died
26 February 1911	Bankside, SE1	Paper and rag warehouse; two firemen killed
3 November 1912	John Barker's, Kensington High Street, W8	Department store; five shop workers killed
30 January 1918	Albert Embankment, SE1	Cattle food warehouse on site of future Brigade HQ; seven firemen killed
15 August 1920	River Thames, Woolwich, SE 18	Motor barge *Dorcas* caught fire and exploded
1 November 1920	Lower Oliver's Wharf, Wapping, E1	Explosion and fire; two firemen killed
11 April 1923	Shadwell, E1	Bonded tobacco warehouse; £850,000 loss
26 October 1924	Wardour Street, Soho, W1	Film processing works; £1 million loss; first steps towards increased fire safety in use of celluloid film
10 March 1925	Madame Tussaud's, Baker Street, W1	Waxworks exhibition; £200,000 loss
9 September 1930	Wapping High Street, E1	Warehouses containing cocoa beans, butter and rubber; £600,000 loss
3 April 1933	West India Dock, E14	Bonded warehouse; 1 million gallons of rum involved
25 September 1935	Colonial Wharf, Wapping, E1	Warehouses containing tea and wine; Brigade saved much stock
30 November 1936	Crystal Palace, Crystal Palace Parade, SE19	Paxton's historic building from 1851 Exhibition totally destroyed; 70 LFB pumps involved and 400 firemen

The period of the Second World War brought incendiary and high explosive attacks to the London area, followed by V1 flying bombs and V2 rockets. Enemy action over London began in August 1940 and continued until 27 March 1945. Amongst the most heaviest and concentrated air raids of the Blitz were those of 8 December 1940, 29 December 1940, 11 January 1941, and 10 May 1941. The lengthiest period of continuous nightly raiding upon London and its suburbs was the unbroken period from 7 September 1940 through to 3 November 1940.

Date	Location	Incident
21 December 1951	Broad Street Goods Depot, Eldon Street, EC2	Railway goods transhipment depot; two firemen killed and 12 seriously injured by falling wall; £1 million loss
11 May 1954	Langley Street, Covent Garden, WC2	Three firemen died
23 January 1958	Smithfield Central Meat Market, EC1	Two firemen killed; 40 hours of firefighting to bring under control; 390 pumps and 1,700 firemen attended over a 48 hour period
22 September 1965	Livery Hall, Grocer's Hall Court, EC2	300 firemen with 55 pumps prevented spread into nearby buildings including the Bank of England and the Mansion House
22 September 1966	Grovelands Road, South Tottenham, N15	Large timber yard; crews of 50 pumps prevented fire from spreading to surrounding houses
8 March 1968	Kings Road, Chelsea, SW3	Two firemen killed in flashover in restaurant
6 June 1969	Leinster Towers Hotel, Bayswater, W2	45 residents rescued, many from windows using ladders
17 July 1969	Dudgeon's Wharf, Manchester Road, E14	Five firemen killed in fire and explosion in derelict fuel tanks
11 May 1971	Hills Hotel, Bayswater, W2	Multiple rescues from upper floors
9 August 1971	Wilson's Wharf, Battlebridge Lane, Tooley Street, SE1	Riverside warehouse close to where Braidwood died; 50 pumps; three firemen badly burned
17 June 1974	Westminster Hall, SW1	Terrorist fire bomb; damage confined to roof area
13 December 1974	Worsley Hotel, Maida Vale, W9	Six residents and one fireman killed; three firemen badly burned; 32 persons rescued from upper floors; cause — arson
1 October 1978	St. Pancras Way, NW1	One firemen died when wall of warehouse collapsed onto turntable ladder
19 March 1980	Kilburn, NW6	Nine residents killed in hostel
10 July 1980	Alexandra Palace, N10	200 firefighters restricted damage to part of historic structure
16 August 1980	Denmark Place, Soho, W1	Unlicensed club; 37 fatalities
23 November 1984	Oxford Circus Underground Station, W1	Train and station equipment damaged by fire; 400 passengers rescued from five other trains stranded in smoke
31 March 1986	Hampton Court Palace	Damage confined to apartment block of historic 16th century palace
18 November 1987	Kings Cross Underground Station, NW 1	30 passengers and one fireman killed

Date	Location	Incident
31 March 1990	Trafalgar Square, WC2	Arson hit office block during poll tax riots
7 August 1991	Minster Court, Mark Lane, City, EC1	Fire in roof space at 10th floor level; 20 pumps and aerial ladders
13 April 1996	Smithfield, EC1	Cinema club; 11 members dead
12 December 1997	Terminal 1, Heathrow Airport	Fire in fast food bar spread into service ducting; crews prevented serious fire spread
16 July 2000	Garrett Lane, Wandsworth, SW18	Storage warehouse with no sprinklers, windows or ventilation. Crews from 25 stations attended
21 May 2001	City University, EC1	Caused by arson; crews restricted damage to upper floors of building
7 December 2003	Industrial Estate, Zennor Road, Balham, SW12	Factory units, 12 pumps and three aerial ladders

One of the first tests for the newly formed London Fire Engine Establishment came on 16 October 1834 when fire broke out at the Palace of Westminster and spread to both chambers of Lords and Commons. Superintendent Braidwood summoned all his manual pump resources and although both chambers were badly damaged, Westminster Hall was saved.

The remains of one of the Dennis pumps that attended a fire involving the petrol barge *Dorcas* on the River Thames at Woolwich. The blazing barge burned through its mooring ropes and drifted with the tide, colliding with and setting fire to two tugs, Woolwich Pier, nine other barges, a ferry boat and several buildings before grounding on the river shore. Here ten LFB pumps were waiting for the *Dorcas* but as they tackled the flames, the vessel blew up. Fortunately, there were no serious injuries but firemen had to abandon three pumps which were all severely damaged, including the one in this view pictured at Lambeth workshops. 15 August 1920.

With Tower Bridge in the background fire strikes again at a large Thamesside warehouse. This is a view of Colonial Wharf, Wapping High Street, East London, at the height of firefighting operations. The front wall of the warehouse has fallen outwards into the Thames and much of the firefighting water on this frontage is being provided by two London Fire Brigade fireboats just in sight on the left. 25 September 1935.

The scene of devastation the morning after the Crystal Palace conflagration with only part of the east wing and tower left standing amongst the smouldering mass of iron and melted glass. The tower was demolished just before the beginning of the London Blitz for fear of aiding the Luftwaffe's day time navigation. 1 December 1936.

Throughout the Brigade's history, fires in large warehouses have always posed danger and difficulty for London's fire crews. On 21 December 1951 the Brigade were called to smoke issuing from a five floor railway goods depot in Eldon Street, EC2. 20 pumps and five turntable ladders were working to surround the fire when, with little warning, an end wall suddenly crashed outwards down onto a number of firemen working off ladders and around various fire engines in the street. Two firemen were killed and 12 others seriously injured: two turntable ladders and a number of wheeled escapes were badly damaged.

A close up view of one of the crushed turntable ladders at Eldon Street showing the massive fall of brickwork and masonry from the warehouse. 21 December 1951.

An aerial view of the back of the railway warehouse at Eldon Street showing five damaged wheeled escape ladders upon which firemen were working when the tons of brickwork came crashing down. 21 December 1951.

This dramatic view shows one of several London fireman who were overcome by smoke during operations at a serious basement fire in Langley Street, Covent Garden, WC2, in which a station officer and two firemen died. The casualty is being carried towards a waiting ambulance close to the London Fire Brigade's Leyland control unit on the right. 11 May 1954.

Dawn breaks over London's historic Central Meat Market in Smithfield, EC1, showing some of the 30 pumps and 150 firemen in attendance. During the dark hours a station officer and a fireman died in the thick smoke of the market's complicated basement layout when their oxygen supplies ran out. Despite the efforts of fire crews the fire is spreading in all directions via concealed ducting and the thick smoke is intensified by the burning cork insulation of the basement store rooms. 23 January 1958.

Some idea of the difficult conditions facing the breathing apparatus crews working in the basement at Smithfield can be gained from this view in which a station officer (on the left) and a fireman are wriggling through a confined space behind some pipe work to check a fire affected area. 23 January 1958.

This photograph was taken some hours later when the decision had been taken to allow the fire to burn out of the basement. By then the working conditions for breathing apparatus crews in the intense heat and thick smoke of the basement was intolerable and most crews were withdrawn to positions surrounding the island site using cooling water jets. This view shows a large capacity radial branch at work in the foreground, capable of projecting water at a rate of 250 gallons per minute together with one of the LFB's latest dual purpose Dennis F101 pumps. This one is attached to B20, Clerkenwell fire station, one of the first on the scene at Smithfield. These fine machines were powered by a Rolls Royce diesel engine and were the most advanced fire engines of their day. 23 January 1958.

A view of the severe fire damage to the fabric of the historic banqueting room of Grocers' Hall in the City of London following a 55 pump fire, which at one stage threatened to spread into surrounding buildings, including the Bank of England. 22 September 1965.

An aerial view following the huge fire in Bamberger's timber yard, Grovelands Road, South Tottenham, N15. Hundreds of residents had to be evacuated from the houses that surrounded the site, but crews successfully prevented the blaze from spreading into these properties. 22 September 1966.

A dramatic photograph taken during firefighting operations at Bamberger's timber yard showing a crew working two jets into the inferno. 22 September 1966.

This action photograph shows advanced firefighting efforts in progress in rooms and corridors on the top floor of the Leinster Towers Hotel, Bayswater, W2, soon after dawn on 6 June 1969. During the first few minutes after their arrival firemen rescued 45 residents, many down the ladders pitched to the frontage of the hotel. A number of gallantry awards were won by London firemen as a result of their heroic actions at this major rescue incident.

Another Bayswater hotel fire of this period was that at Hills Hotel, W2, where a number of residents were rescued down ladders. This photograph was taken after all the action had died down and the fire was under control. London's Chief Officer, Joe Milner, is looking towards the photographer and no doubt reflecting upon new legislation that was in the pipeline to bring about an increased level of fire safety in hotels. The AEC Merryweather 100 ft turntable ladder in the foreground is from A21 Paddington, one of London's busiest fire stations of that era. 11 May 1971.

A small fire in this riverside warehouse in Battlebridge Lane, near Tooley Street, SE1, rapidly developed into a serious conflagration requiring 50 pumps, two fireboats and 250 firemen. As at the 1958 Smithfield Central Meat Market fire, much of this warehouse was lined with cork, creating huge volumes of swirling thick brown smoke. At one stage it was necessary to wear breathing apparatus even when working outside the building. In this view of the rear of the warehouse, taken about an hour into the fire, the photographer has caught the ferocity of a flashover on the upper floors. Note several vertical cracks in the outer wall through which smoke can be seen emerging. 9 August 1971.

When terrorists fire bombed Westminster Hall on 7 June 1974, the Brigade were soon in attendance in some force. The fire was contained to the roof of the historic Hall at one end and this view shows LFB crews working on the ridge of the roof removing heavy slates to ensure that the fire underneath has been fully extinguished.

The largest fire in London during 1974 was at the Worsley Hotel, Clifton Gardens, Maida Vale, W9, on Friday 13 December. In the early hours of the morning an arsonist lit two fires on separate floors, trapping many residents. The first firemen on the scene rescued 32 people, although six residents died in the blaze. During the final stages of firefighting part of the roof suddenly fell in, trapping a crew of four firemen in a second floor room under burning debris. Here the three hour teamwork rescue operation to release the trapped crew is under way.

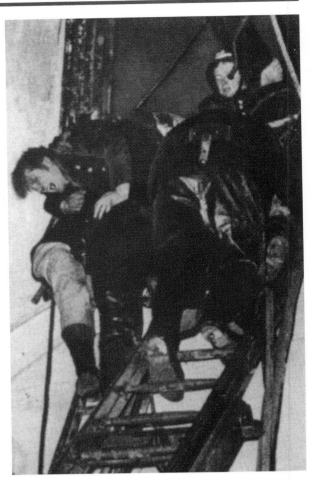

This action view of the Worsley Hotel frontage shows the moment of rescue at second floor level of Fireman Tony Stewart who was one of the firemen who had been buried in the fatal collapse. Friday 13 December 1974.

In this photograph of the aftermath of the Worsley Hotel, Station Officer Colin Searle is being placed in an ambulance after having been extricated from the burning debris at second floor level following a protracted rescue effort of firemen by firemen. The third Brigade casualty, Fireman Martin Walker, was released soon after; both he, Stewart and Searle were badly burned around their lower limbs. Tragically the last of the crew to be released, probationary Fireman Hamish Pettit, was pronounced dead. Friday 13 December 1974.

At the end of the evening rush hour on 18 November 1987 the Brigade were called to Kings Cross underground station where the first crews found a severe fire in progress involving escalators and the entire booking hall area. A massive rescue operation was mounted amid the smoke, but tragically 30 commuters lost their lives. During a heroic rescue attempt Station Officer Colin Townsley also perished and was postumously awarded the George Medal. This photograph shows crews emerging from one of the smoke blackened entrances during the later stages of firefighting.

Prime Minister Margaret Thatcher said that she was shaken and horrified by the Kings Cross disaster and could not speak highly enough of the rescuers. She said: *What you don't get a feeling of, except by being with the firemen, is the intense heat in a limited space. . . . They lived up to the best British tradition.* Here, the Prime Minister talks to some of the first London firemen on the scene at Kings Cross. 18 November 1987.

Some of the fire damage at Kings Cross showing the extensive devastation at the top of the Piccadilly Line escalator under which the fire originated. 18 November 1987.

Thanks to the increasing fire safety work of the modern Brigade large scale fires do not occur as regularly as in the past. However, despite the best efforts of London's firefighters, some outbreaks do still reach major proportions, including this fire in the roof of the City University, EC1, on 21 May 2001. Here the crew in the cage of an aerial ladder are working a powerful cooling jet to help restrict fire spread to unaffected parts of the university building.

CHAPTER FOURTEEN

Special Services

'Special services' is a term used by fire brigades to describe the increasing number of non-fire '999' emergency calls attended by firefighters. Nowadays, these include those to road traffic accidents where persons are trapped in the impacted wreckage of vehicles; machinery and lift accidents; railway crashes and derailments; aircraft incidents; the leakage of toxic chemicals whilst in manufacturing use, storage or in transit; gas leakages and explosions; animals in some dire predicament and the unpredictable effects of adverse and freak weather conditions upon the community at large.

In addition, there are '999' calls to attempted and threatened suicides; sporting and farming accidents; and assistance to the police and ambulance services. The range of special service calls is varied and can often be challenging to firefighters who are frequently called upon to use their expertise and equipment in critical situations where life often hangs by a thread.

The London Fire Brigade began to answer the first special service calls in the early 1900s. These were emergencies involving sewermen overcome by noxious fumes whilst working underground. This was the time when the LFB was first equipped with self contained breathing apparatus and a number of daring rescue attempts were made, although sadly not all successful.

By 1927, the annual total of special service calls in the London County Council area had risen to 61, the highest ever in the Brigade's history. During 1936, the London's annual total reached 201 including an unprecedented day on 8 September when the LFB responded to no fewer than four separate special service calls during a single day. These included a man under a bus in Garratt Lane, Wandsworth; a man trapped in the tipping mechanism of a lorry in Marsham Street, Westminster; a man trapped by a fallen tree in Albany Street, Camberwell; and another casualty under a bus in Greenwich Road, Greenwich.

66 *...Today, London firefighters attend about 50,000 special service calls a year...* 99

66 *For over 90 years and more, the*
London Fire Brigade has rescued
innumerable people at non-fire
emergencies...

From those early years, the general national trend has been towards an inexorable growth in non-fire emergency calls. Today, London firefighters attend about 50,000 special service calls a year, roughly just under a third of all the annual emergency incidents attended by the Brigade. However, nearly 80% of these London non-fire incidents reflect just five of the 27 different types of special service normally provided by the LFB. These include: the release of people shut in lifts; flooding; road traffic accidents; persons locked out of buildings; and making buildings safe. With its high proportion of high rise buildings, London has a unique pattern of calls to people stuck in lifts — around 38% of all annual special service calls in the capital. These calls are usually easily dealt with by the Brigade and those shut inside released. However, the many casualties of road traffic accident calls do frequently involve serious life threatening conditions.

Indeed, the extrication work involved in road traffic accidents means that fire brigades nowadays physically rescue more men, women and children from this type of special services than they do from fire emergencies. Occasionally, a special service call will turn out to be a major accident such as a train crash or derailment where there are likely to be hundreds of casualties. The steady increase in special service work no doubt reflects today's high speed mechanised modern society. Commerce too is constantly trying to meet the demands of the consumer in which manufacturing industry reaches new heights of production and processes. And, of course, accidents still continue to happen.

Since the second half of the 20th century, British fire brigades have increasingly used a discretionary power to respond to the growing number of special service calls, although they never had a legal duty placed upon them unlike the historic requirement to attend and deal with outbreaks of fire. However, in October 2004 under the modernising legislation of the new Fire and Rescue Services Act and the government's earlier National Framework fire authorities were, for the first time, given a statutory responsibility for dealing with rescue from road traffic accidents.

❝ *Occasionally, a special service call will turnout to be a major accident...* ❞

For over 90 years and more, the London Fire Brigade has rescued innumerable people at non fire emergencies and the sophisticated specialist equipment used by firefighters has been progressively improved and developed since the first days of special services. Nowadays, the Brigade's new front line Fire Rescue Units carry a complex range of rescue tools including hydraulic cutting and spreading gear, air bags for lifting, chemical protection suits, inflatable paths for water rescues; and a host of other items to allow crews to deal with rescue from road and rail accidents, water and ice, urban search and rescue operations such as collapsed buildings, and rescue involving ropes and lines.

The following summary is a listing of some of the major non fire emergencies attended by the London Fire Brigade during the past 90 years. A number of these incidents were quickly declared major accidents by virtue of the number of casualties involved.

SOME SIGNIFICANT SPECIAL SERVICE EMERGENCIES ATTENDED BY THE LONDON FIRE BRIGADE		
Date	Location	Incident
18 March 1913	Pembridge Villas, Bayswater, W11	Two firemen died during attempted underground rescue of sewerman overcome by gas
8 April 1926	Marlborough Lane, Charlton, SE7	Rescue of workman from sewer under repair
7 January 1928	Thames Embankment and other riverside locations	River Thames broke its banks causing major flooding over a 24 hour period
10 October 1933	Savoy Hotel, Strand, WC2	Rescue of workman overcome by gas down 250 ft well shaft
4 December 1957	St. John's, Lewisham, SE13	Two trains in collision in fog, bringing down bridge onto wreckage. 93 passengers killed

Date	Location	Incident
5 November 1967	Hither Green, SE12	Train derailment. 49 passengers dead
16 May 1968	Ronan Point, East London	Gas explosion in tower block of flats caused partial collapse
4 May 1971	Tooting Broadway Underground Station, SW17	Train ran into dead end buffers. Driver killed
11 June 1972	Eltham Well Hall Station, SE9	Derailment caused by excessive speed; driver and five passengers killed
19 December 1973	Longfield Avenue, West Ealing, W5	High speed derailment; ten passengers killed
28 February 1975	Moorgate Underground Station, EC2	Crowded train ran through station and crashed into dead end tunnel. 43 persons died; the last surviving casualty removed after 13 hours
10 January 1985	Newnham House, Putney Hill, SW15	Gas explosion partly demolished block of flats; first use of thermal imaging and listening gear to locate buried casualties
12 December 1988	Clapham Junction, SW11	Two trains in collision; 37 passengers killed
4 March 1989	Purley Railway Station	Two trains in collision; five killed
20 August 1989	River Thames near London Bridge	Dredger collides with river cruiser *Marchioness*; 51 persons drowned
8 January 1991	Cannon Street Railway Station, EC4	Train in collision with buffers; two passengers killed
10 April 1992	St.Mary Axe, City, EC3	Terrorist bomb; three dead
24 August 1993	Bishopsgate, City, EC2	Terrorist bomb; many injuries and extensive damage
13 August 1996	A40 Western Avenue, Northolt	Executive jet skidded and ran off runway into A40 traffic
4 February 1997	Bexley High Street, Bexley	Derailed freight train crashed off embankment demolishing buildings
19 September 1997	Near Southall Railway Station	Head on collision between high speed train and freight train; six fatalities
27 October 1997	Thames Barrier	MV *Sand Kite* collided with lock gates and partially sunk
6 October 1999	Ladbroke Grove, North Kensington, W10	Head on collision between high speed and local trains; two drivers and 29 passengers killed

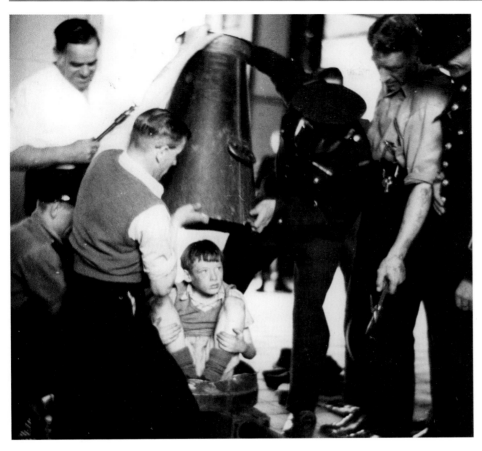

This remarkable photograph records the moment of rescue of a young boy who had climbed in a milk churn in a dairy yard and was unable to get out. A resourceful milkman took the churn and boy to nearby Lambeth fire station where, after some judicious cutting, the top of the milk churn was lifted off to reveal a chastened yet unharmed youngster. 4 July 1947.

The collision between two rush hour trains in fog near St John's station, Lewisham, SE13, on 4 December 1957 was one of the worst railway accidents in British history. 93 people were killed by the collision which also brought down a steel bridge upon the crushed wreckage. Extrication of the casualties was a lengthy process requiring the use of railway heavy cranes. This photograph shows cutting and lifting operations in progress at the scene.

The Hither Green rail crash in south London was caused by a broken rail when all 12 coaches of this London bound train derailed at speed, with many turning over onto their sides. 49 passengers lost their lives and many more were injured. 5 November 1967.

This unusual and dangerous special service occurred high up at 12th floor level of a block of flats under construction when the jib of a tower crane collapsed, trapping the operator in his crushed cabin. Firemen worked for over an hour to free him before carefully easing the casualty down the crane's main column and then into the building to safety and onto hospital. North Kensington. 28 January 1968.

The Brigade were called to Ronan Point, a high rise block of residential flats following the partial collapse of the building structure on one of its corners. The Brigade carried out a number of rescues and this photograph shows the scope of the damage virtually from the top to the bottom of the tower block. East London 16 May 1968.

In this photograph the rescue is in progress of a worker who has been buried following the collapse of shoring at a construction site involving a deep trench at Sutton, south London. An LFB crew are down in the trench carefully digging their way through to the casualty. 2 October 1973.

The camera captures the moment that a horse is brought to safety having been firmly stuck in deep mud for several hours. This crew of firemen are assisting two vets and all concerned have got thoroughly covered with black slime during the operation.

The Moorgate underground disaster ocurred when a rush hour train failed to stop at its terminal station and crashed into a dead end tunnel. This major accident posed a tremendous difficulty for rescue crews due to the compressed wreckage of the train. Taken early on during the incident, this view shows the third carriage jammed into the dead end of the tunnel with the first two carriages ahead in which there were still many casualties trapped. Firemen could only access the front of the train by burrowing through the crushed and twisted structures of the train and this photograph gives a clear idea of the restricted working space. Moorgate Underground station, Northern Line, EC2. 28 February 1975.

Another view of the train involved in the Moorgate disaster. This crew are working at the end of the first carriage which has been pushed up into the roof of the tunnel by the force of the sudden crash into the buffer stops. It was 13 hours before the last surviving casualty was extricated and a further four days before all the fatalities were removed from the front carriage. Chief Fire Officer Joe Milner paid tribute to all his firemen who attended the Moorgate disaster when he called them *'my 1,000 selfless heroes'*. Moorgate Underground station, Northern Line, EC2. 28 February 1975.

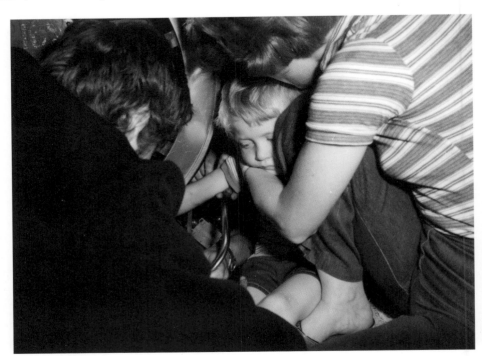

Comforted by his mother, this small boy stoically awaits rescue whilst firemen release his arm from an escalator in a Wembley department store. Remarkably, he was not seriously hurt. 28 July 1976.

This is all that remained of Newnham House in Putney Hill, SW15, south west London, following a massive gas explosion in one of the residential flats. At this stage several residents were still unaccounted for and a carefully controlled digging operation was under way. This involved the senior LFB officer occasionally calling for complete silence in order that any sound from beneath the debris could be detected. The danger from the overhanging structure is obvious. Newnham House was one of the first incidents where the Brigade's new thermal imaging cameras were used. 10 January 1985.

Another major accident involving a considerable amount of extrication work followed the collision of two commuter trains just outside Clapham Junction station, SW11, on 12 December 1988. The Brigade rapidly committed 200 firemen to the scene and working with medical teams, carried out some remarkable rescues from the compacted wreckage. Sadly 37 people died in the crash.

This view of the crash site at Clapham Junction gives some idea of the scale of the wreckage of the two trains and the rescue task involved. 12 December 1988. (*Press Association*)

Motorists on the A40 Western Avenue adjacent to Northolt Airport were lucky when this executive jet skidded off the runway, crashed through the perimeter fence and out onto the carriageway, colliding with a passing van. There were no serious injuries and here firefighters standby awaiting the recovery vehicles, having applied a foam carpet on fuel spilt from the aircraft. 13 August 1996.

When a freight train was derailed on an embankment above Bexley High Street, some of its wagons crashed down onto parked vehicles below. Here a fireman uses sensitive listening equipment to ensure that there are no casualties buried under the debris. 4 February 1997.

Yet another major train crash occurred on 19 September 1997, close to Southall railway station in west London when a high speed train collided head on with a freight train. 130 passengers were led to safety but 25 people were trapped with the last being released four hours after the crash. Seven persons died as a result of the accident.

An unusual special service occurred when the dredger *Sand Kite* collided with the Thames Barrier causing the vessel to sink by the bow. This view is taken from a London fireboat as it stands by, having assisted in the removal of the dredger's crew. 27 October 1997.

Extrication work following road traffic accidents has become a fine science that embraces some sophisticated rescue equipment. Here, working with London Ambulance Service paramedics, firefighters have released the trapped occupants of two cars in collision. Note the considerable amount of power operated cutting and spreading equipment laid out in the left foreground. Walthamstow, EC17. 6 August 1998 (*Walthamstow Guardian*)

The skills of a medical team were needed at this special service in South Street, Mayfair, W1, when a man fell on some railings. This photograph shows the scene before his release and removal to hospital. 19 February 1999.

Yet another serious London rail crash that was quickly declared a major accident bringing in police, ambulance and medical teams, took place when an incoming high speed train collided head on with an outgoing suburban service not far from the terminus at Paddington. Both drivers and 29 passengers were killed and a number of passengers had to be cut free from the wreckage. This view shows the devastation of the accident site some time after all the casualties have been released. Ladbroke Grove, North Kensington W10. 6 October 1999.

This close up view of some of the wreckage of the two trains at Ladbroke Grove gives an idea of the complicated task of rescue for London fire crews. Note the steel cable in the right foreground and the two steel props providing some stability for the rescuers at work within the wreckage of the suburban train. 6 October 1999.

CHAPTER FIFTEEN

The Structure of the London Fire Brigade and its Authority

O n 3 July 2000 the London Fire and Emergency Planning Authority (LFEPA) was born and succeeded the London Fire and Civil Defence Authority. The LFEPA is directly accountable to the Mayor of London, currently Ken Livingstone, who appoints the members of the Authority and sets its budget.

There are a total of 17 members of the LFEPA and this group sets the Authority's policies. This group of 17 members comprises of nine from the London Assembly and eight nominated by the London Boroughs via the Association of London Government. The various appointments reflect the political balance of both the London Assembly and the 33 London boroughs. The Chair of the LFEPA is Val Shawcross, CBE.

This view illustrates one of the considerable number of historic national buildings protected by the LFB as the Brigade command unit pauses outside the Palace of Westminster. This impressive looking vehicle is based at Lambeth Headquarters and normally responds to major incidents in the London area.

❝ *In 2003–04, the Brigade attended over*
180,000 emergency incidents. ❞

The 'Fire' responsibilities of the LFEPA include setting the strategy for the provision of London's fire service and ensuring that: the London Fire Brigade can meet all normal requirements efficiently; members of the Brigade are properly trained and equipped; effective arrangements are in place to receive fire calls and deal with them promptly; information likely to be useful for firefighting is gathered; arrangements for the enforcement of fire safety laws, and general advice and guidance on fire prevention are made. The LFEPA is also responsible for various emergency planning activities assisting the London Boroughs to plan for emergencies.

The London Fire Brigade employs 5,700 uniformed operational fire-fighters and supervisory officers. The majority of uniformed personnel are shift based and attached to the Brigade's 111 fire stations and one river station which are staffed 24 hours a day, 365 days a year. All LFB fire stations are based upon a borough command structure whose boundaries reflect those of each of the 33 London boroughs. Uniformed teams are also located in fire safety offices, the '999' control room and at the Headquarters offices at Lambeth.

The uniformed personnel of the Brigade are supported by 1,100 non-uniformed administrative and technical support staff whose contribution is critical to the efficient round-the-clock work of the Brigade. The civilian teams work in a wide and diverse range of groupings including legal, finance, human resources, equality services, communications, strategy and performance, procurement, information technology, property and democratic services.

In 2003–04, the Brigade attended over 180,000 emergency incidents. This total breaks down to include 57,000 fires, 48,000 special service non-fire emergencies and 77,000 false alarms.

The LFB is organised into three Directorates headed up by the Commissioner for Fire and Emergency Planning, Ken Knight CBE, QFSM, MIFireE. The three Directorates embrace Fire and Community Safety; Resources; and Corporate Services.

The Commissioner for Fire
and Emergency Planning,
Ken Knight (left), pictured
with Val Shawcross, the
Chair of the London Fire and
Emergency Planning
Authority (centre) and
Ken Livingstone, the Mayor
of London (right).

The Brigade's '999' operational services are focused within the Fire and Community Safety Directorate under the Deputy Commissioner. The LFB's administrative support services are provided by the Resources Directorate and the Corporate Services Directorate.

The Commissioner for Fire and Emergency Planning

The most senior LFEPA officer is the Commissioner for Fire and Emergency Planning, Ken Knight. He is also the statutory Chief Fire Officer who chairs the Corporate Management Board (CMB).

The Commissioner has four primary roles. These are: to provide overall co-ordination and promotion of the highest standards of management and operational practice throughout the organisation; to ensure the effective, efficient and economic discharge of the fire and emergency planning responsibilities; give leadership and direction through the provision of sound strategic planning to meet objectives; and to take ultimate responsibility for advising the Authority's elected members on business decisions.

London Fire Brigade male and female firefighters in action during a training session.

Corporate Management Board

The Corporate Management Board (CMB) is the top level officer body. The Commissioner chairs the CMB which normally meets fortnightly and takes decisions or makes recommendations to the LFEPA about policy and resource planning. The Commissioner and the three Directors make up the Board. The Head of Legal Services, Head of Democratic Services, Head of Finance, and the Assistant Commissioner (Service Delivery) are standing advisers to the Board whilst the secretary to the Board is The Head of Strategy, Performance and Planning.

Fire and Community Safety Directorate

The Fire and Community Safety Directorate is responsible for all aspects of the Brigade's service delivery. Roy Bishop, the uniformed Deputy Commissioner for Fire and Emergency Planning, is the Head of this Directorate.

The Director's role is to plan, direct and deliver core fire and community safety policies to maximum effectiveness, ensuring continual improvement in efficiency and performance and compliance with regulations and the law. As a member of CMB he contributes to the corporate management of the Authority.

> 66 *The London Fire Brigade employs 5,700 uniformed operational firefighters and supervisory officers.* 99

The Director is supported by four uniformed Assistant Commissioners (ACs) whose roles cover service delivery, operational response, operational planning and safety. The Deputy Commissioner is also responsible for the Head of Equalities.

Assistant Commissioner (Service Delivery) — Ron Dobson
His responsibilities cover delivering firefighting, rescue and fire safety services to the public. Services are delivered at London borough level by borough teams each working under a borough commander. To support him with service delivery, fire stations in the London boroughs are grouped into six areas, each with an area manager.

Assistant Commissioner (Operational Response) — John Anthony
Responsibilities cover mobilising, including the Brigade's command and mobilising centre handling '999' calls, incident communications, London resilience, incident command policy, chemical policy, water policy and resources, operational staff deployment policy and industrial relations.

Assistant Commissioner (Operational Planning) — Jon Webb
This post covers service delivery planning, equipment specification, private finance initiative liaison, environmental policy and planning, Greater London Authority liaison, health and safety at work, emergency planning, inter-agency liaison, major event planning and operational policy on rivers, railways, airports and utilities.

Assistant Commissioner (Safety) — Malcolm Kelly
His responsibilities cover community and statutory fire safety policy including community fire safety resources, action against arson and deliberate fire-setting, fire investigation, schools liaison and young people's strategy, crime and disorder and equalities and outreach liaison, fire safety legislation, fire safety engineering, railways (including the London Underground), quality assurance and audit, petroleum, local

Two female firefighters of the London Fire Brigade.

authority lead partnerships, liaison with district surveyors and approved inspectors. At the moment, the AC — Safety is also responsible for discipline matters under the Fire Service (Discipline) Regulations and is the designated brigade investigating officer.

Head of Equalities is Pat Oakley. She is responsible for developing and implementing the Authority's Equality at Work policy to make sure equality issues are fully integrated into best value service delivery and performance plans and implemented effectively.

❝ The uniformed personnel of the Brigade are supported by 1,100 non-uniformed staff... ❞

Resources Directorate

The Director of Resources, Barbara Riddell, provides information, advice and expertise to help meet the Authority's strategic objectives through the optimal use of resources. She provides direction and strategy for each of the areas of resource to enable them to contribute to the achievement of overall corporate strategy. She is responsible for five heads of service:

Head of Finance — Colm O'Callaghan is responsible for the proper administration of the Authority's financial affairs and provides for the economic, effective and efficient operation and development of the financial advice and financial management services including accountancy, audit and treasury management, exchequer and payroll.

Head of Human Resources — James Dalgleish who manages and develops the human resources function including local personnel services, employee relations, organisation and human resource planning, recruitment and selection, counselling and advisory services. He provides advice, information and technical expertise on personnel matters to the Authority, its members and senior management.

Assistant Commissioner (Training and Development) — Max Hood leads, develops and supports the Brigade's training and development function and is responsible for securing resources to deliver the function and implements quality assurance systems to continually improve perform-ance. He provides advice, information and technical expertise on training matters and ensures effective design and delivery of training.

Head of Procurement — Terry Brewer manages a central procurement function for all goods, services, clothing, technical equipment and services, including the research and development, provision, repair and maintenance of operational equipment. He is responsible for the vehicle public finance initiative (PFI) contract and acts as a focal point for the project management of all PFI and other projects, including that for corporate property.

Head of Property — Nadim Moge provides property management, development and maintenance service to the Authority. He oversees the

> 66 *All LFB fire stations are based upon a borough command structure...* 99

provision, repair and maintenance of all premises and plant belonging to, or occupied by, the Authority and provides costs effective architectural, surveying, building engineering services, and effective estates management.

Corporate Services Directorate

The Director of Corporate Services, Rita Dexter, is responsible for the service areas which support the delivery of the Authority's business objectives. She leads the development of corporate strategy, develops and leads effective performance management systems and sets best practice and leads innovation in service areas to benefit the Authority. The Director also raises awareness at the highest possible levels of potential corporate opportunities and risks and is responsible for six heads of service:

Nick Collins is the *Assistant Commissioner (Risk)* responsible for risk analysis and management including the Authority's Integrated Risk Management Plan and corporate risk and pre-determined attendance policy.

Head of Strategy, Planning and Performance — Andy Chanin provides strategic planning expertise and co-ordinates planning activity in relation to all projects and capital programmes. He provides strategic planning advice in respect of time, cost and resource in relation to business activities and monitors performance against plans, re-scheduling activities where appropriate in order to achieve best value. Andy co-ordinates management of information systems and provides management information to external agencies, manages the Best Value unit, operations and training performance inspectorate and the Commissioner's secretariat. He is secretary to the Corporate Management Board.

Head of Democratic Services — Jill Lightbown manages and co-ordinates all aspects of the official administrative functions of the Authority relating to the servicing of meetings, committees and panels. She provides and develops services to members.

> ❝ *The LFB is organised into three Directorates...* ❞

Head of Communications — James Flynn is the Brigade's principal adviser in internal and external communication and is responsible for raising the profile of the Authority through the management of media and other methods of communication via press relations, publicity, publications, web, external events and visitors. He also makes sure staff understand the role they play in meeting the Brigade's plans through effective internal communication systems.

A typical modern day London Fire Brigade crew of firefighters.

A female London Firefighter pictured during a pump drill that involves getting lines of hose to work.

Head of Legal Services — Steve Starling ensures legal integrity and sound legal practice in the affairs of the Brigade, securing the provision of economic, efficient and effective legal services (including legal advice, representation, information and technical expertise) for the Authority on the full range of its activities. He acts as the Monitoring Officer within the meaning of the Local Government and Housing Act 1989.

Head of Information Technology — Tony McManus advises on information systems and information technology including business systems, IT operations, technical support networks, radio and telecommunications, help desk and information technology (IT) training. Tony leads the IT service delivery function to make sure it provides cost effective services and develops the IT strategy to meet future needs.

CHAPTER SIXTEEN

Fire Stations of the London Fire Brigade

Fire Station	Address	London Borough
Acton	27 Gunnersbury Lane, W3 8EA	Ealing
Addington	197-199 Lodge Lane, CR0 0QA	Croydon
Barking	Alfreds Way, IG11 0BB	Barking and Dagenham
Barnet	144 Station Road, EN5 1TE	Barnet
Battersea	11 Este Road, SW11 2TL	Wandsworth
Beckenham	8 Beckenham Road, BR3 4LR	Bromley
Belsize	36 Lancaster Grove, NW3 4PB	Camden
Bethnal Green	11 Roman Road, E2 0HU	Tower Hamlets
Bexley	172 Erith Road, Bexleyheath, DA7 6BY	Bexley
Biggin Hill	2 Kingsmead, TN16 3UB	Bromley
Bow	64 Parnell Road, E3 2RU	Tower Hamlets
Brixton	84 Gresham Road, SW9 7NP	Lambeth
Bromley	4 South Street, BR1 1RH	Bromley
Chelsea	264 Kings Road, SW3 5UF	Kensington and Chelsea
Chingford	34 The Ridgeway, E4 6PP	Waltham Forest
Chiswick	2-4 Heathfield Gardens, W4 4JY	Hounslow
Clapham	29 Old Town, SW4 0JT	Lambeth
Clerkenwell	42–44 Rosebery Avenue, EC1R 4RN	Islington
Croydon	90 Old Town, CR0 1AR	Croydon
Dagenham	70 Rainham Road North, RM10 7ES	Barking and Dagenham
Deptford	186 Evelyn Street, SE5 8PR	Lewisham
Dockhead	8 Wolseley Street, SE1 2BP	Southwark
Dowgate	94–95 Upper Thames Street, EC4R 3UE	City of London
Downham	260 Reigate Road, BR1 5JN	Lewisham
Ealing	60–64 Uxbridge Road, W13 8RA	Ealing
East Greenwich	235 Woolwich Road, SE7 7RF	Greenwich
East Ham	210 High Street South, E6 3RS	Newham
Edmonton	99 Church Street, N9 9AA	Enfield
Eltham	266 Eltham High Street, SE9 1BA	Greenwich
Enfield	93 Carterhatch Lane, EN1 4LA	Enfield
Erith	52 Erith Road, Belvedere, DA17 6HR	Bexley
Euston	172 Euston Road, NW1 2DH	Camden

Fire Station	Address	London Borough
Feltham	101 Faggs Road, TW14 0LH	Hounslow
Finchley	227 Long Lane, N3 2RP	Barnet
Forest Hill	155 Stansted Road, SE23 1HP	Lewisham
Fulham	685 Fulham Road, SW6 5UJ	Hammersmith and Fulham
Greenwich	4 Blisset Street, SE10 8UP	Greenwich
Hainault	368-388 New North Road, IG6 3DY	Redbridge
Hammersmith	190-192 Shepherds Bush Road, W6 7NL	Hammersmith and Fulham
Harrow	500 Pinner Road, HA5 5RW	Harrow
Hayes	65 Shepiston Lane, UB3 1LL	Hillingdon
Heathrow	Building 450, Heathrow Airport Northern Perimeter Road, TW6 2RR	Hillingdon
Hendon	91 The Burroughs, NW4 4BL	Barnet
Heston	520 London Road, Isleworth, TW7 4HR	Hounslow
Hillingdon	Uxbridge Road, UB10 0PH	Hillingdon
Holloway	262-268 Hornsey Road, N7 7QT	Islington
Homerton	97 Homerton High Street, E9 6DL	Hackney
Hornchurch	42 North Street, RM11 1SH	Havering
Hornsey	108 Park Avenue South, N8 8LS	Haringey
Ilford	460 High Road, IG1 1UE	Redbridge
Islington	278 Upper Street, N1 2TZ	Islington
Kensington	13 Old Court Place, Kensington High Street, W8 4PL	Kensington and Chelsea
Kentish Town	20 Highgate Road, NW5 1NS	Camden
Kingsland	333 Kingsland Road, E8 4DR	Hackney
Kingston	390 Richmond Road, KT2 5PR	Kingston upon Thames
Knightsbridge	16 Basil Street, SW3 1AL	Kensington and Chelsea
Lambeth	8 Albert Embankment, SE1 7SD (River Thames station also)	Lambeth
Lee Green	9 Eltham Road, SE12 8ES	Greenwich
Lewisham	249/259 Lewisham High Street, SE13 6NH	Lewisham
Leyton	90B Church Road, E10 5HG	Waltham Forest
Leytonstone	466 High Road, E11 3HN	Waltham Forest
Mill Hill	10 Hartley Avenue, NW7 2HX	Barnet
Millwall	461 Westferry Road, E14 3AN	Tower Hamlets
Mitcham	30 Lower Green West, CR4 3AF	Merton
New Cross	266 Queen's Road, SE14 5JN	Lewisham
New Malden	180 Burlington Road, KT3 4RW	Merton
Norbury	1321/1325A London Road, SW16 4AU	Croydon
North Kensington	242 Ladbroke Grove, W10 5LP	Kensington and Chelsea
Northolt	74 Petts Hill, UB5 4JT	Ealing
Old Kent Road	405 Old Kent Road, SE1 5JH	Southwark
Orpington	Avalon Road, BR6 9AX	Bromley

Fire Station	Address	London Borough
Paddington	156 Harrow Road, W2 6NL	Westminster
Park Royal	Waxlow Road, NW10 7NU	Brent
Peckham	78-80 Peckham Road, SE5 8PR	Southwark
Plaistow	145 Prince Regent Lane, E13 8RY	Newham
Plumstead	1 Lakedale Road, SE18 1PP	Greenwich
Poplar	168 East India Dock Road, E14 0BP	Tower Hamlets
Purley	128 Brighton Road, CR8 4DB	Croydon
Richmond	323 Lower Richmond Road, TW9 4PN	Richmond upon Thames
Romford	198 Pettits Lane North, RM1 4NU	Havering
Ruislip	Bury Street, HA4 7TW	Hillingdon
Shadwell	290 Cable Street, E1 0BX	Tower Hamlets
Shoreditch	235 Old Street, EC1V 9EY	Hackney
Sidcup	162 Main Road, DA14 6NZ	Bexley
Silvertown	303 North Woolwich Road, E16 2BB	Newham
Soho	126 Shaftesbury Avenue, W1D 5ET	Westminster
Southall	17-19 High Street, UB1 3HA	Ealing
Southgate	96 High Street, N14 6BN	Enfield
Southwark	94 Southwark Bridge Road, SE1 0EG	Southwark
Stanmore	650 Honeypot Lane, HA7 1JS	Harrow
Stoke Newington	64 Stoke Newington Church Street, N16 0AP	Hackney
Stratford	117 Romford Road, E15 4LY	Newham
Surbiton	31/33 Ewell Road, KT6 6AF	Kingston upon Thames
Sutton	43 St Dunstans Hill, SM1 2JX	Sutton
Tooting	91 Trinity Road, SW17 7SQ	Wandsworth
Tottenham	49 St Loys Road, N17 6UE	Haringey
Twickenham	30 South Road, TW2 5NT	Richmond upon Thames
Wallington	19 Belmont Road, SM6 8TE	Sutton
Walthamstow	343 Forest Road, E17 5JR	Waltham Forest
Wandsworth	45 West Hill, SW18 1RL	Wandsworth
Wembley	591a Harrow Road, HA0 2EG	Brent
Wennington	Wennington Road, RM13 9EE	Havering
West Hampstead	325 West End Lane, NW6 1RR	Camden
West Norwood	445 Norwood Road, SE27 9DG	Lambeth
Westminster	4 Greycoat Place, SW1P 1SB	Westminster
Whitechapel	27 Commercial Road, E1 1LD	Tower Hamlets
Willesden	59a Pound Lane, NW10 2HH	Brent
Wimbledon	87 Kingston Road, SW19 1JN	Merton
Woodford	2 Snakes Lane, IG8 0BS	Redbridge
Woodside	2 Long Lane, Addiscombe Road, CR0 7AL	Croydon
Woolwich	24 Sunbury Street, SE18 5LU	Greenwich

Note: The following list of the Brigade's 111 operational fire stations was correct at the time of going to press in June 2005.

Lewisham Fire Station, 249–259 Lewisham High Street, SE13 6NH.

Wimbledon Fire Station, 87 Kingston Road, SW19 1JN.

Harrow Fire Station, 500 Pinner Road, HA5 5RW.

Edmonton Fire Station, 99 Church Street, N9 9AA.

Romford Fire Station, 198 Pettits Lane North, RM1 4NU.

Clerkenwell Fire Station,
42–44 Rosebery Avenue
EC1R 4RN. Clerkenwell has
the distinction of being the
oldest fire station in the
London Fire Brigade having
been opened in 1870 during
the days of the Metropolitan
Fire Brigade.

Westminster Fire Station,
4 Greycoat Place, SWIP ISB.

One of the Brigade's newest
fire stations is Hammersmith.
Located at 190–192 Shepherds
Bush Road, SW6 7NL, the
new station was opened in
2004 to replace an outdated
building opened in the early
1900s, and incorporates a
community fire safety centre.

CHAPTER SEVENTEEN

Handling London's '999' Fire Calls

Today, the London Fire Brigade is the biggest fire and rescue service in the United Kingdom and the Brigade's central '999' control room in Docklands currently receives in excess of 300,000 '999' emergency calls each year. In addition, the control room also takes 750,000 operationally urgent calls per annum, for example, changes in the availability and status of fire engines and supervisory officer resources. Not surprisingly, handling this enormous number of emergency calls makes London's fire control room the busiest single fire control in the world.

It is interesting to reflect upon the historic manner in which an alarm of fire has been dealt with in London since the beginning of organized fire-fighting from 1833 and the days of the London Fire Engine Establishment. The normal method of raising an alarm in case of fire at this time was by

This photograph shows the Brigade's first centralised '999' control room located in the basement of Lambeth Headquarters. Commissioned in 1948, this new control coincided with the phased abolition of street fire alarms which meant that the vast majority of fire calls were received through the '999' telephone system, rather than at individual fire stations.

> ❝ ...*London's fire control room is the busiest single fire control in the world.* ❞

means of a messenger on foot or horseback, or even taking a cab to the nearest fire station. It was not until 1880 that electrical methods of calling out the Brigade were first introduced. One innovation authorised by the Metropolitan Fire Brigade Act 1865 was the establishment of 'telegraphic communication' that allowed communication between each local station, its District Station and the Brigade Headquarters. A fire station receiving a call to a fire could notify other stations and obtain support far quicker than the days of having to despatch a runner to the next nearest station.

In 1878, Brigade Headquarters moved to Southwark Bridge Road, the site of the Brigade's present Training Centre. The speed and effectiveness of the Brigade's response was further enhanced by the introduction in 1880 of street fire alarms, which were to become a London feature for some 70 years, although even as early as 1881, false alarms were becoming more numerous. About the same time, the telephone was being introduced and after some hesitation by the postal authorities to allow the telephone to be used for giving an alarm of fire, or for summoning the Brigade when the fire was not on the subscriber's own premises, the Postmaster General eventually allowed the new apparatus to convey information 'concerning the outbreak of fire or rioting'.

Upon the outbreak of the First World War in 1914, all inner London fire stations were linked by special telephones in order to receive warning of approaching enemy Zeppelins and aircraft. Then, again with war looming in 1938, arrangements were put in place for the co-ordination and mobilisation of resources to large incidents, including a telephone network connecting all London's 360 Auxiliary Fire Service sub stations with the central control room at Lambeth. These arrangements continued to work throughout the period after August 1941 when the fire service was nationalized. Towards the end of the war, a number of fire engines based at London fire stations began to have radios fitted.

When in 1948 the service was denationalized, the Fire Services Act 1947 placed the responsibility for maintaining efficient fire brigades upon the County Councils and County Boroughs and with effect from 1 April 1948,

A late 1960s view of the Eastern Command control room at Stratford, showing the teleprinter mobilising system in use at that time.

when the London County Council (LCC) once again became responsible for the London Fire Brigade. Post war improvements were made to the methods by which the Brigade handled emergency calls from members of the public. Until 1948, each fire station had its own street fire alarm system and calls were received at five District Headquarters. A growing post war problem was the increasingly high number of malicious calls being received via street fire alarms, and after some deliberation, the LCC requested the Post Office to replace the street alarms with telephone boxes. At the same time a free calling system for the fire brigade, police and ambulance services using the '999' number was introduced. This important development required a '999' call centre and as the radio system had to be operated from a central point, it was operationally imperative to mobilise London's fire engines from the same location. Consequently, in 1948 a new control room was opened at Brigade Headquarters at Lambeth where all '999' calls were received and from where all London's 60 fire stations could be mobilised. As a result of this, 1949 saw the beginning of the abolition of the capital's street fire alarms.

The new computer aided centralised Command and Mobilising Centre was opened in February 1990 and for some 14 years served as the focal point of the fire and rescue work of the Brigade. Some of the touch screen control operator positions can be seen beneath the dynamic wall map of fire engine and personnel resources. 25 July 1997.

At this time, fire station watchrooms were continuously staffed so that emergency calls could be received from the central control room, fire engines turned out and various items of communications equipment operated. In 1963, a new telecommunications system was planned that involved the transmission of calls from the control room at Lambeth to stations by teleprinter. This ambitious scheme became operative in 1965 and eliminated the need for watchrooms to be continuously manned, an arrangement that still applies today.

In April 1965, the Greater London Council (GLC) was formed with its new enlarged London Fire Brigade organised into three commands, sub-divided into 11 divisions with a total of 120 fire stations and nearly 7,000 personnel. The enlarged Brigade's control and communications network was designed to deal with upwards of 60,000 emergency calls each year. London's '999' fire calls were handled at four control rooms manned by 196 control room personnel. One control remained at Headquarters at Lambeth taking calls from the central London area, whilst the new controls at Croydon, Stratford and Wembley were each responsible for a geographically discreet area of London.

> ❝ *The annual emergency call rate at this time was a remarkable 148,737.* ❞

When a '999' call was received, a street index card for the appropriate thoroughfare held on rotary drums was located, enabling the Control Officer to identify the nearest number and type of fire engines to be despatched to the incident. The mobilising message was then sent to the appropriate station(s) via the teleprinter network that was also used to transmit administrative messages throughout the Brigade.

In 1972, an Operations Room was set up at Brigade Headquarters responsible for co-ordinating the operational workload of the Brigade and two years later, the control room at Lambeth was closed with mobilising responsibility for the central London area being divided between the other three control centres which from this time were equipped with new visual display unit systems.

During 1980 the Brigade conducted a feasibility study into future mobilising arrangements and this identified the need for change, with a recommendation of a computer-aided despatch system based in a single centrally located control room. In December 1981, the contract to deliver this system was awarded to GEC Marconi Radar and Defence Systems.

In 1986 the abolition of the Greater London Council saw the transfer of the London Fire Brigade to the control of the London Fire and Civil Defence Authority (LFCDA). Simultaneously, the Brigade re-organised into a five area operational structure, comprising 114 fire stations. The annual emergency '999' call rate at this time was a remarkable 148,737.

The Brigade's new computer aided centralised control room at Lambeth Headquarters, known as the Command and Mobilising Centre (CMC) and manned by 135 uniformed control room personnel, was finally opened in February 1990. Some functions were not enabled until some time after such as the completion of the software for senior officer mobilising, which was delivered in April 1990. By December 1997, the CMC had received and dealt with a staggering 2,114,303 emergency calls, at that time making it the busiest fire brigade control room in the United Kingdom.

Another view of the computer aided Command and Mobilising Centre at Lambeth that handled all London's fire calls and mobilised the Brigade's fire engines to emergencies from 1990 to 2004.

Following a staff and shift review in 1997, a number of changes were made to the CMC working arrangements which resulted in a workforce total of 93 control room personnel.

By then, with the global growth and development of IT, the CMC system was increasingly becoming obsolescent and unable to meet the Authority's need for management information. A further review resulted in a decision to procure a new '999' mobilising system that would be

> 66 *By December 1997, the CMC had received and dealt with a staggering 2,114,303 emergency calls...* 99

flexible to change and, as far as possible, able to exploit new and emerging technology. A second generation project team was formed consisting of control room, operational and other personnel to oversee the procurement process and implementation of the new system. In 2002, the contract to deliver the new system was awarded to Motorola (Integrated Systems Division).

In 2002, following the consideration of a range of options, the Authority decided to reorganise Brigade Headquarters on the Albert Embankment site. This required a new location to be found for Brigade Control. Following a thorough and robust evaluation process and taking into account a range of factors including staff location, communication links and affordability, a site in Docklands was identified as having the necessary potential from which the Authority could satisfactorily conduct its emergency call handling and mobilising function.

At 0200 hrs on 20 April 2004, the new Brigade Control became fully operational and continuously staffed by approximately 100 uniformed control officers working on a shift basis, supported by a further 30 operational, non-operational and other specialist personnel providing address management, technical support and various administrative functions.

CHAPTER EIGHTEEN

London's Firefighting Teams

Historically, London's firefighters have always been a professional full time force on call from fire stations staffed 24 hours a day throughout the year. As the hours of the working week were progressively reduced, the virtually constant on call duty system of firemen in the 19th century days of the London Fire Engine Establishment gave way to two shifts of manpower, or watches, as they are called.

After the Second World War came a third watch meaning that the firefighting resources of the capital were spread evenly across three shifts known as the Red, White and Blue watches. Finally, in late 1975 came the introduction of a national agreement accepting the 42 hour week for

This photograph shows firefighters on a trainees course undertaking ladder and hose drills using a specially constructed training building at the Brigade's Training Centre at Southwark.

66 *Historically, London's firefighters have always been a professional full time force...* 99

operational firefighters. For the London Fire Brigade this involved a mammoth recruiting and training exercise to implement the change and as a result, a fourth shift (the Green watch) was created. Nowadays, a number of specialist personnel who do not normally respond to emergency incidents work a day based rota, whilst certain supervisory officers perform a flexible duty system that provides for cover across the London area during weekdays, night time and at weekends.

New Role Based Structures

In 1998, the national negotiating body of the fire service finally agreed a new role-based structure to replace the existing ranks within fire brigades. In London local consultation with union officials began in early 2004 to implement these important changes within the LFB. As a

This pair of London firefighters is displaying the new firefighting uniform, introduced from late 1998 onwards. The design of this personal protective equipment was evolved following an extensive trial of a number of types of uniform and the LFB was the first brigade in the country to introduce a fully co-ordinated kit embracing everything from helmet to boots.

A London firefighter handles a high pressure water jet during a drill session. A control valve allows him to select a water jet, a fine atomised spray for maximum cooling purposes and protection from radiated heat, or a combination of both.

London firefighters regularly undergo continuation training in breathing apparatus. Here, a crew member is negotiating part of a multi-level crawling gallery which contains various obstacles and confined space restrictions. This training would normally be undertaken with the building full of non-toxic cosmetic smoke.

result, in spring 2005, the London Fire and Emergency Planning Authority took the first steps towards the creation of a flexible fire and rescue service for London by planning to switch the existing 11 ranks within the LFB with seven role-based positions.

The future new structure will mean that the existing ranks of firefighter, leading firefighter and sub officer will change to two roles, namely crew and watch manager. Each watch at a London fire station will be managed by a watch manager supported by a number of crew managers, depending upon the number of fire engines at a particular station. Personnel will take the responsibility for their personal performance and development of their skills to improve their own performance and will be expected to provide support to colleagues. Under the new arrangements, it is likely that a firefighter trainee should, on average, be confirmed as reaching a competent stage within three years. Apart from the requirement to save and preserve endangered life, a number of other elements of the firefighter role emphasise the contribution being made to community fire safety,

> ❝ ...the Brigade aims to have the right
> people, with the right skills, in the
> right place at the right time. ❞

including providing advice and information as well as undertaking fire safety inspections of premises to minimise the risks to people, property and the environment.

The new role-based titles will be:

Existing Rank	New Role
Firefighter	Firefighter
Leading Firefighter	Crew Manager
Sub Officer	Watch Manager A
Station Officer	Watch Manager B
Assistant Divisional Officer	Station Manager B
Divisional Officer 2	Group Manager B
Divisional Officer 1	Area Manager A
Senior Divisional Officer	Area Manager B
Assistant Commissioner	Brigade Manager
Deputy Commissioner	Brigade Manager
Commissioner	Brigade Manager

Each role has an agreed map that identifies core functions that staff need to carry out and points to those areas where they need to be more competent to work effectively within those roles. The role maps are designed to encourage effective teamwork and are the same across the entire British fire service. The new arrangements will change the manner in which firefighters are appointed and promoted with the introduction of the integrated personal development scheme (IPDS). This has, in fact, been in use within the LFB for some time through various assessment and development programmes for uniformed personnel.

The new role-based structure recognises the changing work of firefighters in a service that aims to become more responsive to the risks and the needs of the communities served by the London Fire Brigade. Put simply, the Brigade aims to have the right people, with the right

Two views of firefighters at work during a training session on a fire station drill tower with a pump, hose and ladders in use. In this case, the drill simulates a fire in the first floor of a domestic property.

The London fireboat *Fire Dart* is dwarfed whilst moored under the Queen Elizabeth Bridge at Dartford carrying the M25 over the River Thames as an LFB crew carefully descend one of the bridge's supporting pillars from the road level with a stretcher and 'casualty' during a line rescue exercise.

Firefighting is all about teamwork and here there is plenty in evidence in this action shot of a crew working an external cooling water jet during a serious fire in 2004 at an empty commercial premises in West London.

skills, in the right place at the right time. This will allow the Brigade to use its people, equipment and fire stations in the most effective manner to ensure the future safety of Londoners.

Recruitment into the Brigade

Potential recruits to the London Fire Brigade no doubt see themselves as sliding down a pole, jumping onto a gleaming red fire engine and then racing off into the night, with blue lights flashing and sirens blaring. Nowadays in the modern LFB, the reality is somewhat different. Today's

Divisional Officer Dany Cotton, is the most senior female firefighter in the London Fire Brigade having joined the Brigade in 1988. After serving at various fire stations in south east London, Dany became a Station Commander, then progressed through several specialist roles before being appointed to her current post as Head of Firefighter Development at Southwark Training Centre in 2005.

emphasis for everyone connected with the Brigade is on preventing fires occurring in the first place and this means that firefighters help to educate the community in which they work about the vital importance of fire safety.

This is, of course, not to say that the Brigade is less than prepared to deal with emergencies. Clearly, being ready to tackle '999' situations whenever they occur at all times of the day or night and in all weather, is still critical. These incidents can be fires or other life threatening emergencies such as road, rail and air traffic accidents along with chemical spillages, floods, or rescue work where people are trapped in lifts or tunnels. Looking back over a long and distinguished history, the men and women of the modern London Fire Brigade have never been better trained and equipped.

One of the Brigade's new Mercedes Fire Rescue Units pictured during its equipment fitting out stage.

Aspiring trainees to the London Fire Brigade need to satisfy the necessary selection tests and can then look forward to a career that gives the chance to form incredibly strong bonds with the rest of the fire station 'family' team of which they will be an integral part. A key priority for the Brigade is to develop its services in a manner that is sensitive to the differing needs and aspirations of different parts of London's diverse communities and to be exemplary employers. The LFB carefully monitors information by racial group about its staff and those who apply to join the Brigade and there has been good progress made already in increasing the number of black and minority ethnic and women firefighters who serve in the LFB.

Once the Brigade commences a period of recruiting activity, the selection process for firefighters is a phased one and involves the following stages:

(i)   Application form and questionnaire. Aspiring trainees complete an application form and questionnaire and this enables the Brigade to assess if a candidate meets the basic eligibility criteria.

(ii)   Written tests. A candidate is required to complete tests involving learning information, understanding information, using numbers and observation.

(iii) Physical fitness assessments. These include a strength test, a shuttle run test and work related tests.

(iv)   Interview and Team Exercise. A candidate is required to attend an interview with two experienced interviewers and answer questions that help the Brigade judge how the applicant would perform in

different situations. Prospective trainees will be asked to give examples from their own experience, whether from work, home or school/college, to establish how they might cope with the varied role of a firefighter. In the team exercise, candidates work with each other and are given a topic to discuss.

(v)   Medical. If a candidate passes the interview and physical tests, they then attend a medical at the Brigade's Occupational Health Unit and need to arrange an eye examination with an appropriately qualified ophthalmologist. Only those considered fit by the Brigade's Medical Examiner are accepted as a trainee firefighter.

(vi)   Reference Checking. All offers of employment are subject to the receipt of satisfactory references covering the last three years. The LFB operates a strict absence policy and information concerning sickness records are closely scrutinised.

(vii)   Induction. Finally, those successfully passing the selection process are invited to attend an induction session at the Brigade's Training Centre in Southwark. Here trainees are measured for their various uniforms and may invite a partner or a close family member to join in

The Brigade is progressively replacing a number of its high rise fire engines with new aerial ladder platforms such as this Mercedes/ Magirus seen here at an exhibition in 2004.

" ...the men and women of the modern LFB have never been better trained..."

the visit. This gives trainees the opportunity to meet their trainers and other members of the group, have a good look around the Training Centre and learn a little more about the training course.

Trainee Firefighter Course

This is of 18 weeks duration and is a mix of both intensive theory and practical training. The theory includes a basic understanding of fire science and combustion, hydraulics, electricity, and chemistry. The practical work includes hose running, ladder handling, working safely at heights, pump operation, extinguishers, ropes and lines, special service rescue equipment, first aid and basic casualty care skills, as well as equipment used in dealing with emergency incidents involving hazardous materials. Before posting to an operational station, a trainee also undertakes a course to qualify to wear breathing apparatus.

Once trainee firefighters have successfully completed the initial 18 week course at Southwark Training Centre, they are posted to an operational London fire station to serve a probationary period whilst gaining operational experience attending fires and other emergencies as a member of a crew. After satisfactory completion of the probationary period, a firefighter then becomes eligible to undertake a series of progressive assessments and courses that in time opens the way to proceed right through to the most senior ranks in the fire service.

CHAPTER NINETEEN

The London Safety Plan

Every year, fire authorities are required to produce an Integrated Risk Management Plan (IRMP) for their area. The London Fire Brigade call this the London Safety Plan. The London Safety Plan aims to create a modern fire and rescue service for the capital that works hard to stop emergencies happening in the first place. Although the London Fire Brigade has always responded very rapidly and effectively to a fire or other emergency, prevention is clearly better than cure. By reducing the number of fires that break out in the first place the Brigade is aiming to reduce the danger, suffering, damage and economic loss that fires can cause.

The changes contained in the Safety Plans constitute what are probably the most significant transformation of London's fire and rescue services since the Second World War. Many of these changes have come about as the direct result of the government's modernisation plans contained in the Fire and Rescue Services Act of 2004 and the National Framework structure. Amongst other things, the new arrangements give

The Work of Statutory Fire Safety

The Authority's statutory fire safety responsibilities are discharged by some 214 inspecting officers, including 45 non-uniformed officers. These officers are based in Borough Teams at 24 office locations across London and are in the main responsible for ensuring compliance with fire safety legislation in some 300,000 premises in the capital.

The principal legislation under which the Authority has enforcement responsibility are the Fire Precautions Act 1971, and the Fire Precautions (Workplace) Regulations 1997 as amended, which require certain fire safety standards to be met in premises such as offices, shops, hotels and other places of work. The Brigade's inspecting officers also respond to consultation from the London Boroughs to give advice on fire safety matters under the Building Regulations, in respect of licence applications for places of entertainment and in relation to standards for houses in multiple occupation. The Authority is also the petroleum licensing authority for London and is therefore responsible for issuing licences and ensuring safety standards are maintained in all the capital's petrol filling stations.

Having turned off the gas supply, this lady is tackling a burning chip pan by carefully replacing the lid to exclude the oxygen. Note she has not attempted to move the chip pan or use water to try to extinguish the flames.

fire authorities additional responsibilities for responding to road traffic accidents and other emergencies, including major accidents and acts of terrorism. Fire authorities also now have more flexibility to plan how best to respond to its risks. Under the old standards of fire cover, attendance times for fire engines were determined on the perceived danger to property rather than to people.

The first London Safety Plan was approved by the London Fire and Emergency Planning Authority in January 2004. The second Plan builds upon the consultation responses and a summary of the phased approach to delivering improvements described fully in the London Safety Plan includes the following:

The government wants all fire authorities to produce integrated risk management plans and using an improved understanding of risk and its role, the Brigade will provide a better standard of service to more people. As a result of London's Plan, more Londoners will get a second fire engine to their home or workplace faster than before as 10 fire engines will be moved to other stations in London where they can make the most difference to attendance times.

““ *The changes in the Safety Plan constitute probably the most significant transformation of London's fire and rescue services...* ””

The Plan also takes steps to free more firefighter time to work with local communities and households to make them safer.

London firefighters will continue to have the training and equipment they need to respond to acts of terrorism or other major disaster. Over the last two years there has been a very significant investment in new equipment and staff and the range of rescue services the Brigade can deliver has been expanded.

Fire Risk Assessment: The Modern Approach to Fire Safety

Since 1989 a European Directive has required the United Kingdom and other member states to incorporate fire safety legislation that was risk based and transfer ownership of this responsibility to the employer, there has been a change in the way the subject of fire safety is approached.

This Directive, which was eventually transferred into the Fire Precautions (Workplace) Regulations 1977 (Amended 1999), has led to the transfer of responsibility for determining adequate fire safety provision in the workplace from fire authorities to employers.

Following a number of multiple fatality fires especially in hotel and hostel accommodation in the late 1960s, the Fire Precautions Act 1971 was introduced as the principal legislation relating to fire safety. Since then, it has proved extremely successful in reducing fire casualties in the particular premises it has controlled. The government has just introduced a new Fire Safety (Regulatory Reform) Order replacing the existing Fire Precautions Act 1971 and the more recent Fire Precautions (Workplace) Regulations 1997 (amended 1999).

The new Fire Safety Order should go a long way towards creating one fire safety regime. Existing guidance including the various codes of practice will be replaced by a series of 11 guidance documents relating to different types of risk. The new Order will also continue the movement towards risk based fire safety and one of its most significant effects will be that all future fire safety should follow a fire risk assessment approach. This will mean the abolition of fire certificates issued by the fire authority.

Employers will remain responsible for fire safety in the workplace except where there is no employer. On these occasions, a 'defined responsible person' will be held accountable for the safety of all occupants, including members of the public and visitors, rather than just employees as is currently the case.

> 66 *Fire authorities also now have more flexibility to plan how best to respond to risks.* 99

One of the major causes of accidental fire is smoking and the carelessly discarded use of smoking materials. This fire has originated on a coffee table upon which two ash trays are full of cigarette ends and has spread up the wall to cause serious smoke damage to the remainder of the property.

> 66 *The first London Safety Plan was approved by the LFEPA in January 2004...* 99

Chip pan fires are the second most common cause of accidental fire in the home and according to the latest annual national fire statistics for 2003 were responsible for 33 deaths and 3,200 injuries in the United Kingdom. This is a typical devastating aftermath of a chip pan fire when the occupier has attempted to pour water onto the burning contents. The subsequent violent reaction has ignited the surrounding area of the cooker and spread fire to the rest of the kitchen. The person using the chip pan was badly burned.

> **❝** *...in 2005/06 it is planned that firefighters will make 25,000 visits to people's homes.* **❞**

Arson Task Force

In April 2004 the LFEPA received a grant of £530,000 spread over two years from the Office of the Deputy Prime Minister through the Arson Control Forum, to establish an Arson Task Force. The aim of the Team is to reduce the number of non-accidental fires in the top 60 wards in London with the aim of supporting one of the Brigade's 2004/2005 Best Value Performance Indicators: 'To reduce by 10% the number of deliberate fires by March 2010'. The Arson Task Force Team consists of one manager and six practitioners. Put simply, the work of the Team is to 'get the fuel off of the streets' in order to prevent opportunist arson as well as to liaise, communicate and educate the community, local authority and other public services about the problems associated with arson. The Team has so far spent nine months actively working in six out of the 18 Boroughs which house the top 60 wards in which arson is a particular problem. So far the results have been very positive and in comparison to the year-on figures, the top 10 wards on average have seen a reduction in fires by 50%.

In recent times, the Brigade has increased the number of firefighters in London. Improvements to the way the Brigade works and a reduction in the number of days lost to sickness mean that the number of firefighters at some stations can be reduced without affecting the number of available fire engines. The speedy response to '999' calls, including terrorist incidents, is as it has always been but there will now be greater efficiency.

The Brigade will work with the London Ambulance Service to get speedy help to victims of cardiac arrest in a pilot scheme in Tower Hamlets. This will mean that when Londoners in Tower Hamlets ring '999', both a fire engine and an ambulance may be sent if a person is having a cardiac arrest.

The Brigade will continue to rescue people from road traffic accidents thus fulfilling the Brigade's new statutory duty.

The Brigade will maximise its various activities to reduce the number of '999' calls received such as false alarms caused by automatic fire alarm systems, hoax '999' calls and calls to lift breakdowns.

The Brigade's home fire safety programme will continue and in 2005/06 it is planned that firefighters will make 25,000 visits to people's homes.

The London Fire Brigade Fire Investigation Search Dog Unit

The Brigades Search Dog Unit came into being in August 2000 following several years of research and field trials. It is an integrated part of the Brigade's Fire Investigation Group and as such provides Fire Investigators with the most accurate and sensitive bio scanner known to man. The use of the dog's olfactory senses in detecting traces and residues of ignitable liquids used by the arsonist not only provides a confirmation to the Fire Investigator of a probable intent of arson, but also assists the Police Service with a strong evidential trail to advance the subsequent criminal investigation. The dog is able to discriminate between the introduced ignitable liquids in the fire scene and the naturally occurring ignitable hydrocarbon products which are present as a by-product of man-made fibres affected by fire. The London Fire Brigade Fire Investigation Search Dog Unit was fortunate to have been supported by generous sponsorship of £30,000 from Zurich Financial Services UK for the provision of the Unit's first dog, Odin, the Unit's training programme, and ongoing dog expenses. ADT Tyco also provided valuable sponsorship of £30,000 for the provision of a suitable search dog team carrying vehicle, whilst food sponsorship totalling £500 per annum for the Team's second dog (Simba) is kindly provided by Nestle Purina ProPlan for the life of the dog. Simba was a 'gift' dog and as such attracted no financial burden to the Brigade, and her training was undertaken by the Brigade's first handler in house on a 'nil cost basis' to the Brigade. This use of these valuable sponsorships has allowed Brigade funding to be used in other important Community Fire Safety project areas to make London a safer place to live and work for both residents and visitors.

The Team's motto is '*To Detect and Deter*' and as such the team is an important tool to the both the fire and criminal investigator and a powerful public relations tool in the Brigade's work within the community to reduce and combat arson in London.

In August 2000 the Brigade commissioned its first dog search unit to work in conjunction with existing fire investigation teams. Based at New Cross, the team's first canine member was black Labrador Odin, whose primary role as sniffer dog was to trace accelerants used in suspected arson fires. Led by Station Officer Pat Lyon, the dog team was successful from its inception and was established with some commercial support from Zurich Financial Services and subsequently ADT Tyco. In more recent times a second dog, named Simba, has joined the team and this view shows Station Officer Lyon with Odin on the right and Simba on the left.

Home Fire Safety Checks

Most fire deaths in London occur in the home and a key aim of the London Safety Plan is to reduce the number of accidental fire related deaths in the home by 20% over the next five years. One of the Authority's main community fire safety campaigns for some considerable time has been to install and maintain domestic smoke alarms. As recent statistics show, this simple and relatively low cost investment has been proven to be a major factor in reducing death and injury from fire in the home. Since November 2003, the Brigade has had a programme of carrying out home fire safety checks (HFSCs) and there is a target for London firefighters to carry out 25,000 HFSCs in 2005/6. Just over 11,000 such safety visits were completed in 2004/5. The Authority's programme has been boosted by two Government grants aimed at expanding activity in this area. The latest grant totalled £5 million spread over four years and is aimed at geographically defined risk groups. It will involve working in close partnership with other agencies, including local authorities and the voluntary sector, toward the common goal of improving public safety. All this work is intended to complement the excellent work being undertaken by the London Boroughs to install smoke alarms in their own housing stock. A good example of this is the London Borough of Southwark where over 44,000 smoke alarms have now been fitted in Southwark's residential properties at no cost to tenants, as part of a two-year 'Fire Angel' project.

This London firefighter is demonstrating the workings of a domestic smoke alarm and no doubt extolling its value to two ladies of an over 60's group during a fire safety exhibition staged by the Brigade.

> *In the London Borough of Southwark, over 44,000 smoke alarms have now been fitted...*

Partnerships with other agencies will be developed so that they can also offer fire safety advice to those most at risk. In addition, the problems of antisocial behaviour and arson will also be a priority.

Schools will remain the focus of the Brigade's fire prevention work so that children learn at an early age what they can do to make themselves and their families safer from the risk of fire.

This London Fire Brigade officer and two crew members answer questions from the audience following a fire safety presentation to a group of school children.

In July 2004 the London Fire Brigade entered a unique partnership to reduce the number of injuries and death caused by fire to children in London. In the presence of HRH Prince Michael of Kent, Patron of the Children's Fire and Burn Trust (CFTB), the LFB signed a joint project with the Chelsea and Westminster Healthcare NHS Trust and the CFTB to share information and draw upon their extensive experience and research. This photograph shows (back row, left to right) Ken Knight, Commissioner for Fire and Emergency Planning; Heather Lawrence, Chief Executive of Chelsea and Westminster Healthcare NHS Trust; HRH Prince Michael of Kent; Carolyn Cripps, founder and Director of the CFTB; and Colin Tandy, Vice-Chair of the London Fire and Emergency Planning Authority, together with a representative group of children who have helped to promote the aims of the CFTB.

The Brigade will expand its work with young persons outside school settings. The aim of this work is to help them understand what happens if cars or property are set on fire. This provides an outlet for their curiosity in a safer environment, and helps them to develop a sense of responsibility.

The Brigade will continue to work with its partners including the police and other agencies to reduce the number of deliberate fires that occur in London.

The existing risk-based inspection programme for 300,000 places of work and entertainment will be developed and extended as a further 300,000 premises are added as a result of the proposed Fire Safety (Regulatory Reform) Order. These inspections will focus on identifying the highest risk premises and maker them safer.

The London Fire and Emergency Planning Authority has also set new main targets that will run to March 2010. These aim to achieve the following reductions:

Accidental fires in people's homes by 5%

Accidental fire-related deaths in the home by 20%

Deliberate fires by 10%

Hoax calls (malicious false alarms) by 5%

A final aim up to 2010 is to improve the time that it takes a second fire engine to attend incidents across the London area. The effect of this will be that over 1,000 more of these incidents will now get a second fire engine within eight minutes.

With the focus of the Brigade increasingly upon working more closely through the Boroughs, a major new project has been to convert a number of key fire stations into flagship stations for the local community. Here members of the public and businesses are encouraged to see their local fire station as somewhere they can visit if they have questions about fire safety. One of the first of the flagship stations was Edmonton with others following in Brent, Lewisham, Newham, Croydon, Hammersmith and Fulham, and Hilllingdon.

For some years the Brigade has supported the work of Prince's Trust, and in May 2005 nine young people from Hounslow successfully completed the Brigade's 12th personal development programme. Similar 12 week programmes have been staged in Tower Hamlets and Islington. Here, the successful Hounslow youngsters show their completion certificates after presentation by Assistant Commissioner Malcolm Kelly (back row, centre).

The London Safety Plan includes a programme of community fire safety visits by firefighters to promote a greater awareness of the dangers of fire to a wide age range. Here, during a fire station visit, a firefighter is showing a domestic smoke alarm to a group of children.

Early feedback from some of the many new initiatives in the London Safety Plan would suggest that there has already been a dramatic reduction in fire deaths across London. During the period from April 2004 to the end of February 2005, fire fatalities more than halved compared to figures from the same months in 2003/04. A total of 36 people died in fires during these months in 2004/05 and 28 of the 34 fatal fires were in domestic properties. This compares to 77 fatalities for the same period in 2003/04 when 60 of the fatal fires were in people's homes.

There is more detailed information on the various aspects of the London Safety Plan readily available in the various publications of the LFEPA or on the London Fire Brigade's website: www.london-fire.gov.uk

Breakdown of fire incidents by borough 2004/05

Deaths from Fire 2004/05

Fire Deaths 2004/05

- 2
- 1

Fire station grounds

Borough boundary

Fire station

Fire related incidents 2004/05

Borough	Accidental firess in the home	Deliberate fires	Hoax calls	Borough	Accidental firess in the home	Deliberate fires	Hoax calls
Barking	118	1531	342	Hounslow	145	872	151
Barnet	237	648	245	Islington	183	766	265
Bexley	102	999	119	Kensington	162	235	135
Brent	247	628	312	Kingston	100	338	65
Bromley	139	1200	182	Lambeth	376	695	348
Camden	314	553	266	Lewisham	242	784	324
City	9	42	18	Merton	126	412	65
Croydon	222	897	140	Newham	233	1250	447
Ealing	251	806	234	Redbridge	144	741	135
Enfield	191	989	327	Richmond	92	272	35
Greenwich	197	1441	307	Southwark	312	1291	385
Hackney	258	918	368	Sutton	118	494	65
Hammersmith	195	273	131	Tower Hamlets	163	2154	513
Haringey	208	722	390	Waltham Forest	170	693	263
Harrow	114	349	222	Wandsworth	239	556	196
Havering	98	1035	114	Westminster	279	397	300
Hillingdon	145	835	168				

Fire deaths by cause with breakdown of accidental fatal fires (April 1996 - March 2004)

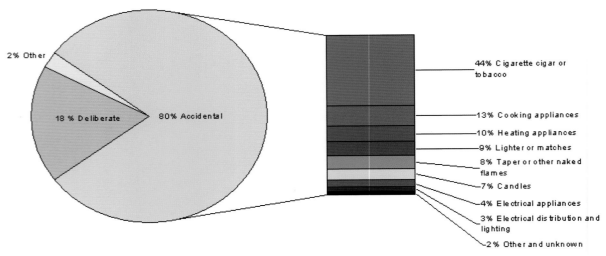

Data source: LFEPA Real Fire Library

Accidental fire deaths by age (April 1996 - March 2004)

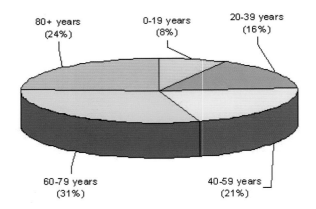

CHAPTER TWENTY

London Resilience, Emergency Planning and New Dimensions

The disastrous attack by terrorists on the World Trade Centre in New York and in Washington on 11 September 2001 was also a tragic turning point for fire and rescue services and all those involved in emergency planning. From that terrible moment onwards, governments across the world regarded their large cities as potential terrorist targets.

As the capital city of the United Kingdom, London is the centre of government and has a resident population of over 7 million with over three million persons commuting into London to work. London is the largest city in Europe and is equal with Paris as the world's most popular tourist destination, attracting over 13 million overseas arrivals and 17 million domestic visitors every year.

However, it would be wrong to assume that London is the only target and one effect of modern terrorist attacks, particularly since 9/11, has been a complete review of the role of the British Fire and Rescue Service role in preparedness and response. The arrangements, procedures and equipment now in place in London are similar in every region and for each British fire brigade.

New Dimensions Emergency Vehicles

The New Dimension equipment programme provided through the New Dimensions programme of the Office of the Deputy Prime Minister includes two principal types of emergency vehicles, the Incident Response Unit (IRU) and the High Volume Pump (HVP). Both types of vehicle are based upon a Man 6×4 rigid chassis. The IRU carries mass decontamination equipment likely to be needed at the scene of a conventional, chemical, biological, radiological or nuclear incident, either caused by terrorist action or by an accident. Each IRU is able to provide decontamination for a combined total of 400 persons per hour. High Volume Pumping (HVP) is a term used when there is a need to move very large quantities of water over long distances. HVP equipment is likely to be needed when there is serious flooding or the need to provide considerable quantities of water for firefighting. The HVPs carry two modules; one is a submersible pump and hose box with 6 inch (150 mm) diameter hose, whilst the second contains two hose boxes. HVPs are able to extract and pump up to 1,542 gallons (7,000 litres) per minute, about three times the capacity of ordinary pumping fire engines.

One of the ten new Incident Response Units operated by the London Fire Brigade. These fire engines carry a full range of equipment sufficient to decontaminate up to 400 persons per hour in the event of a Hazmat incident.

The arrangements to protect London from major international terrorism are termed the London Resilience Programme, in which preparedness for terrorist attack over the past three years has seen some very significant steps. In recognition of the specific risk of attack against London, the government initiated a London Resilience Team (LRT) to assess and co-ordinate improvements in the resilience of the capital to withstand terrorist attack. This team was required to: '*undertake "an immediate and urgent review" of the preparedness of London's key services to cope with an incident on the scale of the events of 11 September.*'

From the very earliest stages of the exercise, it became clear that no single government department or agency had the capability to plan for and deal with the hazards and risks posed by the threat of international terrorism, or the effects of a major natural disaster all on its own. The London Resilience Forum now provides the London Fire Brigade with an effective framework and allows it to be prepared in two ways.

Firstly, the Brigade has the flexibility to adjust its response as new hazards arise, and secondly, can manage more effectively the traditional hazards with which firefighters are familiar. At a local level, the

> ❝ *...the Brigade has the flexibility to adjust its response as new hazards arise...* ❞

overwhelming likelihood is that the challenges which local emergency responders will be called upon to face are the everyday hazards of modern life, not terrorism. However, it is terrorism that poses a major risk to London, the United Kingdom and, indeed, anywhere in the world.

An enhancement of the Brigade's general resilience capabilities, such as in search and rescue, decontamination or handling large scale incidents is also needed to deal with the potential threat from international terrorism. This has been provided via New Dimensions and the London Resilience programme. In the United Kingdom, the threat of terrorism coupled with other national emergencies, such as the widespread foot and mouth disease in cattle and the extensive floods of 2000–2001, has been the stimulus to redress the deficiencies in national and local contingency planning.

In July 2000 a major exercise publicly tested London's counter terrorism response plans. Shortly afterwards, the events of 11 September 2001 provided the governmental impetus for investment in change and in the Fire and Rescue Service, this is most clearly seen in the 'New Dimensions' work that has been undertaken so far and continues to be developed.

As a multi-agency team, the London Resilience Team was able to call on a wide range of experience to produce a comprehensive report that was delivered in February 2002. This recognised that London, as the capital city and the seat of national government, was considered to be a principal target for terrorist attack. There was also recognition of a special focus on the resilience of London and for the Government Minister responsible for London and the Mayor of London to have a direct overview of London's preparedness and recovery, giving a clear and direct political focus.

Significant steps have been taken towards achieving this, notably the establishment of the London Resilience Forum (LRF), chaired by a Government Minister with the Mayor of London as Deputy Chair. In turn the London Resilience Team provides regular and detailed briefings to Ministers and the Mayor on specific elements of London's preparations for the response to a catastrophic incident.

In 2003, the Brigade took part in an exercise to test the emergency services response to a simulated terrorist chemical attack on a train at the Bank station on the London Underground. Here, two firefighters rigged in chemical suits are briefed before their descent into the underground station. Note the officer on the right has the breathing apparatus control board in which are personal tallies of a crew who have already entered the incident.

Whilst a number of firefighters rigged in chemical suits were carrying out rescues down in the Bank underground station, other crews at street level were assembling decontamination shelters and equipment, carried on the Incident Response Units.

One of the strongest messages from the London Resilience Team review, was the need for an overarching region wide strategic emergency planning role to support the planning of the 33 local councils in London and other key agencies by co-ordinating their roles, responsibilities and capacities. The London Resilience Forum also has representatives, at a principal level, of London's emergency services and other key organisations.

The London Resilience Forum provides practical supervision and strategic guidance to emergency planning. Of particular significance is the formal inclusion of the health services, utility companies (gas, electricity, and water), transport operators, security services and business community in regional planning. London already had some advantage in planning for both the new terrorism threat and regional resilience. Uniquely in England, London is a region in its own right with a single focus; a principal police authority, the Metropolitan Police; one fire brigade (the London Fire Brigade); a single ambulance service (the London Ambulance Service) and an integrated local council structure for the whole of the London Region.

London also has a valuable 30 year history of planning for major incidents and their execution through the London Emergency Services Liaison Panel, established following activity during the 1970s and 1980s arising from Northern Ireland terrorism. With the strategic governance

Down at underground railway line level, two firefighters in chemical suits remove a casualty from the affected train on a stretcher, watched by three LFB observers. The casualty will immediately be taken up to street level, undergo triage and decontamination.

❝ ...*London's preparedness has undoubtedly been enhanced by a number of improvements.* **❞**

measures now in place, London's preparedness has undoubtedly been enhanced by a number of improvements.

These improvements include a new strategic emergency planning regime; regional command and control arrangements for a catastrophic incident; a programme of multi-agency exercises; individual organisation/ sector improvements; business continuity planning awareness campaign; frameworks for transport and evacuation of key areas; and a review, analysis and major ongoing reinforcement of chemical, biological, radiological and nuclear capability and recovery.

The London Fire and Emergency Planning Authority has provided individual training to the chief executives of all of the 33 London boroughs. The role of London's Borough councils at the time of a terrorist attack is to manage the collective London Local Government response to a Catastrophic Incident; advise the emergency services and other agencies on local authority issues and capabilities; liaise after the incident about the return to normality; and compile and disseminate information for local authorities across London.

However, the growing threat of the new style of terrorism, illustrated very dramatically in the USA on 11 September, identified a significant number of resilience challenges which must also be prepared for. These included matters such as an attack of multiple sites, loss of public communications, electricity and water infrastructure. During 9/11 disruption to transport systems affected service provision across a much larger area of Manhattan than that directly affected by the immediate collapse of the World Trade Centre. All of these had serious implications for the strategic command and service provision of the emergency services. The challenges faced by New York, with whom London and other cities share similar risks, were therefore used in the development of strategic plans to manage the consequences and effects of a catastrophic incident occurring in London. The London Resilience Forum has also adopted a revised command and control protocol as a result of lessons learnt from a number of strategic exercises in London.

The Brigade is frequently called to assist in the aftermath of flooding incidents in the London area, usually following a prolonged period of rain. Here, an elderly lady is carried to safety during flash flooding in Islington. At the same time, emergency planning staff will also be working to minimize the effect of the flooding to the community.

As part of the strategic protocols produced by the London Resilience Forum a 'catastrophic incident' has been defined and agreed by all the emergency and support services. A 'catastrophic' incident is where following the advice of the emergency services, the Minister for Civil Resilience, or in his absence the Home Secretary, is of the opinion that it is of such magnitude that it will require a specific or exceptional response from members of the London Resilience Forum.

Key characteristics of the response are the involvement from the outset of a large number of agencies and not just the emergency services, and the involvement of central government in the incident management stage. A catastrophic incident will be managed from a newly established Strategic Co-ordination Centre where other strategic decision makers from the responding agencies will be co-located and together form the Strategic Co-ordinating Group. The primary role of this Group is to provide strategic support and co-ordinate the activities of the various agencies and not as a substitute for the existing emergency control facilities.

It is important that the Strategic Co-ordinating Group is capable of effective decision making, probably for long periods over many days, whilst still ensuring that input is received from all appropriate agencies. 'Strategic cells' will therefore be formed with representatives of agencies

*❝ This enables agencies to share
information, discuss and
co-ordinate... ❞*

from the same sector (such as health, water, social services, and the business sector) in order to include as many agencies as required, whilst retaining a manageable sized Co-ordinating Group. This enables agencies to share information, discuss and co-ordinate their strategic response but importantly each one to have a single representative at the Strategic Co-ordinating Group itself.

After the rescue phase of the incident the emergency services will no longer be the focus of the response, and management of the incident will pass from the strategic Co-ordinating Group to a multi-agency 'Recovery Management' Group. The Recovery Management Group will act from the very beginning of an incident in planning and advising on the co-ordinated recovery phase following a catastrophic incident.

For the London Fire Brigade, recognition of the fire and rescue service role in responding to the terrorist threat in the capital has resulted in considerable new funding being allocated to support the required investment. The Brigade has received new funding for the provision of new vehicles and equipment from central government, provided to all British Fire and Rescue Services on a Regional basis.

The new equipment includes public mass decontamination units, new supplies of gas tight suits, chemical agent detection and identification equipment, radiation detection equipment, extended duration breathing apparatus equipment and urban search and rescue vehicles. This will result in some 60 new specialist vehicles including 10 Incident Response Units and six High Volume Pumps arriving in the London Fire Brigade fleet alone over this period. In addition, the Brigade have been required to provide new mobile command facilities, increased numbers of fire rescue units with extended duration breathing sets, mobile hazardous materials laboratories, personnel and equipment carriers, specialist transport and equipment for the London Underground. A range of other equipment and training to support the response to the new terrorist threat, new training requirements for firefighters, and multi-agency initial assessment teams are also essential.

Proper decontamination of operational crews is a vital part of dealing with hazardous chemicals that have become either involved in fire or accidental spillage. This photograph records part of the decontamination procedure of firefighters who have been removing leaking drums of chemicals to safe storage. Each of the firefighters is wearing breathing apparatus inside the chemical suits and has to pass through the high pressure water sprays of the special cleansing unit in the background.

The new multi-agency initial assessment team is called MAIAT and the partnership working can be amply demonstrated by the introduction in July 2004 of a unique multi-agency operational response team. As part of the continuing work to improve the capability to deal with major incidents, the government has funded a one year trial of the MAIAT team across the London region. This team provides a permanently staffed operational capability using two jointly crewed vehicles comprising a total of eight officers from the London Fire Brigade, the Metropolitan Police Service, City of London Police and the London Ambulance Service. All personnel in the team wear non-service specific clothing and incident ground personnel protective equipment. Dependant upon the nature of the incident, MAIAT also has a London-wide response.

" *...new specialist vehicles include*
10 Incident Response Units and six
High Volume Pumps... **"**

MAIAT's core purpose is to bring together the expertise of all of the emergency services and support the incident commander at the very earliest opportunity, by providing an independent integrated operational assessment of an incident where the scale, complexity or apparent hazard indicates a multi-agency assessment would enhance the emergency service's response. MAIAT will also provide an initial assessment of potential chemical, biological, radiological or other major incidents. The team will deploy into the 'Hot Zone' or inner cordon with a range of detection, identification and monitoring equipment for the purpose of making an initial assessment of the hazards involved, which will then be communicated to the incident commander. The MAIAT team has already been deployed to over 500 incidents since it was set up.

In addition to all the foregoing work, the Authority's emergency planning officers perform an important role in protecting Londoners from the consequences of major, or even catastrophic, incidents. Working in partnerships with others, the emergency services, the government, the Greater London Authority and the Boroughs, the aim is to improve London's resilience and ability to respond to and deal with these incidents. The range of legal responsibilities of the Authority relating to emergency planning includes the following areas:

Assisting local authorities to meet their responsibilities to prepare emergency plans, to train their staff in preparing those plans, and to exercise the plans to make sure they work.

Working with businesses and the other emergency services to prepare emergency plans as required under the Control of Major Accident Hazard Regulations.

Preparing and exercising plans in partnership with others in line with the Radiation (Emergency Preparedness and Public Information) Regulations 2001. Under these regulations, emergency planners ensure, in case of a radiological emergency in London, that information is available about the emergency and what measures Londoners should take to minimise the risk to themselves.

Working with relevant businesses and other agencies to secure the safe operation of 219 miles (350 kilometres) of pipelines running through, or under, London, in line with the Pipelines Safety Regulations 1996.

Emergency planning officers provide support for an arrangement known as 'Local Authority Gold' through a 24 hours a day, seven days a week 'Gold office'. In a crisis, one Chief Executive would represent all 33 local London authorities.

London's emergency planners also sponsor, organise and facilitate multi-agency events which bring together key players from across the public, private and voluntary sectors to increase awareness about emergency planning issues, to make sure all of those agencies understand their responsibilities to prevent major disasters.

Emergency planning officers work closely with the other emergency services, the London boroughs and other agencies. Currently there is an officer seconded to the London Resilience Team — a strategic partnership working to make sure London is prepared for major incidents or catastrophes. It embraces all the key organisations and bodies in the capital in both the public and private sectors.

Prolonged heavy rain in the Hounslow area in 1999 caused flash floods and a number of calls for assistance to the Brigade. Here, a crew are ferrying mothers and children away from the worst affected area.
(*Hounslow Chronicle*)

*❝ The MAIAT team has already been
deployed to over 500 incidents. . . ❞*

The Authority also has representatives on various groups:

The London Emergency Services Liaison Panel. Chaired by the Metropolitan Police, this group is made up of all London's emergency services and local authorities to help plan for, and respond to, a major incident in the capital.

The London Voluntary Aid Societies Emergency Committee. This group consists of representatives of the Salvation Army, British Red Cross, St. John's Ambulance Brigade and the Women's Royal Voluntary Service.

Mutual Aid Groups drawn from the 33 London boroughs. They are divided into five mutual aid groups, southwest, southeast, northeast, north and northwest and each group has a lead borough.

The London Local Authority Emergency Planning Group on which each of the London boroughs are represented.

London Resilience sub-committees and working groups.

The Regional approach through the London Resilience Forum, its partnership and the joint regional capability has allowed the London Fire Brigade to work together to develop innovative response options to face the emerging threat. This has been and continues to be a huge and exhausting programme with many dedicated staff working in areas unthinkable only three years ago. Current London regional plans agreed at a strategic level of the Forum are at the final stages of consideration and the implications for Local Authorities, mass fatalities and temporary mortuary arrangements, removal of mass building collapse debris and site clearance, advice to help organisations with planning and decontamination of buildings and infrastructure following a chemical, biological, radiological and nuclear incident.

By the end of 2005, some 350 London firefighters will have had firefighters urban search and rescue training. Perhaps some idea of the commitment of the emergency services to the new challenges can be seen in that the nominations on the American course were offered on a purely voluntary basis, yet the response from the London Brigade alone was overwhelming.

" The LFB is now better prepared than it has ever been..."

The London Fire Brigade is now better prepared than it has ever been in relation to the new challenges it faces, although there is still further detailed work needed to provide new capabilities. The new expectations of the LFB in delivering this new role following a terrorist attack are vast. So too are the training and resources and the consequent impact on budgets. The new equipment will not only benefit the community during a terrorist attack, it will also be deployed to a range of other incidents such as road and rail accidents, building collapse and flooding, as well as the accidental release of hazardous chemicals — improving the overall service in general to the communities throughout London.

CHAPTER TWENTY-ONE
Remembrance
The Peacetime Roll of Honour

This chapter commemorates all those who have died on duty since 1840 in the peacetime service of the London Fire Engine Establishment, the Metropolitan Fire Brigade and the London Fire Brigade. These names are inscribed on the Memorial at Brigade Headquarters at Lambeth presented by Lloyds of London.

Rank and Name	Location	Date
Fireman Robert Loader	Ratcliffe Highway	26 December 1840
Junior Fireman Richard Wivell	Tower of London	30 October 1841
Junior Fireman Henry J Parkes	Blackfriars Road	14 November 1841
Junior Fireman William Webb	Blackfriars Road	14 November 1841
Junior Fireman James MacLean	Upper Grosvenor Street	28 January 1843
Senior Fireman Benjamin Cummings	Denmark Street	31 March 1847
Senior Fireman John Piercey	New Crane Wharf	28 July 1848
Junior Fireman James Y Hancock	New Crane Wharf	28 July 1848
Engineer Alfred Wilson	Haydon Square, Minories	15 July 1852
Senior Fireman John Crampton	Haydon Square, Minories	15 July 1852
Senior Fireman John Eilbeck	John Street	27 September 1859
Superintendant James Braidwood	Cotton's Wharf, Tooley Street	22 June 1861
2nd Class Fireman Joseph A. Ford	Grays Inn Road	7 October 1871
3rd Class Fireman Stanley M. Guerny	Upper Thames Street	10 November 1872
4th Class Fireman George Lee	St. John Street, West Smithfield	26 July 1876
4th Class Fireman Patrick Fitzgerald	Charlton Street, Somers Town	21 April 1880
1st Class Fireman Thomas G. Ashford	Alhambra Theatre, Leicester Square	7 December 1882
4th Class Fireman Henry Berg	Alhambra Theatre, Leicester Square	7 December 1882
4th Class Fireman Richard J. Long	Greenwich Road	Injured 24 July 1883 Died 25 July 1883

Rank and Name	Location	Date
4th Class Fireman Joseph G. Thatcher	Hamsell Street, City	14 December 1883
3rd Class Fireman John C. Barrett	Upper Marylebone Street	24 October 1888
3rd Class Fireman William G. Jacobs	Bell Lane, Wandsworth	12 September 1889
4th Class Fireman Sydney A. H. Crowe	Felix Street, Westminster Bridge Road	18 February 1890
4th Class Fireman William B. Smart	Hargrave Park, Upper Holloway	10 June 1892
4th Class Fireman William J. Abernethy	Hargrave Park, Upper Holloway	10 June 1892
4th Class Fireman Frederick J. Fielder	4 Agar Street, Strand	26 November 1892
Coachman Robert Schulz	Hurstbourne Road, Forest Hill	31 July 1895
4th Class Fireman Martin E. Sprague	New Church Court, Strand	29 October 1895
4th Class Fireman Charles Wilcox	Vanbrugh Fields, Blackheath	Injured 29 July 1896 Died 30 July 1896
3rd Class Fireman Samuel E. Handley	Southwark HQ	3 January 1900
3rd Class Fireman Fredrick Black	Brixton Road	15 April 1901
3rd Class Fireman Herbert White	Lots Road, Chelsea	Injured 19 October 1904
Fireman George Willan	Bridge Wharf, Bankside	26 February 1911
Fireman John H. Webster	Bridge Wharf, Bankside	26 February 1911
Superintendent Charles E. Pearson	Sidney Street, Mile End	Injured 3 January 1911 Died 9 July 1911
Fireman Robert F. Libby	Pembridge Villas, Bayswater	18 March 1913
Fireman William McLaren	Pembridge Villas, Bayswater	18 March 1913
Fireman William H. E. Martin	Knightsbridge Fire Station superintending hook ladder drill	Injured 17 September 1913 Died 18 September 1913
Fireman William H. Mott	Vanbrugh Park, Blackheath	21 June 1914
Sub Officer William W. Spensley	Bridewell Place, City	Injured 6 May 1915 Died 7 May 1915
Fireman John S. Green	Lambs Conduit Passage, Holborn	Injured 8 September 1915 Died 17 September 1915
Fireman. Alfred H. H. Vidler	Whitechapel Fire Station	Injured 13 June 1917 Died 15 June 1917
Fireman Henry B. Summers	Greycoat Place, Westminster	Injured 26 January 1918 Died 31 January 1918
Sub. Officer William E. Cornford	Albert Embankment	30 January 1918
Sub. Officer Walter W. Hall	Albert Embankment	30 January 1918
Fireman Edmund J. Fairbrother	Albert Embankment	30 January 1918
Fireman William E. Nash	Albert Embankment	30 January 1918

Rank and Name	Location	Date
Fireman John W. C. Johnson	Albert Embankment	30 January 1918
Fireman Arthur A. Page	Albert Embankment	30 January 1918
Fireman James E. Fay	Albert Embankment	30 January 1918
Fireman John Coleman	Lower Olivers Wharf, Wapping	1 November 1920
Fireman Alfred Best	Lower Olivers Wharf, Wapping explosions, stationed Shadwell	1 November 1920
Fireman Harry J. Green	Lower Olivers Wharf, Wapping	1 November 1920
Fireman John T. Scholes	Southwark HQ	Injured 27 May 1924 Died 12th July 1924
Fireman Alfred H. Parsons	Kingsbury Road	23 August 1924
Sub Officer Valentine G. Sinden	Finsbury Street, City	18 September 1925
Fireman Joseph G. Schubert	Stoke Newington Fire Station escape drill	11 April 1928
Fireman Arthur J. Stillman	Southwark HQ hook ladder drill	Injured 3 January 1933 Died 5 January 1933
Station Officer Cecil J. Dickinson	Southwark HQ drill display	Injured 13 June 1934 Died 14 June 1934
Fireman Arthur J. Putt	Edgware Road Fire Station hook ladder drill	13 June 1935
Station Officer Alfred J. H. Diehl	Orchard Place, Blackwall	7 July 1935
Fireman Edward W. Netley	Orchard Place, Blackwall	7 July 1935
Fireman Charles P. Sweetlove	Camomile Street, City	4 April 1938
Fireman Percy J. S. Baker	St. Paul's Churchyard	21 February 1940
Station Officer Charles Fisher	Covent Garden, WC2	20 December 1949
Fireman Edward James Harwood	Eldon Street, EC2	21 December 1951
Fireman Thomas Albert Joy	Eldon Street, EC2	Injured 21 December 1951 Died 23 December 1951
Fireman Leslie Williams Skitt	Eldon Street, EC2	21 December 1951
Station Officer Fredick E. Hawkins	Langley Street, WC2	11 May 1954
Fireman Arthur J. Batt Rawden	Langley Street, WC2	11 May 1954
Fireman Charles George Gadd	Langley Street, WC2	Injured 11 May 1954 Died 23 May 1954
Sub. Officer John Skinner	King Street, W6	29 July 1954
Leading Fireman Fredrick Charles Willoughby	Kensington High Street	22 February 1956
Fireman Robert Stiles	Downham Fire Station hook ladder drill	Injured 28 May 1956 Died 1st June 1956
Station Officer Jack Fourt-Wells	Smithfield, EC1	23 January 1958

Rank and Name	Location	Date
Fireman Richard Daniel Stocking	Smithfield, EC1	23 January 1958
Fireman Albert Hunt	Brixton Fire Station escape drill	17 March 1961
Station Officer Thomas Carter	Wyndham Road, SE5	12 February 1962
Fireman James Anthony Bardens	Wyndham Road, SE5	12 February 1962
Fireman Daniel Michael O'Donovan	Hilldrop Lane, N7	11 March 1964
Fireman Donald E. Owen	Wembley Fire Station — turntable ladder drill	3 August 1965
Fireman Ronald Charles Wiggins	Southwark Training School — extension ladder drill	Injured 23 August 1965 Died 2 September 1965
Sub. Officer Leslie Arthur Tucker	Ealing Fire Station — accident at station	Injured 4 December 1966 Died 12 December 1966
Fireman Colin Coomber	Kings Road, SW3	Injured 8 March 1968 Died 11 March 1968
Fireman Brian P. O'Connell Hutchins	Kings Road, SW3	Injured 8 March 1968 Died 11 March 1968
Sub. Officer Michael William Gamble	Manchester Road, E14	17 July 1969
Fireman John Victor Appleby	Manchester Road, E14	17 July 1969
Fireman Terence Breen	Manchester Road, E14	17 July 1969
Fireman Trevor Paul Carvosso	Manchester Road, E14	17 July 1969
Fireman Alfred Charles Smee	Manchester Road, E14	17 July 1969
Leading Fireman Michael William Lee	Goswell Road, EC1	29 September 1969
Fireman Hamish Pettit	Clifton Gardens, W9	13 December 1974
Fireman Stephen Michael Neill	St. Pancras Way, NW1	1 October 1978
Leading Fireman Stephen Thomas Maynard	Regents Canal Dock, E12	25 January 1980
Fireman Anthony Marshall	The Broadway, Wimbledon	30 April 1981
Fireman Barry Charles Trussell	Blackshaw Road, SW17	Injured 21 April 1981 Died 24 May 1981
Fireman Derek Thomas Potts	Compton Road, N1	26 June 1983
Station Officer Colin James Townsley	Euston Road, NW1	18 November 1987
Firefighter David John Stokoe	Gillender Street, E3	10 July 1991
Firefighter Terence James Hunt	Gillender Street, E3	10 July 1991
Sub. Officer Kevin John Power	Scrubs Lane, NW10	30 September 1992
Firefighter Michael David Hill	Villiers Road, NW2	10 May 1993
Firefighter Bill Faust	Bethnal Green Road, E2	20 July 2004
Firefighter James Meere	Bethnal Green Road, E2	20 July 2004

The peacetime Roll of Honour in the foyer of Brigade Headquarters at Lambeth donated by Lloyds upon which are inscribed all the names of those London firefighters who have died on duty since 1840.

LONDON FIRE SERVICE
ROLL OF HONOUR — SECOND WORLD WAR

Commemorating those who died on active service with the London Fire Service 1939–1941 and theNational Fire Service (London Region) 1941–1945

Rank	Name	Base Brigade
Fireman	Alfred G. Abahart	London
Fireman	Percy A. Aitchison	Beckenham
Fireman	Thomas C. Aldsworth	London
Fireman	Edwin W. Ambridge	London
Fireman	Cecil R. Andreazzi	London
Fireman	David Appleby	London
Fireman	Albert E. Arber	London
Leading Watchroom Attendant	Richard E. Archer	London
Sub Officer	Arthur Ash	West Ham
Fireman	Derek E. Aust	London
Fireman	John A. Axcell	London

Rank	Name	Base Brigade
Fireman	Maurice C. Ayers	London
Fireman	Edward W. Badland	West Ham
Fireman	Ronald M. Bailey	Beckenham
Firewoman	Lilian S. Baker	London
Fireman	Victor Baldesarre	London
Fireman	Douglas B. Baldwin	London
Fireman	Alan C. Barber	Beckenham
Fireman	John C. Barrell	London
Leading Fireman	Charles W. Barrow	London
Firewoman	Joan F. Bartlett	London
Fireman	Arthur E. Batchelor	London
Leading Fireman	Jack Bathie	London
Fireman	Richard Beacon	Beckenham
Fireman	Ernest R. Beadle	Beckenham
Company Officer	William Beard	London
Fireman	George A. Bell	London
Fireman	William F. Belton	London
Fireman	William T. Benney	London
Fireman	Joseph C. Bines	London
Fireman	Herbert T. Blundell	London
Fireman	Henry J. Bouch	London
Leading Fireman	George Bowen	London
Fireman	Kenneth J. Bowles	Beckenham
Fireman	John W. F. Brazier	London
Fireman	Christopher J. Briggs	London
Fireman	Henry C. Brightwell	London
Fireman	Albert S. Brooker	Wembley
Fireman	Thomas W. Brown	London
Fireman	William H. Brown	London
Fireman	William G. Brum	London
Fireman	John H. Burch	London
Station Officer	Charles H. Burden	London
Fireman	Henry H. Butcher	London
Fireman	Richard H. Butler	London
Fireman	Patrick J. Campbell	London
Fireman	Henry J. C. Carden	Beckenham
Fireman	Eric B. Cartwright	London
Leading Fireman	David J. Chalmers	Beckenham
Fireman	Oliver C. Cheater	London
Fireman	Walter H. Childs	London
Fireman	Benjamin E. Chinnery	London
Fireman	Cecil R. S. Chopping	London
Fireman	Albert E. Clarke	London
Fireman	David Clatworthy	London

Rank	Name	Base Brigade
Fireman	Harold G. Coleridge	London
Fireman	Alexander W. Collins	London
Fireman	Stanley T. Conniff	Wembley
Fireman	Herman H. Conrad	London
Fireman	George J. Cook	London
Fireman	Percy Crane	London
Fireman	Frederick W. Crowe	London
Fireman	John Culley	London
Fireman	Alfred Cumberland	West Ham
Senior Fireman	Thomas W. Curson	London
Fireman	James Daly	London
Fireman	Henry J. Davidson	London
Firewoman	Marjory W. Davies	London
Fireman	Robert J. Deans	Beckenham
Fireman	Frederick W. Dell	West Ham
Fireman	Israel Deutch	London
Fireman	Hugh Dicken	West Ham
Fireman	John Dilworth	London
Fireman	James W. N. Dinwoodie	London
Fireman	Henry A. C. Dixon	London
Fireman	Bernard J. Donner	London
Fireman	William Downes	London
Fireman	Charles L. M. Drew	Beckenham
Fireman	Reginald H. Driver	London
Fireman	Stanley G. DuVergier	London
Firewoman	Hilda Dupree	London
Fireman	James A. C. Durling	London
Fireman	Edward B. East	London
Fireman	Cecil A. Ellman	Mitcham
Fireman	Herbert T. W. Ellis	London
Fireman	Edmund F. Emmett	London
Fireman	Frank J. Endean	Beckenham
Fireman	Albert B. Evans	London
Fireman	Albert C. Eyre	West Ham
Fireman	Cecil Farley	Beckenham
Fireman	Arthur Farnin	London
Fireman	Hyman Feldman	London
Messenger	Percival H. Field	London
Fireman	Denis G. Fitzgerald	Beckenham
Fireman	Henry G. Flegg	London
Fireman	James Fletcher	London
Deputy Commandant	Arthur T. Ford	Barnet
Fireman	Robert Forrester	London
Station Officer	Thomas Forrow	London

Rank	Name	Base Brigade
Fireman	Edward J. Fox	London
Fireman	Alfred J. Francis	London
Fireman	Leonard J. Freeman	London
Fireman	William Fuller	London
Fireman	Frederick G. Gage	West Ham
Fireman	David W. Garrick	London
Senior Fireman	Albert Gentry	London
Fireman	Robert W. George	London
Fireman	Harold C. Gillard	London
Fireman	Bernard J. Godfrey	London
Leading Fireman	Herbert B. H. Golden	London
Fireman	George E. Goldsmith	London
Leading Fireman	Lionel A. Gothard	London
Fireman	James S. Gower	London
Leading Fireman	Arthur H. Grant, GM	London
Fireman	Samuel J. Gray	London
Fireman	Barnet Greenburg	London
Fireman	Joseph Greenburg	London
Fireman	Frank L. Greenway	London
Fireman	William G. Grieve	London
Fireman	Albert W. Griffin	London
Fireman	George J. J. Hall	Beckenham
Senior Fireman	George W. Hall	London
Sub Officer	Henry W. Halliday	London
Fireman	John S. Hammersley	West Ham
Fireman	Bertie J. F. Harris	London
Section Officer	James C. Harris	London
Fireman	Walter C. Hart	London
Fireman	Christopher E. Hartwell	Banstead
Fireman	Alfred R. Hayden	London
Fireman	Frederick W. Hayward	London
Fireman	Leslie T. Healey	Beckenham
Fireman	James H. Heath	London
Fireman	Ernest A. Hemming	London
Sub Officer	Ernest J. Henley	London
Fireman	Herbert E. Henley	London
Fireman	William H. Herbert	London
Fireman	George A. Hickey	London
Fireman	George W. Hill	London
Fireman	John J. Hill	London
Station Officer	John W. Hill	London
Fireman	Sydney A. Holder	London
Sub Officer	Edward A. Hollett	London
Fireman	George H. Holloway	Mitcham

Rank	Name	Base Brigade
Fireman	Edward W. Hoskins	London
Fireman	Walter G. Hubbard	London
Fireman	Stanley R. Hudders	Beckenham
Fireman	Harold Huggett	West Ham
Fireman	Albert Hughes	London
Fireman	A. S. Humphreys	Erith
Fireman	Frank W. Hurd	London
Fireman	Ernest Hutton	London
Firewoman	Frances E. Huxley	London
Fireman	Ernest W. Hyde	London
Fireman	Leslie J. H. Hyde	London
Fireman	Leslie W. Issacs	London
Fireman	Sydney H. Jarvis	London
Fireman	Harold G. Jerome	Bromley
Leading Fireman	James A. Johnson	London
Fireman	Arthur H. Jones	London
Fireman	Evan M. Jones	London
Fireman	Sydney B. Jones	London
Fireman	Sydney G. Jones	London
Fireman	Charles S. Kelly	London
Fireman	Robert L. Kerr-Lindsay	London
Fireman	Frederick G. Kiefer	London
Fireman	Charles T. King	London
Leading Fireman	David A. King	London
Fireman	Reginald F. King	London
Fireman	J. D. Kirkland	London
Fireman	Albert V. Kite	Beckenham
Station Officer	Henry W. Knight	London
Fireman	John T. Knight	London
Fireman	Reginald F. W. Knight	London
Fireman	William F. Knight	Wembley
Fireman	Eric W. Lambert	Bromley
Fireman	Marcel Lavelli	London
Fireman	Charles L. Layton	Bromley
Fireman	Clifford M. Leake	London
Fireman	Thomas C. Leaver	London
Fireman	Victor H. Legg	London
Fireman	Ascher D. Lettner	London
Fireman	Abraham Lewis	London
Fireman	Eric D. Lewis	London
Fireman	John J. Lewis	London
Fireman	John W. Lewis	London
Fireman	William H. Long	West Ham
Fireman	Donald MacKenzie	London

Rank	Name	Base Brigade
Fireman	Vincent L. Mander	London
Fireman	Benjamin Mansbridge	London
Fireman	Harold Marriott	West Ham
Fireman	Harry R. Marshall	London
Fireman	Richard J. Martin	London
Messenger	Francis P. McDonough	London
Fireman	Daniel B. McEvoy	London
Fireman	Ewen S. McEwen	West Ham
Fireman	Henry J. Mead	London
Fireman	John F. Mead	London
Fireman	Leslie C. Medhurst	London
Fireman	Victor Michaelson	London
Fireman	Vernon J. Middleditch	London
Fireman	Arthur W. Miller	London
Firewoman	Josephine J. Miller	London
Fireman	Percy Millett	London
Leading Fireman	Frank K. Mills	London
Fireman	Alfred E. Minter	Beckenham
Fireman	Frederick Mitchell	London
Section Officer	G. L. Moor	Kingston upon Thames
Fireman	Charles E. Moore	London
Fireman	Frederick W. Moore	Beckenham
Fireman	William B. Moore	London
Section Officer	Sydney A. Morris	London
Fireman	William G. Morrow	London
Fireman	Norman R. C. Mountjoy	Beckenham
Fireman	John J. Munday	London
Fireman	C. W. Murphy	London
Fireman	Arthur E. Murray	West Ham
Fireman	Sydney J. Newbold	London
Fireman	Charles E. Nightingale	London
Fireman	George R. Norris	London
Fireman	Maurice P. O'Neill	London
Fireman	Horace V. Olney	London
Fireman	Albert E. Owen	London
Sub Officer	Harry Page	London
Fireman	Leslie J. Palmer	Beckenham
Fireman	Walter J. Palmer	West Ham
Fireman	Frederick G. Parcell	Beckenham
Leading Fireman	Martin C. Parfett	Beckenham
Fireman	William F. Parfey	London
Fireman	Harold C. Parkes	Mitcham
Fireman	Edward J. Pattenden	London
Fireman	Albert E. Pearton	London

Rank	Name	Base Brigade
Firewoman	Violet I. Pengally	London
Fireman	Edward E. G. Pepper	Mitcham
Firewoman	Winifred A. Peters	London
Fireman	John Phelan	London
Fireman	Henry Piller	London
Fireman	William C. Plant	Beckenham
Fireman	Cyril B. Porter	London
Fireman	Edward Preston	London
Fireman	James H. Purslow	London
Fireman	Frederick A. Rae	London
Fireman	William T. Randall	London
Fireman	Stanley H. Randolph	London
Fireman	William T. Rashbrook	London
Fireman	Henry C. Rathbone	London
Fireman	William Rawlings	Erith
Fireman	George Reardon	London
Firewoman	Joan M. Ridd	London
Fireman	Ernest F. Robinson	Mitcham
Fireman	Arthur H. Rogers	London
Leading Fireman	Leonard Roots	Beckenham
Fireman	William R. Roots	London
Fireman	Richard C. Roullier	London
Fireman	Edward Sackie	London
Section Officer	Frederick C. Salkeld	London
Senior Fireman	Laurence W. Sander	London
Fireman	Stanley Sargant	London
Fireman	Herbert C. J. Saunders	London
Fireman	Albert A. Saville	London
Fireman	Frederick Scates	London
Fireman	Ernest A. Schneider	London
Fireman	Arthur Seaby	London
Fireman	Reginald A. L. Seymour	London
Fireman	Benjamin J. Sheldon	London
Leading Fireman	Stanley Short	Beckenham
Fireman	Jack A. Shrimpton	London
Section Officer	James Simpson	London
Station Officer	Richard W. Sinstadt	London
Fireman	Harry R. Skinner	London
Fireman	Alexander Smith	London
Fireman	Edward H. Smith	London
Fireman	Frederick C. Smith	London
Fireman	Frederick J. Smith	London
Fireman	Thomas J. Snowdon	London
Fireman	Romeo C. Sorrenti	London

Rank	Name	Base Brigade
Fireman	Walter J. Spence	London
Leading Fireman	A. H. Spiller	Mitcham
Fireman	Harry J. Stangroom	London
Fireman	Oliver J. Steele	London
Fireman	George R. Steers	London
Fireman	Stanley R. Stevens	London
Fireman	Albert H. Strange	London
Fireman	Eric C. Stringer	London
Fireman	Charles Strutton	London
Fireman	Alfred C. Sturk	London
Sub Officer	Frederick C. Sutherland	London
Fireman	Robert Tanner	London
Leading Fireman	John J. Taylor	Bromley
Fireman	Mervin J. B. Taylor	London
Fireman	John Teague	London
Fireman	Sydney S. Tidy	London
Section Officer	Frederick Tierney	London
District Officer	Joseph L. Tobias	London
Fireman	George H. Tonkin	London
Station Officer	Ernest A. Tooke	London
Fireman	Walter Turley	West Ham
Fireman	Albert A. Turner	London
Fireman	Albert D. Umney	London
Fireman	Mathys Van Hulst	London
Fireman	James Vernon	London
Fireman	Harry C. Vesey	London
Leading Fireman	Edgar W. Vick	Beckenham
Fireman	Ronald V. Waghorne	London
Fireman	Reginald B. Wakeham	London
Fireman	Walter W. Wallis	London
Fireman	Myer Wand	London
Fireman	George A. Waterman	London
Fireman	Frederick J. Watkins	London
Fireman	Henry H. Wayte	London
Fireman	Arthur H. Wenbourne	London
Fireman	William Westwood	London
Fireman	Charles W. Whipps	London
Fireman	Frederick N. Williams	London
Fireman	Ronald Wilson	London
Station Officer	Leslie W. G. Wilson, BEM	London
Fireman	Francis J. Wingfield	London
Fireman	Herbert T. Wolff	London
Fireman	Walter H. Wooder	London
Leading Fireman	Walter J. Woodland	Beckenham
Fireman	Victor G. Wratten	London

During his service as London's Chief Fire Officer, Gerry Clarkson established the Guild of Firefighters and one of its first projects was to raise sufficient funds for a permanent memorial to wartime Blitz firefighters. On 4 May 1991, the Queen Mother unveiled the new memorial sited in Old Change Court, close to St. Paul's Cathedral, and this photograph shows Her Majesty admiring the fine sculpture, together with the names of all those firefighters who lost their lives during the Second World War.

A smaller version of the Blitz memorial sculpture was presented to the London Fire Brigade by Cyril Demarne, former wartime Chief Fire Officer of West Ham Fire Brigade. The sculpture is now part of the foyer of Lambeth Headquarters, alongside the peacetime roll of honour.

Epilogue

W hen back in 2004 I first approached Ken Knight, London's Commissioner for Fire and Emergency Planning, to seek his support for *In Case of Fire*, I knew full well that from a standpoint as a London Fire Brigade 'old boy', my task as a writer was, in part, going to be a nostalgic one.

And indeed it certainly has been during the past busy months of researching and chronicling various aspects of the life and times of the London Fire Brigade and its origins, back into the days of the insurance company brigades of the 18th century. In many ways, penning *In Case of Fire* has involved a personal journey through some of the most memorable and fiery times in London's long and proud history. Aided by some remarkable photographs from the Brigade's pictorial archives, I have travelled in time from James Braidwood to Massey Shaw, and from Freddy Delve right up to the new century with all the changes set out in the

A study of concentration as this female firefighter carefully adjusts her breathing apparatus facemask before joining a crew to undertake a training exercise. Nowadays with the regular presence of toxic smoke even in small domestic fires, a breathing set is a firefighter's personal life support system.

> *London's Fire Brigade has always enjoyed an enviable international reputation...*

A firefighter of the London Fire Engine Establishment, c.1850.

London Safety Plan, now being introduced into the role of the modern London Fire Brigade.

A firefighter of the London Fire Brigade, 2005.

A small part of my research and writing coincided with my own service in the Brigade and re-awakened a few vivid memories of the days in the 1960s and 1970s as one of a crew of four on the pump escape or three on the pump, noisily going to some of the incidents described in the pages of *In Case of Fire.*

Now as my book approaches completion, it is extremely pleasing to learn that the modern Brigade is already having some impressive success in reducing the fatal toll caused by fire in the capital through the initiatives set out in the London Safety Plan.

Although firemen back in my days undertook some very basic fire safety work in the community, its scope and scale was not the same as today's wide ranging effort to make London a safer city through the more flexible use of operational resources and range of innovative fire prevention activities.

Nevertheless, a detailed survey of the causes of all fire deaths in London between 1996 and 2004 revealed the nature of the challenge for the men and women of the LFB that still lies ahead. Of all the fire deaths over this period, 44% were caused by cigarettes, cigars or other tobacco; 13% by cooking appliances; 10% by heating appliances; and 9% by lighters

The cap badge of the London Fire Brigade 1904–1941.

The cap badge of the National Fire Service 1941–1948.

The cap badge of the London Fire Brigade 2005.

or matches. A total of 7% of fire deaths were caused by candles; 4% by electrical appliances; 3% by electrical distribution and lighting; and 2% by other or unknown sources. The survey also revealed that in over half of the fatal fires of this period, no smoke alarm was fitted. Another outcome of this work was to illustrate the scourge of arson in London — 18% of all these fire deaths were caused by deliberate ignition by some means.

On top of this recent London fire deaths survey come the latest available annual figures showing that the overall economic cost of fire in England and Wales is running at the staggeringly high total of £7.7 billion. No less than £2.8 billion of this figure is directly attributable to arson.

The pages of *In Case of Fire* clearly illustrate how the risks faced by those who live and commute to work in London have significantly changed during the last 50 years or so. What has not changed, however, is the self-less commitment of all those connected with the London Fire Brigade around the clock, day and night and in all weathers.

Having had the privilege of working in close contact with various members of the Brigade over the last few months, I can honestly say that Londoners could not be better served by the men and women of its highly professional firefighting and rescue force, either in various preventive safety roles within the community, or when crews are called to action amid the smoke and flames of a fire or to deal with the aftermath of a tragic road traffic accident. London's Fire Brigade has always enjoyed an enviable international reputation for its firefighting and rescue work and looking back over distant and more recent times, this accolade could not be more justly deserved.

London's Chief Fire Officers 1833–2005

London Fire Engine Establishment

1833–1861 James Braidwood

1861–1865 Captain Eyre Massey Shaw, KCB

Metropolitan Fire Brigade

Metropolitan Board of Works

1866–1891 Captain Sir Eyre Massey Shaw, KCB

1891–1896 James Sexton Simonds

1896–1903 Captain Sir Lionel de Latour Wells, CB CMG CBE RN (retd)

London Fire Brigade

London County Council

1903–1909 Rear Admiral James de Courcy Hamilton, MVO RN (retd)

1909–1918 Lieut-Commander Sir Samson Sladen, KBE RN (retd)

1918–1933 Arthur Reginald Dyer, AMICE

1933–1938 Major Cyril Clark Boville Morris, CBE MC MIMechE

1938–1939 Commander Sir Aylmer Newton George Firebrace, CBE RN (retd)

1939–1941 Major Frank Whitford Jackson, CBE DSO
(Deputy Chief Officer Commanding the London Fire Brigade)

NATIONAL FIRE SERVICE 1941–48

London Fire Brigade

London County Council

1948–1962 Sir Frederick William Delve, CBE

1962–1965 Leslie William Thomas Leete, CBE

London Fire Brigade

Greater London Council

1965–1970 Leslie William Thomas Leete, CBE

1970–1976 Joseph Milner, CBE

1977–1980 Sir Peter Howard Darby, CBE

1981–1986 Ronald Alfred Bullers

London Fire Brigade

London Fire & Civil Defence Authority

1986–1987   Ronald Alfred Bullers

1987–1991   Gerald Dawson Clarkson, CBE

1991–2000   Brian Gordon Robinson, CBE

London Fire Brigade

London Fire & Emergency Planning Authority

2000–2003   Brian Gordon Robinson, CBE (Commissioner)

2003–   Kenneth John Knight, CBE (Commissioner)

Acknowledgements

In a long list of thanks my sincere appreciation must first go to the Commissioner of the London Fire and Emergency Planning Authority, Ken Knight, CBE, QFSM, MIFireE, for his unfailing and enthusiastic support without which *In Case of Fire* would simply not have happened. I must, too, thank James Flynn, London Fire Brigade's Head of Communications for his encouragement and Steve Cox, the LFB Press Office Manager who organised my many visits to Lambeth Headquarters and various parts of the Brigade over the past months.

My appreciation is also due to Rita Dexter and Barbara Riddell, the two Directors of the Brigade, who together with the Assistant Commissioners made time to meet me in order that I could fully understand the workings of the modern London Fire Brigade. Dave Scott, the Borough Commander of Southwark and Jeff Powell, the Principal Controller at Brigade Control were also most helpful in this regard.

My gratitude is also due to Terry Jones and Pauline Drummond of the Brigade's photographic section during my selection of many images from the photographic archives. Then my thanks must go to the following Brigade personnel: Kelly Fairman, the Commissioner's Staff Officer; Justina Leitão, Head of Design; Julie Marshall, Deputy Information Manager and Paul Eady; Richard Howat, Editor of *London Firefighter*; Esther Mann, the Curator of the Brigade Museum at Southwark; Jill Carey, Dick Nye and Kate Warren of Fire Safety.

It would also be appropriate for me to recognise the outstanding work of the Brigade's photographers that grace the pages of *In Case of Fire*. For almost 100 years, the uniformed photographers of the LFB have captured the action and drama of major fires and emergencies and many other significant events. This amazing collection of photographic images of the Brigade at work in peace and war forms a historic panorama of the life and times of the capital since Victorian times. My special thanks are therefore due to all modern day Brigade photographers including Les Lockwood, Steve Hall, Simon Gridley, Chris Hart, Keith Watt, Marc Downing, Darren Barnett and Andy Brown, together with their talented

❝ It is also appropriate to recognise the outstanding work of LFB photographers...❞

predecessors of past years for many of the superb illustrations that appear on the pages of *In Case of Fire*. In addition, I appreciate the use of several images from Keith Wardell's excellent photographic collection.

I should also like to record my recognition of the work of my good friend and fellow writer Sally Holloway. Over the years Sally has rightly been recognised as a learned authority on the history of the Brigade and her advice on all things London Fire Brigade continues to be much appreciated.

Then I must pay tribute to my publisher, Jeremy Mills, for having the commercial confidence to produce *In Case of Fire* and for his professional input into matters of design and layout. Finally, to my dear wife Susie who has, as usual, supported me indomitably with her outstanding administrative and proof reading skills often undertaken against the most pressing deadlines, and generally kept me up to my writing task.

Further Reading

Blackstone, G. V., *A History of the British Fire Service*, Routledge and Kegan Paul, 1957

Demarne, Cyril, *The London Blitz — A Fireman's Tale*, After The Battle, 1992

Fire and Water — The London Firefighters' Blitz 1940–42 Remembered, Firestorm Publications, 1992

Firebrace, Sir Aylmer, *Fire Service Memories*, Andrew Melrose, 1948

Arthur Nicholls, *Going to Blazes*, Hale, 1978

Henham, Brian, *True Hero: The Life and Times of James Braidwood*, Brian Henham, 2000

Holloway, Sally, *London's Noble Fire Brigades*, Cassell, 1973

Holloway, Sally, *Moorgate: Anatomy of a Railway Disaster*, David & Charles, 1987

Holloway, Sally, *Courage High,* HMSO, 1992

Holloway, Sally and Wallington, Neil, *Fire and Rescue,* Patrick Stephens, 1994

Honeycombe, Gordon, *Red Watch*, Hutchinson, 1976

Jackson, Eric W., *London's Fire Brigades,* Longmans, 1966

Morris, C. C. B., *Fire*, Blackie & Son, 1939

Shaw, Sir Eyre Massey, *Fire Protection — A Complete Manual of the Organisation, Machinery, Discipline and General Working of the Fire Brigade of London*, Charles and Edwin Layton, 1976.

Wallington, Neil, *Fireman — A Personal Account,* David and Charles, 1979

Wallington, Neil, *Firemen at War*, David and Charles, 1982

Wallington, Neil, *Images of Fire,* David and Charles, 1989

Wallington, Neil, *Firefighter!* Firestorm Publications, 1992

Wallington, Neil, *Out of the Flames*, Fire Services National Benevolent Fund, 2003

Wassey, Michael, *Ordeal By Fire*, Secker & Warburg, 1941

While, Jack, *Fifty Years of Firefighting in London*, Hutchinson, 1931

Index